The
Johannine
Writings

The Biblical Seminar
32

The
JOHANNINE
WRITINGS

edited by
**Stanley E. Porter &
Craig A. Evans**

Sheffield
Academic Press

Published by
Sheffield Academic Press Ltd
Mansion House
19 Kingfield Road
Sheffield, S11 9AS
England

Typeset by Sheffield Academic Press
and
Printed on acid-free paper in Great Britain
by The Cromwell Press
Melksham, Wiltshire

British Library Cataloguing in Publication Data

A catalogue record for this book is available
from the British Library

ISBN 1-85075-729-1

CONTENTS

Preface to the Series

This Series, of which *The Johannine Writings* is one, collects what the Series editors believe to be the best articles on the topic published in the first 50 issues (1978–1993) of *Journal for the Study of the New Testament*. Founded in 1978, with one issue in its inaugural year, *JSNT* was produced from 1979 to 1990 in three issues a year, and then, from 1991 to the present, in four issues a year. The continuing success of the journal can be seen in several ways: by its increasing circulation, by its increased publication schedule, by its fostering of a significant supplement series, which has now reached its one-hundredth volume (JSNT Supplement Series), by its public exposure and influence within the scholarly community, and, most of all, by the quality of the essays it publishes. This volume contains a representative group of such articles on a specific area of New Testament studies.

Once it was decided that such a Series of volumes should be issued, the question became that of how the numerous important articles were going to be selected and presented. The problem was not filling the volumes but making the many difficult choices that would inevitably exclude worthy articles. In the end, the editors have used various criteria for determining which articles should be reprinted here. They have gathered together articles that, they believe, make significant contributions in several different ways. Some of the articles are truly ground-breaking, pushing their respective enquiry into new paths and introducing new critical questions into the debate. Others are assessments of the critical terrain of a particular topic, providing useful and insightful analyses that others can and have built upon. Others still are included because they are major contributions to an on-going discussion.

Even though back issues of *JSNT* are still in print and these essays are available in individual issues of the journal, it is thought that this kind of compilation could serve several purposes. One is to assist scholars who wish to keep up on developments outside their areas of specialist research or who have been away from a topic for a period of time and wish to re-enter the discussion. These volumes are designed to be representatively selective, so that scholars can gain if not a thorough grasp of all of the developments in an area at least significant insights into major topics of debate in a field of interest. Another use of these volumes is as textbooks for undergraduates, seminarians and even graduate students. For undergraduates, these volumes could serve as useful readers, possibly as supplementary texts to a critical introduction, to provide a first exposure to and a sample of critical debate. For seminary students, the same purpose as for undergraduates could apply, especially when the seminarian is beginning critical study of the New Testament. There is the added use, however, that such material could provide guidance through the argumentation and footnotes for significant research into a New Testament author or topic. For graduate students, these volumes could not only provide necessary background to a topic, allowing a student to achieve a basic level of knowledge before exploration of a particular area of interest, but also serve as good guides to the detailed critical work being done in an area. There is the further advantage that many of the articles in these volumes are models of how to make and defend a critical argument, thereby providing useful examples for those entering the lists of critical scholarly debate.

Many more articles could and probably should be re-printed in further volumes, but this one and those published along with it must for now serve as an introduction to these topics, at least as they were discussed in *JSNT*.

Craig A. Evans
Trinity Western University
Langley, B.C. Canada

Stanley E. Porter
Roehampton Institute London
England

ABBREVIATIONS

AB	Anchor Bible
AGJU	Arbeiten zur Geschichte des antiken Judentums und des Urchristentums
ANRW	*Aufstieg und Niedergang der römischen Welt*
ATR	*Anglican Theological Review*
BETL	Bibliotheca ephemeridum theologicarum lovaniensium
Bib	*Biblica*
BJRL	*Bulletin of the John Rylands University Library of Manchester*
BNTC	Black's New Testament Commentaries
BR	*Biblical Research*
BTB	*Biblical Theology Bulletin*
BZ	*Biblische Zeitschrift*
CBQ	*Catholic Biblical Quarterly*
CJT	*Canadian Journal of Theology*
ConBNT	Coniectanea biblica, Old Testament
DTT	*Dansk teologisk tidsskrift*
ETL	*Ephemerides theologicae lovanienses*
EvQ	*Evangelical Quarterly*
ExpTim	*Expository Times*
FFNT	Foundations and Facets: New Testament
HibJ	*Hibbert Journal*
HNT	Handbuch zum Neuen Testament
HNTC	Harper's NT Commentaries
HTKNT	Herders theologischer Kommentar zum Neuen Testament
HTR	*Harvard Theological Review*
HTS	Harvard Theological Studies
IB	*Interpreter's Bible*
IBS	*Irish Biblical Studies*
ICC	International Critical Commentary
JAC	Jahrbuch für Antike und Christentum
JBL	*Journal of Biblical Literature*
JEH	*Journal of Ecclesiastical History*
JJS	*Journal of Jewish Studies*
JQR	*Jewish Quarterly Review*
JR	*Journal of Religion*
JRH	*Journal of Religious History*
JRS	*Journal of Roman Studies*
JSJ	*Journal for the Study of Judaism in the Persian, Hellenistic and Roman Period*
JSS	*Journal of Semitic Studies*

JTS	*Journal of Theological Studies*
KD	*Kerygma und Dogma*
LCL	Loeb Classical Library
LThJ	*Lutheran Theological Journal*
MNTC	Moffatt NT Commentary
NCB	New Century Bible
NHS	Nag Hammadi Studies
NICNT	New International Commentary on the New Testament
NovT	*Novum Testamentum*
NovTSup	*Novum Testamentum* Supplements
NRT	*La nouvelle revue théologique*
NTS·	*New Testament Studies*
PEQ	*Palestine Exploration Quarterly*
PG	J. Migne (ed.), *Patrologia graeca*
PL	J. Migne (ed.), *Patrologia latina*
RB	*Revue biblique*
REJ	*Revue des études juives*
RivB	*Rivista biblica*
RSR	*Recherches de science religieuse*
SBLDS	SBL Dissertation Series
SBLSP	SBL Seminar Papers
SJ	Studia judaica
SJT	*Scottish Journal of Theology*
SNTSMS	Society of New Testament Studies Monograph Series
SPB	Studia postbiblica
Str.–B.	H. Strack and P. Billerbeck, *Kommentar zum Neuen Testament aus Talmud und Midrasch*
TBl	*Theologische Blätter*
TDNT	G. Kittel and G. Friedrich (eds.), *Theological Dictionary of the New Testament*
TLZ	*Theologischer Literaturzeitung*
TRu	*Theologische Rundschau*
TS	*Theological Studies*
TSAJ	Texte und Studien zum antiken Judentum
TU	Texte und Untersuchungen
TynBul	*Tyndale Bulletin*
TZ	*Theologische Zeitschrift*
VC	*Vigiliae christianae*
VT	*Vetus Testamentun*
VTSup	*Vetus Testamentum*, Supplements
WBC	Word Biblical Commentary
WUNT	Wissenschaftliche Untersuchungen zum Neuen Testament
ZNW	*Zeitschrift für die neutestamentliche Wissenschaft*

THE GOSPEL OF JOHN AND ITS INFLUENCES

JSNT 13 (1981), pp. 83-101

DISCOURSE AND TRADITION:
THE USE OF THE SAYINGS OF JESUS IN THE DISCOURSES OF THE
FOURTH GOSPEL

Barnabas Lindars, S.S.F.

I

The Johannine discourses are a unique feature of the Fourth Gospel, but
they include elements which have a close connection with the Synoptic
sayings. These are not sufficiently numerous to warrant the suggestion
that John had a discourse-source, comparable to the sayings-source Q.[1]
If we have to suppose that the discourses are drawn from a previous
source, it is better to stick to Bultmann's *Offenbarungsreden-Quelle*,
and to assume that the evangelist has made use of items from the
sayings tradition in reshaping the source as utterances of Jesus. But this
would give to the sayings a very subordinate place in the composition of
the discourses as a whole. In fact, though they are few in number, they
occupy a crucial place in the construction of the discourses. For this
reason it is much more likely that there never was a written source for
the discourses. They are the free composition of the evangelist, building
upon a careful selection of traditional sayings of Jesus. But although this
means that the sayings tradition is the only source of the discourses in
the strict sense, the meaning and purpose of the discourses are not dictated by the sayings, but relate closely to the conditions of Johannine
Christianity at the time when the evangelist is writing, probably late in
the first century. It may be said that John uses the sayings simply as a
jumping-off place for what he really wants to say, in much the same way

---

1. For a recent survey of theories concerning the sources of the discourses,
cf. S.S. Smalley, *John: Evangelist and Interpreter* (Exeter: Paternoster Press, 1978),
pp. 108-12.

as many preachers use (or mis-use) a text of Scripture. But John uses them much more purposefully than that. It is part of his intention in writing a Gospel at all to uphold the claim that Johannine Christianity is directly related to Jesus himself. Thus the characteristic Johannine doctrines must be seen to be implied by the words of Jesus. This must be shown, in spite of the fact that the sayings tradition is extremely poor in christological material. So what John does is to select a saying in which he can perceive a principle suitable to his purpose. He draws out the principle in the typical cut and thrust of the argument of the discourses, and so leads up to his desired christological conclusion.

The point may be illustrated from Jn 8.28-29: 'When you have lifted up the Son of Man, then you will know that I am he, and that I do nothing on my own authority but speak thus as the Father taught me. And he who sent me is with me; he has not left me alone, for I always do what is pleasing to him.'

This is the climax of a very long and complex argument about the true identity of Jesus. The theme was enunciated in the parable of the apprenticed son in 5.19,[2] after a carefully prepared introductory narrative and transitional dialogue in 5.1-18. The parable states that a son can do nothing on his own authority, but depends upon his father's instructions. If the parable is authentic, it would admirably suit Jesus' ironic style of self-defence, which can be seen so often in the Synoptic Gospels. Just as he defends his slackness about fasting by means of the parable of the bridegroom in Mk 2.18-19, so with this parable he defends his bringing of the gospel to the common people by pointing out that he is only copying the practice of 'your Father who is in heaven, for he makes his sun rise on the evil and on the good, and sends rain on the just and on the unjust' (Mt. 5.45). From this parable John has deduced the principle of Jesus' exact conformity to the will of God. He refers to it with reference to judgement in 5.30. He picks it up again with regard to

2.   The parable should not be taken to include 5.20a, as suggested in my commentary (*The Gospel of John* [NCB; London: Oliphants, 1972]), following C.H. Dodd ('A Hidden Parable in the Fourth Gospel', in *More New Testament Studies* [Manchester: Manchester University Press, 1968], pp. 30-40) and P. Gächter ('Zur Form von Joh. 5,19-30', in *Neutestamentliche Aufsätze* [ed. J. Blinzler, O. Kuss and F. Mussner; Regensburg: Pustet, 1963], pp. 65-68). Verse 20a begins John's exposition of the parable, using words ('the Father loves the Son') almost identical with 3.35. It is possible that John intends to refer to the creation at this point (πάντα...ἃ...ποιεῖ, cf. v. 17 ἐργάζεται). Then the 'greater things' of v. 20b prepare the way for the eschatological functions in vv. 21-22.

teaching in 7.16-17. In 8.12-20 he shows that this conformity to the will of God is witness to Jesus' status as Son of the Father. In the following verse there is a dark hint that this will become plain only in the cross (8.21). In 8.25 Jesus is directly challenged concerning his identity. Then comes the climax in 8.28, which not only picks up the phrases of 5.19, 30 and 7.16-17, but relates the substance of the claim to the revelatory character of the cross, referring back to the lifting up of the Son of Man which had previously been enunciated in 3.14. But as that also depends upon the sayings tradition, it is fair to say that not only the opening of this great christological dispute comes from the tradition (5.19), but also the conclusion (8.28, based on 3.14 and 5.19, etc.). The conclusion is that Jesus is God's agent, and as such he has a special relationship with God, which corresponds with the father/son relationship commonly employed in statements about Jesus. Thus the Christian claim that Jesus is the Son of God is here supported by an explanation of one aspect of the father/son relationship, based on a saying from the tradition from which the principle can be deduced.

It is not without significance that the saying in this case is unknown from the Synoptic Gospels. It has been suggested that a variant of the parable of the apprenticed son lies behind Mt. 11.27 = Lk. 10.22.[3] If so, we must think of more than one channel of tradition, and the saying has the warrant of double attestation. This also strengthens the contention that John had access to traditions comparable to those used by the Synoptic writers, but not identical with them. John may have known and used one or more of the Synoptic Gospels. But he was not solely dependent upon them for his historical tradition.

The vexed question of the relationship between John and the synoptics is not our concern here. The point at issue is the place of traditional material in the composition of the discourses. What I want to emphasize is that recognition of this is essential to a correct understanding of the discourses themselves. This has already been indicated in connection with the unwieldy composition of ch. 5, and its continuation in 7.16–8.29. This will now be applied to the discourse with Nicodemus (ch. 3), the discourse on the bread of life (ch. 6), and the discourse on slave and son (8.31-58). The last case includes a new assessment of the nature of the underlying tradition which leads to a much more satisfactory analysis of the discourse than has previously been possible.

3.   J. Jeremias, *New Testament Theology*, I (London: SCM Press, 1971), p. 58.

II

The discourse with Nicodemus begins with a saying from the tradition
(Jn 3.3, 5): 'Amen, amen, I say to you, unless one is born ἄνωθεν (v. 5:
from water and Spirit), he cannot see (v. 5: enter) the kingdom of God'.

This saying is a variant of the synoptic saying on becoming a child,
which is found in independent versions in Mt. 18.3 and Mk 10.15. I have
argued elsewhere that, when stripped of Johannisms, this saying can be
seen to be an independent Greek translation of the same Aramaic saying
which lies behind the other two versions.[4] There are thus three different
Greek versions of the saying. The cardinal point is that Matthew's 'turn
and become as children' is a Semitic idiom, meaning 'become again as
children'. This idiom is represented differently in Jn 3.3, if ἄνωθεν is
understood to mean 'again'.[5] It may be said in favour of this suggestion
that it is most unlikely that John's text was the same as Matthew's, and
he has deliberately expressed the idiom differently, because the same
idiom occurs in a quotation at Jn 12.40, apparently unrecognized by
John. On the other hand, even though John in all probability took
ἄνωθεν to mean 'from above', the fact that it is capable of being a rendering of the idiom preserved by Matthew can scarcely be mere
coincidence.

John, however, has understood it to mean 'from above' (cf. v. 2,
'from God'), and this is the basic principle of the discourse which
follows. Entry into the kingdom of God (= eternal life, vv. 15, 16, 36)
requires birth (i.e. renewal) from above (= from water and Spirit, v. 5;
from the Spirit, v. 8). But the crucial point is that such renewal is possible only through belief in the one who is from above (= descended from
heaven, v. 13; the one whom God gave, v. 16; the one whom God sent,
v. 17; the one who comes ἄνωθεν, v. 31; the teacher from God, v. 2).
Thus the whole point of the discourse is to prove that, just as salvation
requires action from God, and cannot be obtained by human exertion,
so the agent of salvation requires origination from God, and no earthly

4.   'John and the Synoptic Gospels: A Test Case', *NTS* 27 (1981), pp. 287-94.

5.   The meaning 'again' occurs in Gal. 4.9, but there it is in conjunction with
πάλιν (= 'all over again'). Thus it does not denote mere repetition, but renewal 'from
the start', so that it is an excellent translation of the Aramaic idiom. Comparable
examples from the papyri are cited by J.H. Moulton and G. Milligan, *The Vocabulary
of the Greek Testament* (1914–29; repr. Grand Rapids: Eerdmans, 1965), s.v.
ἄνωθεν.

teacher can be a substitute for him (v. 13).

This is the main drift of the discourse. But there is another factor of the greatest importance to John, which is expressed with the aid of another saying of Jesus from the tradition (3.14-15): 'And as Moses lifted up the serpent in the wilderness, so *must the Son of man be lifted up*, that whoever believes in him may have eternal life'.

The motif of the serpent is peculiar to John, and the final clause follows his typical mode of expression. But the italicized words reflect the passion predictions of Mark, and are probably to be accepted as a variant of them. We may compare John's ὑψωθῆναι δεῖ τὸν υἱὸν τοῦ ἀνθρώπου with Mk 8.31, δεῖ τὸν υἱὸν τοῦ ἀνθρώπου πολλὰ παθεῖν. But if we also take into account that the verb παραδοθῆναι is much better attested for the passion predictions (Mk 9.30; 10.33; cf. 14.21, 41), it becomes possible to see that the variable verb belongs to a pattern of interpretation which explains John's text here.[6] The underlying saying of Jesus (which cannot be reconstructed with certainty) has been interpreted in the light of the passion prophecy of Isa. 52.13–53.12. The verb παραδοθῆναι is an obvious link, because this verb occurs three times in the Septuagint, including the crucial verse 53.12. There is no need to doubt that John was aware of the link. His variation of the verb can thus be explained as the deliberate choice of a different verb from the same prophecy, i.e. 52.13, in order to bring together the concepts of death by crucifixion and exaltation, as suggested by the symbolism of the serpent (cf. Jn 12.33; 18.32). The reason for this is a central position of John's theology. The cross to John has revelatory significance, because it demonstrates the unity of the Father and the Son. Acceptance of the fact that Jesus must die is therefore indispensable to saving faith.

It can now be seen that this verse (and the subsequent reflections on it in Jn 3.16-21) plays a vital part in the argument of the discourse. If Jesus is the agent of the birth from above, then belief in him as one who originates from God is a matter of the first importance. But belief in him will be defective, if it does not include acceptance of the necessity of his

---

6. I have analysed the passion predictions in 'The New Look on the Son of Man', *BJRL* 63 (1981), pp. 437-62, and more fully in *Jesus Son of Man* (London: SPCK, 1983), ch. 4, 'The Passion Predictions'; see also ch. 9, 'The Son of Man in the Theology of John'. John's use of this material is given very full treatment in F.J. Moloney, *The Johannine Son of Man* (Rome: Pontifical Biblical Institute Press, 2nd edn, 1978).

death on the cross. Thus the verse introduces a secondary, but indispensable, element into the argument. And, like the opening verse, it takes the form of an authentic saying of Jesus, which John has exploited for his theology. This was not necessarily derived directly from Mark, although Mark is our only source for the passion predictions as such. For they have clearly been subject to adaptation and expansion on Mark's part, and their relation to primitive formulae (e.g. 1 Cor. 15.3) suggests that they go behind Mark to earlier tradition. Seeing that the Son of Man in this saying (both in Mark and in John) operates only as a self-reference, and not as a title of honour, it is to be accepted as an original feature. But what was its meaning on the lips of Jesus in this connection is a question which lies outside the scope of this article.[7]

III

The discourse on the bread of life is primarily an exposition of the miracle of the manna, introduced by the feeding of the five thousand from the Jesus tradition. Hence it is not to be expected that sayings of Jesus will play such an important part in the argument. On the other hand two sayings from the tradition can be detected in the discourse, and their function is quite similar to what we have seen in the discourse with Nicodemus.

The discourse starts with the contrast between the gift of the manna ('as it is written, He gave them bread from heaven to eat', 6.31) and the true bread from heaven which the Father gives. As 6.31 is an adapted quotation of Exod. 16.15 or of Ps. 78.24,[8] it can be claimed that the vocabulary of the discourse is derived from the quotation material. So when the audience say 'Lord, give us this bread always' (6.34), it is unnecessary to look for any further allusions. On the other hand there is a striking similarity between πάντοτε δὸς ἡμῖν τὸν ἄρτον τοῦτον and the Lord's prayer, τὸν ἄρτον ἡμῶν τὸν ἐπιούσιον δὸς ἡμῖν

---

7.   The idiomatic *bar enasha*, which lies behind the Son of Man title, is neither an exclusive self-reference (G. Vermes, *Jesus the Jew* [London: Collins, 1973], pp. 160-91) nor a general statement (Maurice Casey, *Son of Man: The Interpretation and Influence of Daniel 7* [London: SPCK, 1979], p. 232), but a generic usage denoting a class with which the speaker identifies himself, in this case a man faced with betrayal or arrest (see my works mentioned in the last note).

8.   The latter is to be preferred, because the psalm provides the means of linking the expositions of *seder* and *haphtarah*, as explained below.

σήμερον (Mt. 6.11). Seeing that John has other probable allusions to the Lord's prayer in the prayer of Jesus before his arrest (πάτερ... δόξασόν σου τὸν υἱόν, ἵνα ὁ υἱὸς δοξάσῃ σε, 17.1; ἵνα τηρήσῃς αὐτοὺς ἐκ τοῦ πονηροῦ, 17.14), it is likely that he was familiar with it, even though he does not reproduce it formally. For John, the prayer of Christians for daily bread (πάντοτε corresponding with ἐπιούσιον in his allusion to it) is a prayer for Jesus himself, because Jesus is the bringer of the true nourishment, which consists in belief in him as the agent of God (6.40). If this discourse was composed originally as a homily at the Christian eucharist it would very naturally include allusion to the Lord's prayer, which may have been recited in the course of the liturgy.[9] The homily is based on the Jewish lections, taken over from the synagogue. So it is an exposition of the *seder*, Exodus 16, interpreted in the light of the *haphtarah*, Isa. 54.9–55.5, quoted in Jn 6.45.[10] But John's Christian interpretation of the theme is already presupposed in the eucharist itself, in which fellowship with Jesus, the risen Lord and mediator of the new covenant, is experienced. Thus the petition for 'daily bread', no doubt generally taken in the obvious practical way as a prayer for physical sustenance (cf. Mt. 6.25-26), is applied to Jesus himself as the true spiritual food, for which he had instructed his followers to pray. The main principle of the discourse is that Jesus is the true bread, by contrast with the Jewish law, of which the manna was the symbol. John is able to anchor this principle in the words of Jesus by referring to the prayer which he gave to his followers.

The second allusion to the words of Jesus is also a liturgical reference in 6.53: 'Amen, amen I say to you, unless you eat the flesh of the Son of man and drink his blood, you have no life in you.' The relationship

9. *Did*. 8, the earliest reference to the Lord's prayer outside the New Testament, orders recital three times a day. The eucharistic thanksgiving immediately follows this instruction. But the earliest witness to its actual use in the eucharist does not appear until the fourth century (Cyril of Jerusalem).

10. This can be claimed only with due caution, because the reconstruction of the Jewish lectionary in the first century is far from secure. A. Guilding (*The Fourth Gospel and Jewish Worship* [Oxford: Clarendon Press, 1960], p. 63) asserts that Isa. 54.9–55.3 (or 5) was the *haphtarah* to Gen. 6.9ff., but she includes both these and Exodus 16 within the second half of Nisan, so that the connection between them was clearly recognized. All that can be said is that John 6 gives the appearance of being based on this connection of *seder* and *haphtarah*, and that no evidence has yet been produced which would make the supposition that they were used together in the synagogue in John's day impossible.

with the eucharistic words is obvious. But its significance will be missed
if it is not observed that the same tradition has already been referred to
in v. 51c: 'And the bread which I will give is my flesh for (ὑπέρ) the
life of the world'.[11] John's ὑπέρ links up with 1 Cor. 11.24 (τὸ σῶμα
τὸ ὑπὲρ ὑμῶν) and Mk 14.24 (τὸ αἷμά μου...ὑπὲρ πολλῶν). It
establishes his intention to use this reference in order to bring in the
notion of the sacrifice of Christ. This is confirmed by the Son of Man
title in v. 53. As far as John is concerned, this is not a title of honour, but
a self-designation used by Jesus in speaking of his sacrificial death. It
refers to him specifically as the one whose cross reveals his true relationship with God, as we have already seen in connection with 3.14. The
Son of Man title is derived from the passion predictions, and so properly
belongs to the traditional material used there. It does not belong to the
underlying words here, but has been introduced here by John, because
he is using the eucharistic words to make the same point as he made in
3.14. Acceptance of Jesus as the true bread is defective unless it includes
acceptance of the necessity of the passion. If it is John's purpose to persuade his readers that all the spiritual benefits, which Jews have found
through meditation upon the law, can be gained through Christ, then he
must make it clear that this is possible only through his death. That
reveals his unique relationship with the Father, and acceptance of it
enables the believer to live within that relationship (6.57).

IV

Our last example is the discourse on slave and son in Jn 8.31-58.[12] This
is more difficult to unravel than the other discourses, because it does not
appear to have a consistent theme. In the others which we have considered the traditional saying employed by John at the outset embodies a

---

11. For the order of words, which varies in the manuscripts, cf. C.K. Barrett, *The
Gospel according to St John* (London: SCM Press, 2nd edn, 1978), ad loc. The
addition of ἣν ἐγὼ δώσω in some texts is comparable to the addition of διδόμενον
to the text of 1 Cor. 11.24 in Lk. 22.19, and this fact enhances the fundamental
similarity of the traditions.

12. What follows is an abbreviated version of an article on 'Slave and Son in
John 8.31-36', in W.C. Weinrich (ed.), *The New Testament Age* (Festschrift
B. Reicke; 2 vols.; Macon, GA: Mercer University Press, 1984), I, pp. 271-86. A
preliminary analysis on the same lines was given in a lecture 'Freedom in the Gospel
according to St John' given at the Presbyterian Conference Centre, Massanetta
Springs, Virginia, USA, in August 1976, from which it may be borrowed on tape.

principle which is worked out in various ways in the succeeding development of the discourse, and the concluding section recalls the opening clearly enough to constitute a literary inclusion, which enables the reader to think of the discourse as a whole. In the present case the figure of Abraham provides an inclusion (vv. 33 and 56-58), but his role is ancillary to the main argument. The purpose of the discourse is very similar to that of ch. 3, where John wished to prove the origination of Jesus from God, and did so by pointing to the necessity of the divine initiative for salvation. If God alone can give salvation, then the agent of salvation must come from God. Here John wants to prove the pre-existence of Jesus. His argument is that, if Jesus is the giver of eternal life, then he must himself be the possessor of eternal life. He therefore has to prove that Jesus does give eternal life, and only after that can he reach the conclusion that Jesus is pre-existent.

The matter is complicated, because John writes against a background of thought in which the means of gaining eternal life is believed to be already available in the Jewish law. There is no appeal to this belief in the course of the argument, but it is the unspoken *tertium comparationis* in this discourse, just as much as it is in the discourse on the bread of life. There is a reference to the commandment not to kill in vv. 37 and 40 (cf. 7.19), and Abraham is invoked precisely because he is the founder of the covenant people who possess the law. It might be expected that John would argue on this basis that the law cannot give life. But John never repudiates the law. Like Paul, he regards the law as containing the revelation of God which reaches its true application in Christ (cf. 5.46-47). The rejection of Jesus is not, as one might suppose, a positive decision in favour of the law in preference to Jesus. John regards it as nothing less than transgression of the law, because it is in his eyes equivalent to killing Jesus. So Abraham and the law are on the side of Jesus, and the wish to kill him stems not from the law but from the devil. Even on the Jews' own terms of reference, then, belief in Jesus is essential for the obtaining of eternal life.

John's argument is thus more logical than appears at first sight, and it is conducted with exceptional verve and dramatic skill. But what has been said so far throws into relief a problem which is sure to trouble the attentive reader, that John starts off with a contrast between slave and son, but drops it after a few verses, and never refers to it again. There are plenty of sharp contrasts in what follows, but the concepts of freedom and slavery play no part in it. In fact, John has confused the issue at the outset by making use of the idea of slave and son, because he is actually concerned only with sonship, and the contrast from v. 38 onwards is put in terms of different fathers. All are sons, whether they are sons of Abraham or sons of the devil or even the Son of God. There really seems to be no point in mentioning slaves at all.

This problem could be dismissed as carelessness on John's part. He has begun the discourse with the idea of slave and son in his mind, but then the issue of sonship claims all his attention, and he forgets to follow through his initial plan.[13] But closer observation of the text suggests a more cogent explanation. John very occasionally uses the concept of slavery (cf. 13.16; 15.15), but he never uses the concept of freedom outside this passage. The word ἐλεύθερος and its cognates occur only here in the Fourth Gospel. It is foreign to John's diction. It thus seems likely that John has used it here rather unwillingly, and abandons it as soon as he has established the terms of reference which he needs for the subsequent argument. If this is so, there must have been a certain constraint upon him to use it in the first place. Our previous observations of John's technique in constructing the discourses point to the conclusion that this constraint comes from his use of traditional material containing this word.

As before, John wishes to use an item from the sayings tradition which embodies the principle which is essential to his argument. But he must have found it no easy matter to hit upon one that was suitable to his purpose. If we were in John's position, with only Q before us, what would we have chosen? But John does not seem to have had access to Q, at any rate in the form used by Matthew and Luke. His saying on renewal in 3.3, 5 has come through a separate channel. Similarly, the parable of the apprenticed son in 5.19 may be a variant of the Q saying in Mt. 11.27 = Lk. 10.22, but it is not derived from it. Now he is able to reproduce another parable, which could perhaps be taken from the same collection as 5.19. It is the parable of the slave and the son in 8.35: 'A slave does not continue in a house for ever; a son continues for ever'. In isolating this verse as a parable derived from the tradition, Dodd recognized that it was open to question, because the phrase μένει εἰς τὸν αἰῶνα is characteristic of John's diction.[14] But he found that these

13. Such changes are characteristic of Paul; see now the analysis of Paul's exegetical argument in 2 Cor. 3 in M.D. Hooker, 'Beyond the Things that are Written? St Paul's Use of Scripture', *NTS* 27 (1981), pp. 295-309.

14. Cf. C.H. Dodd, *Historical Tradition in the Fourth Gospel* (Cambridge:

words occur just sufficiently often in the rest of the New Testament to persuade him that they could belong to the underlying material.

Our argument, however, suggests a different answer. If ἐλεύθερος is, by contrast, foreign to John's vocabulary, then it is likely to be the original word which John has replaced with his own phrase in reproducing the parable itself. Thus the underlying material can be reconstucted as follows: ὁ δοῦλος οὐκ ἐλεύθερός ἐστιν ἐν τῇ οἰκίᾳ· ὁ υἱὸς ἐλεύθερός ἐστιν.

Two things may be said in favour of this reconstruction. First, it fits well into one side of the ethical teaching of Jesus, who not only recognized God as his Father, but also taught his disciples to regard themselves as God's sons, unenslaved by worldly possessions (cf. Mt. 5.45; Lk. 6.32-35). The motif occurs in the parable of the prodigal son (Lk. 15.17-29). It is also a feature of Paul's cosmic understanding of the new status of those who acknowledge Jesus, who have been freed from the πνεῦμα δουλείας and have received the πνεῦμα υἱοθεσίας (Rom. 8.15). This is the cosmic process, by which αὐτὴ ἡ κτίσις ἐλευθερωθήσεται ἀπὸ τῆς δουλείας τῆς φθορᾶς εἰς τὴν ἐλευθερίαν τῆς δόξης τῶν τέκνων τοῦ θεοῦ (Rom. 8.21). Paul in this chapter is certainly building on a tradition of exposition of the Abba address, mentioned in Rom. 8.15 and also Gal. 4.6. Similar traditions lie behind John's exploitation of the father/son correlation in connection with his christology. It is thus not surprising to find that his resources include a saying on sonship as opposed to slavery, which belongs within this general range of teaching.

Secondly, the second, positive half of the saying as reconstructed actually occurs in plural form in Mt. 17.26: ἄρα γε ἐλεύθεροί εἰσιν οἱ υἱοί.[15] It is the unique pericope of the temple tax (Mt. 17.24-27). Critical opinion on the historical value of this pericope is much divided, but there seems to be no good reason to doubt the authenticity of the central core. The mention of Peter may be due to Matthew, and the question concerning payment of the tax may be an artificial setting for the saying, completed with a 'fishing story' derived from a well known theme of folk-lore. But the saying itself is a parable, and has nothing to do with the temple tax: 'From whom do kings of the earth take toll or tribute? From their sons or from others? (Do they not take it) from

Cambridge University Press, 1963), pp. 379-82.

15. Dodd drew attention to this parallel, but failed to observe its value for reconstruction of the actual text used by John.

others? Then the sons are free.' If Jesus gave general teaching along
these lines, it would be likely to belong to his teaching on the nature of
the coming kingdom. The Q material in Lk. 12.32-34 provides a good
parallel.

Now, if this is the tradition which came to John, we can see why he
uses ἐλεύθερος in the context, even though he has altered it in the
saying itself. The alteration is, of course, a carefully chosen midrashic
explanation. The singular ὁ υἱός in John's text was intended, like ὁ
δοῦλος, to be generic. But John has picked out this saying precisely
because it is capable of christological interpretation. The son in the
parable is Jesus, and he it is who is free. But to be free in John's thought
is to have eternal life, and it is essential for the subsequent argument that
Jesus should actually say this concerning the son.

In order to understand this, it is necessary to analyse the sequence of
verses more closely. John first sets out the form of the argument in
vv. 31-32, using the vocabulary of the saying: 'If you continue
(μείνητε) in my word, you are truly my disciples, and you will know
the truth, and the truth will make you free'. This establishes the principle
of cause and effect, which is fundamental to the following argument.
Here the principle is put in terms of truth and freedom. Jesus conveys
the truth, and the truth effects freedom. John is going to drop the
concept of freedom from the argument, but the concept of truth will be
an essential ingredient (vv. 39-47). In v. 32 the audience make the
typically Johannine response of supposing that Jesus is speaking of
freedom in the political sense. This allows John to introduce Abraham,
who also will figure in the following argument.

It is tempting to suppose that John is here dealing with Stoic concepts
of truth and freedom. But this is completely foreign to John's purpose.
Truth has been introduced because it is one side in John's essentially
Jewish dualism, which comes to open expression in vv. 44-46. This dualism is thus another basic feature of the argument, along with the principle of cause and effect. John has deduced both these features from the
saying on slave and son. One of the values of the saying from his point
of view is that the contrast between slave and son makes a splendid basis
for his central position, in which sonship to the devil is contrasted with
Jesus' sonship to God. But the principle of cause and effect is also contained in the parable because, in John's view, the possession of freedom
carries with it the right to confer freedom.

This point is made clear in vv. 34-36, which need to be considered as an integrated whole, in spite of the fact that the core of it is the parable from the tradition, which is both preceded and followed by midrashic exposition:

> Amen, amen I say to you,
> every one who commits sin is a slave.[16]
>> A slave does not continue in a house for ever;
>> a son continues for ever.
> So if the Son makes you free, you will be free indeed.

The contrast, then, is between the one who commits sin (identified with the slave of the parable) and the Son (identified with, and indeed incapable of being distinguished from, the son of the parable). The one who commits sin does not continue for ever. In other words, his sinfulness leads to death, or exclusion from eternal life and the authority to confer it. This double interpretation depends upon the oscillation in the meaning of the parable, which at one level concerns the sons of God in general, as intended by Jesus in the original saying, but at another level can be applied to Jesus as the unique Son of God. As such he is the agent of God for the salvation of God's people. In this application of the parable it is essential that John should make it unmistakably plain that what he is talking about is the capacity for eternal life, and this is why he has altered the parable. But he values the reference to freedom in the original, because it allows him to make the distinction between having freedom and conferring freedom, which he uses as the basis of v. 36. Here we have the principle of cause and effect, already laid out in vv. 31-32, where the idea of freedom was used. But we can see now that freedom denotes eternal life as far as John is concerned, although eternal life is a phrase which is never actually used in this discourse.

After these preliminaries John can indicate the unique position of Jesus by following through the principle which he has enunciated, along with a rigorous application of the dualism suggested by the contrast of slave and son. The essential requirement for eternal life is to believe in Jesus. The refusal of the Jews to believe in him is identified with their intention to kill him. Their wish to kill him is the result of an attitude of falsehood,

---

16. Nearly all texts add τῆς ἁμαρτίας, but it is omitted by D b sy^s; Clem. This is evidence that texts without it were current in the second century, and it is very likely that we have here a genuine case of 'western non-interpolation'. Though the insertion does not affect the sense, it introduces a personification of sin which is foreign to the context, and breaks the artistic balance between slave (v. 34) and free (v. 36). But it was an obvious addition to make, possibly under the influence of Rom. 6.20.

and falsehood comes from the devil. This represents one side of the con-trast. On the other side there is Jesus who conveys truth which leads to life. Thus life is the result of truth, and truth comes from God. This argument is set out briefly in v. 38, and then worked out in detail in vv. 39-47.

So far John has been concerned with the dualistic contrast and the sequence of cause and effect on either side. But he has still not reached the point which he really wished to make when he selected the saying on slave and son from his stock of traditional material. He has shown how the Son channels freedom, or life, but he has not explained what it means to possess it by right. This aspect of the argument is taken up in the remaining verses. To make the point, John introduces another saying from the tradition (v. 51): 'Amen, amen I say to you, if any one keeps my word, he will never see (v. 52: taste) death'. Here again it is possible to strip the text of Johannisms and relate it to a synoptic parallel (Mk 9.1):

Mk 9.1	Jn 8.51-52
ἀμὴν λέγω ὑμῖν	ἀμὴν ἀμὴν λέγω ὑμῖν
ὅτι εἰσίν τινες	ἐάν τις
ὧδε τῶν ἑστηκότων οἵτινες	τὸν ἐμὸν λόγον τηρήσῃ,
οὐ μὴ γεύσωνται θανάτου	οὐ μὴ γεύσηται θανάτου
ἕως ἂν ἴδωσιν τὴν βασιλείαν	εἰς τὸν αἰῶνα.
τοῦ θεοῦ ἐληλυθυῖαν ἐν δυνάμει.	

John has two substantial differences from Mark. In the first place he has substituted for the subject of the verb 'taste' a conditional clause based on the opening words of the discourse in v. 31 (ἐὰν ὑμεῖς μείνητε ἐν τῷ λόγῳ τῷ ἐμῷ). This, of course, did refer to 'some of those standing here', as in Mark. Thus this change can be regarded as merely explana-tory, elucidating the terms of the original in relation to the present dis-course, without requiring an underlying text different from Mark.[17] In

17. It is not my intention to claim that the saying used by John was identical with Mk 9.1, though the argument shows that all the differences from it in Jn 8.51 can be explained from John's editorial work. There are several other instances of ἀμὴν λέγω ὑμῖν...οὐ μὴ...ἕως...in both Mark and Q, cf. Mt. 10.23b; 23.39; 24.34 (= Mk 13.30, which uses μέχρις); Mk 14.25; Lk. 22.16, 18; Lk. 22.34 = Jn 13.38 (cf. Mt. 26.34 = Mk 14.30); cf. also Lk. 2.26. As all these sayings have a good claim to be considered authentic on other grounds, it would seem that we have here a stylistic feature of Jesus' speech. There is thus again no reason to assume that John was actually dependent on Mark here.

the second place, John has abandoned the reference to the coming of the kingdom of God, simply finishing the saying with εἰς τὸν αἰῶνα, which recalls the other saying in v. 35. It is easy to see that John would not wish to speak of the coming of the kingdom. The kingdom to John is a static concept, which can almost be identified with the truth (18.36-37). He has retained it in the traditional saying of 3.3, 5, because it is there a state which can be entered. But the discourse of ch. 3 soon shows that the proper concept from John's point of view is eternal life. It thus seems necessary to suppose that οὐ μὴ ... εἰς τὸν αἰῶνα in the present verse is more than the idiomatic strong negative so frequently used by John, and refers to the coming age. On the other hand it is not followed up in this way, and all the emphasis goes on the idea of not dying. This is the point which John needs. In the past men have always died, including Abraham himself. But Jesus surpasses Abraham. He is not limited by the normal span of life, which ends in death. In the same way his life from the beginning cannot be measured in terms of years (v. 57). Therefore he can say, ἀμὴν ἀμὴν λέγω ὑμῖν, πρὶν Ἀβραὰμ γενέσθαι ἐγὼ εἰμί (v. 58).

The last stages of the argument are extremely tortuous. John has not found it easy to produce such a statement on the basis of the sayings of Jesus that are known to him. In particular, the background of v. 58 is not easily determined. Like the sayings from the tradition in vv. (34) 35 and 51-52, it is solemnly introduced with the Amen formula, but it scarcely seems likely that John is indebted to the sayings tradition on this occasion. On the other hand the absolute ἐγώ εἰμι has been used at the end of the preceding discourse in 8.24, 28. Though the meaning was different there (I am he), it was almost certainly derived from Scripture (cf. Isa. 43.10), and the same may apply in this case. Here we have to find parallels to the exceptional use of ἐγώ εἰμι to denote 'I am in existence'.[18] The best parallel (noted by Bultmann) is Ps. 90.2, though there it is in the second person (LXX Ps. 89.2): πρὸ τοῦ ὄρη γενηθῆναι καὶ πλασθῆναι τὴν γῆν καὶ τὴν οἰκουμένην καὶ ἀπὸ τοῦ αἰῶνος ἕως

---

18. It is possible that ἐγώ εἰμι should be construed here as in 8.24, 28, i.e. 'Before Abraham came into existence, I am he', i.e. 'I am the same' (cf. Isa. 43.10). In any case there seems to be no direct reference to the divine name of Exod. 3.14 (ἐγώ εἰμι ὁ ὤν), except in so far as the notion of existence in a context dealing with origination from God (cf. v. 47) would easily bring it to mind. But the point of v. 58 is not to assert that Jesus is the abiding expression of God, but that he exists from before creation.

τοῦ αἰῶνος σὺ εἶ.[19] The thought here is close to that of Wisdom in Sir. 24.9: πρὸ τοῦ αἰῶνος ἀπ᾽ ἀρχῆς ἔκτισέν με, καὶ ἕως αἰῶνος οὐ μὴ ἐκλίπω. There is a Hebrew parallel with the first person in Prov. 8.27 (*bhkynw šmym šm 'ny*), but the Septuagint differs here. But we may note also Prov. 8.23 and 25 (πρὸ τοῦ αἰῶνος ἐθεμελίωσέν με ἐν ἀρχῇ...πρὸ τοῦ ὄρη ἑδρασθῆναι, πρὸ δὲ πάντων βουνῶν γεννᾷ με). The idea of the time span from aeon to aeon is a striking feature of these texts, and reminds us that the Son μένει εἰς τὸν αἰῶνα. Against this background the sleight of hand, whereby John changes from continuance into the future to continuance from the past, begins to seem less arbitrary. When he says 'Before Abraham was', he is substituting Abraham for an expression of the creation (cf. πρὸ τοῦ ὄρη γενηθῆναι).[20]

The first saying from the tradition in this discourse (v. 35) gave a static view of Jesus as the possessor of eternal life, though the underlying saying itself provided the principle of cause and effect by using the concept of freedom (v. 36). The second saying (vv. 51-52) concentrated attention on the effect, the capacity of Jesus to give eternal life. This enabled John to move his argument in such a way that he could finally adapt a Wisdom Scripture to express the pre-existence of Jesus, which was what he had set out to demonstrate. Thus, unlike 3.14 and 6.53, the second saying does not introduce the theme of the passion, even though it is concerned with death. But it has helped John's purpose, because the opening saying on slave and son did not really contain the theme of eternal life at all, and it needed to be supplemented by another traditional item in which this theme was actually stated. This is what John has been able to do by drawing on a saying comparable to Mk 9.1.

19. MT *'attah 'El*. But LXX has read *'El* as the negative *'al*, and taken it with the next verse.

20. If 8.58 is modelled on the Wisdom sayings, with Abraham replacing the mountains as a symbol of antiquity, we may suspect that John's thought has been assisted by Isa. 51.1-2: ἐμβλέψατε εἰς τὴν στερεὰν πέτραν, ἣν ἐλατομήσατε... ἐμβλέψατε εἰς Ἀβραὰμ τὸν πατέρα ὑμῶν... For John's debt to Deutero-Isaiah (not, however, referring to this possible connection), see G. Reim, *Studien zum alttestamentlichen Hintergrund des Johannesevangelium* (SNTSM, 22; Cambridge: Cambridge University Press, 1974), pp. 162-82.

V

The four discourses with which we have been concerned in this article do not exhaust the evidence for the use of traditional sayings in the Johannine discourses. But they provide excellent examples of the relationship of John to the common tradition. John values the tradition, because he honestly believes that his christology is consistent with it, and indeed is the truth which it contains. It is a great mistake to suppose that John is at odds with the tradition on which he depends. The disputes in John are against the unbelieving Jews, not against fellow-Christians of differing views. John is not arguing against an inferior christology, but against a high and sophisticated regard for the Jewish law as the complete embodiment of the will of God. The claim that the law has been superseded from this point of view by the act of God in Christ had a profound effect upon the development of christology. The beginnings of this effect can already be seen in the writings of Paul. In John we see the same situation at a later stage. Christian claims concerning Jesus have developed, and the breach between church and synagogue has widened into an almost impassable gulf. Meanwhile the corporate memory of Jesus has moved away from the direct and vivid familiarity with his historic origins which can still be seen in Mark, and which is so skilfully evoked by Luke. The idea of Jesus as the Son of God has begun to take over from the memory of him as a man. John wishes to bring his readers into vital relationship with Jesus, because this is the means of salvation. He is less concerned with presenting Jesus as a model for moral example, and he does not seek to expound the teaching of Jesus by means of a commentary upon the tradition. Hence he is concerned to establish an intellectual position, maintained in the mind by a deeply felt emotion. It only confuses the issue to refer to this as mysticism. But, seeing that the point of importance to John is the mental attitude of the believer, it is inevitable that his position should appear to constitute a step in the direction of gnosticism. It is thus not surprising that the opening words of the *Gospel of Thomas* should be an adaptation of Jn 8.51-52, which we have considered in this study.[21]

21. *Gos. Thom.*, Pref. and 1: 'These are the secret words which the living Jesus spoke, and (which) Didymus Judas Thomas wrote. And he said: He who finds the explanation (ἑρμηνεία) of these words will not taste death' (cf. P.Oxy. 654, ουτοι οι λογοι οι (...) λησεν Ιης ο ξων κ (...) και Θωμα. και ειπεν (...) α ν των λογων τουτ (...) ου μη γευσηται); *Gos. Thom.* 18 and 19: '...Blessed

In spite of these developments, which simply reflect the transition of Christianity from the apostolic age to the second century scene, John did make a notable effort to ground the beliefs of his time and milieu in the actual sayings of Jesus. The way in which he adapted them for his purpose may not seem strictly legitimate to us today. But he believed in the continuity of the faith which he had received, and he was not intentionally an innovator. The issues which he had to face in the debate with the synagogue could not be answered simply by quoting the tradition. John thus attempted to seize the essential meaning of the sayings of Jesus which were available to him, and adapted them to meet the actual situation which was pressing upon him. This is the reason for the historical tension of the Fourth Gospel,[22] which appeals to the truth of the tradition, but at the same time treats it in a highly creative and original manner. One facet of this work is John's method of structuring the discourses, in which his theological positions are advanced, around the sayings of Jesus himself.

(μακάριος) is he who will stand at the beginning (ἀρχή), and he will know the end and will not taste death. Jesus said: Blessed (μακάριος) is he who was before he became. If you become my disciples (μαθητής) (and) hear my words, these stones will minister (διακονεῖν) to you...He who will know them will not taste death.' There seem to be allusions to Jn 8.31, 51-52, and perhaps even 58, here.

22. See the essay on this subject in E.C. Hoskyns and F.N. Davey, *The Fourth Gospel* (London: Faber and Faber, 2nd edn, 1947), pp. 58-85.

JSNT 23 (1985), pp. 83-97

THE FAITH OF THE BELOVED DISCIPLE AND THE COMMUNITY IN JOHN 20

Brendan Byrne

Among the many distinctive features in the Fourth Gospel's treatment of the resurrection of Jesus is the presence of 'the other disciple, the one whom Jesus loved' alongside Peter in the first episode at the empty tomb (20.1-10). The scene, in fact, reaches its climax in the Johannine account when we are told (v. 8) that this disciple, upon entry into the tomb, 'saw and believed', and so became, according to this Gospel, the first believer in the resurrection of Jesus. Scholarly study and comment upon this episode has tended to be arrested by the 'race' to the tomb on the part of this disciple and Peter and has dwelt heavily on the relationship between the two figures in the mind of the evangelist and of the community from whom and for whom he wrote. Far less attention has been paid to what the two disciples actually saw in the tomb and how what they saw brought at least one of them, the 'Beloved Disciple', to faith in the resurrection. This is despite the fact that the evangelist goes to considerable lengths in his description of what was to be seen in the tomb and seems, with the simple but dramatic phrase, 'he saw and he believed', to want to associate this vision very closely with the disciple's coming to faith. In the present study I should like to re-examine this episode, paying particular attention to the link between vision and faith, and to do so within the broader context of John 20, since, as I shall argue, various details in the account and the structure of the chapter as a whole suggest that the faith of the Beloved Disciple is to be seen as both precursive and typical of that of later generations of believers.

In making this study of John 20 and of the first episode at the tomb in particular, I am writing to some extent in response to an article on the same chapter by the Australian scholar, Francis Moloney.[1] In recent years Moloney has made the investigation of 'journeys of faith' in John and their reflection in the structure of the Gospel a subject of particular concern.[2] His pursuit of this theme with respect to faith in the resurrection of Jesus in ch. 20 represents a noteworthy contribution to the scholarly literature on John 20, especially in its treatment of the appearance to Mary Magdalene and to Thomas. Because his study appeared in a publication unlikely to be accessible to a wide audience, I shall give a summary of Moloney's thesis, as well as indicating where I see it standing in need of correction and further development.

For Moloney the episodes in John 20 featuring the Beloved Disciple (vv. 1-10), Mary Magdalene (vv. 11-18) and Thomas (vv. 24-29) show persons who passed through stages of faith to complete a journey from unbelief to full faith in the risen Lord and so serve to remind later generations of believers that they too have a journey to make which will enable them to enter fully into the experience of those who actually knew Jesus.[3] The analysis of the episodes with Mary Magdalene and Thomas shows a three-stage growth in faith.[4] Both pass from a state of complete disbelief in the resurrection to an intermediate stage where, in differing ways, there is a desire to impose conditions and to control. Mary (v. 16) recognizes the Jesus she has known and seems to want to stay simply with the restored relationship, as is indicated by the address, 'Rabboni', and the attempt to cling to him. Thomas (v. 25) on hearing the disciples' report, 'We have seen the Lord', does not reject the resurrection out of hand, but lays down his conditions of belief. In both cases Jesus moves to indicate that faith must go further than this. Mary must allow him to ascend to the Father and inaugurate a new relationship between God and believers (v. 17), of which she is to be the proclaimer. Thomas is challenged (v. 27) by an offer, first of all, to fulfil his conditions, followed by an invitation to 'cease his doubting and believe'. This

1. 'John 20: A Journey Completed', *Australasian Catholic Record* 59 (1982), pp. 417-32.

2. Cf. F. Moloney, 'From Cana to Cana (Jn 2.1–4.54) and the Fourth Evangelist's Concept of Correct (and Incorrect) Faith', in E.A. Livingstone (ed.), *Studia Biblica 1978*. II. *Papers on the Gospels, Sixth International Congress on Biblical Studies, Oxford 3–7 April* (JSNTSup, 2; Sheffield: JSOT Press, 1980), pp. 185-213.

3. 'John 20', p. 426.

4. For analysis of these episodes see Moloney, 'John 20', pp. 427-31.

elicits from him the supreme christological confession of the gospel: 'My Lord and my God' (v. 28). In these two cases, Moloney has, it seems to me, most convincingly and fruitfully established the pattern of the three-stage growth in faith. That is the lasting and substantial contribution of his study.

The attempt, however, to bring the faith of the Beloved Disciple into this scheme is far more problematic. Moloney makes a great deal of the actual 'race' to the tomb and builds this into the Disciple's 'journey of faith'.[5] But in so doing he pays very little heed to what the Disciple actually saw in the tomb and the part this vision played in his coming to faith. In these and other respects, notably the interpretation of v. 9, this analysis seems to me to miss the central thrust of this first episode at the tomb and so misconstrues the link between the faith of this Disciple and that of the subsequent community—a link which Moloney himself is anxious to forge.

In the present study my thesis will be that what the Beloved Disciple sees in the tomb constitutes a 'sign' for him and that this makes his believing something truly anticipatory of that of subsequent believers, those upon whom the Lord pronounces the blessing in v. 29b. I shall also devote more consideration to the evening appearance of the Lord to the disciples (vv. 19-23) and argue that this episode also can be drawn into the three-stage faith pattern which Moloney correctly identifies in the appearances to Mary Magdalene and Thomas. In this way I hope to establish for John 20 a structural symmetry with respect to faith tighter even than that proposed by Moloney himself.

The Faith of the Beloved Disciple at the Tomb (John 20.1-10)

It is generally agreed from comparison with Synoptic material that the Fourth Evangelist's account of the episodes at the tomb of Jesus is based on traditions about the discovery of the empty tomb by the women disciples.[6] Traces of this material are probably to be detected in the plural 'we do not know...' placed upon the lips of Mary Magdalene

5.   Moloney, 'John 20', p. 424, actually entitles the whole episode described in vv. 2-10 as 'The race to the tomb'.

6.   See the lengthy analysis given by R.E. Brown, *The Gospel according to John XIII–XXI* (AB, 29A; New York: Doubleday, 1970), pp. 996-1004; also R. Schnackenburg, *Das Johannesevangelium*. III. *Kommentar zu Kap 13–21* (HTKNT 4.3; Freiburg: Herder, 2nd edn, 1976), pp. 355-61.

at the end of v. 2. Luke 24.12 preserves a tradition where Peter runs to the tomb on hearing the women's report, sees the situation there much as in the Johannine account, but leaves 'wondering at what had happened', that is, without coming to faith.[7] What is really novel and distinctive about the Johannine version of the episode is the provision of a companion for Peter in his running and his discovery, the Beloved Disciple, whose coming to faith (v. 8) becomes the climax of the whole affair.[8] In this first episode at the tomb, as distinct from the events described in vv. 11-18, Mary Magdalene serves only to set the story in motion with her report about the disappearance of Jesus' body. Peter, though worsted in the race, enters the tomb before the other disciple and is the first to see the full disposition of the burial clothes. But, in contrast to what we are soon to be told concerning his companion, we are not told anything about his state of faith at this point. He is yoked together with the Beloved Disciple in the plural statements of vv. 9-10 and one could perhaps argue from this that he is implicitly included in the statement about coming to faith in v. 8. Scholars divide upon this point.[9] But one thing is clear: the evangelist, while retaining the tradition about Peter's presence at the tomb, chose to be silent concerning his state of faith. To the question of Peter's faith I shall return later on. For the present I should like simply to underline the way in which the evangelist gives the Beloved Disciple centre stage.

Moloney in his concern to find a 'journey of faith' in these resurrection accounts of John 20 includes the 'race to the tomb' as an element in the Beloved Disciple's journey of faith.[10] This is surely misleading. The race to the tomb on the part of the two disciples shows both their anxiety and their deep residual love for the Master they have lost. The

---

7.   For an excellent discussion of the relationship between the Lukan and Johannine traditions with respect to this common feature of having Peter at the tomb of Jesus, see B. Lindars, *The Gospel of John* (NCB; London: Oliphants, 1972), p. 602.

8.   Cf. Schnackenburg, *Johannesevangelium*, III, p. 368: 'In dem klaren und festen Glauben des beliebten Jüngers liegt die Pointe der Erzählung'.

9.   See the list given by Schnackenburg, *Johannesevangelium*, III, p. 369 n. 33. Brown, *John XIII–XXI*, pp. 1004-05, argues strongly against any suggestion that Peter comes to faith at this point since in his view such an interpretation destroys the contrast the evangelist wants to make between Peter who does not believe and the Beloved Disciple who does.

10.   See 'John 20', pp. 424, 426-27.

faster running of the Beloved Disciple (vv. 4, 8) shows, presumably, his greater degree of love and in the mind of the evangelist this greater love seems to imply a keener predisposition to faith. But the race itself is not undertaken with any flickering of faith in the resurrection. To suggest that such is the case is to ignore the clear statement made in v. 9 explaining why only at that point, that is, when confronted with the full sight of the abandoned grave clothes, could the Beloved Disciple come to faith.[11] Before that, since they had not understood the Scripture's witness that Jesus must rise from the dead, there was simply no stirring of resurrection faith. John seems to me to want to make this very clear. To build the race into a journey of faith obscures the evangelist's detailed description of what precisely brought the Beloved Disciple to the instantaneous, yet mature, act of faith expressed in the firm aorists, 'and he saw and he believed'.[12] It is now appropriate to examine in greater detail what it is that brings this disciple to faith according to the Johannine account.

In the verses immediately preparatory to the statement about the Beloved Disciple's seeing and believing, that is, in vv. 5-7, the evangelist distinguishes very clearly between what can be seen from outside the tomb looking in and what one sees upon actual entry into the tomb. In v. 5 the Beloved Disciple, who has arrived first at the tomb, bends down, looks in and sees 'the linen cloths lying there (*keimena ta othonia*)'. But, the evangelist explicitly tells us, he does not enter the tomb. Peter then comes up, enters the tomb and sees what the other

11. Moloney's handling of v. 9 is confusing. In most cases where he makes allusion to the statement it contains ('John 20', pp. 426, 427, 430, 431) he finds an indication that the journey of faith must go on. This must refer primarily to the faith of the Johannine community, since for Moloney the Beloved Disciple arrives at perfect faith in v. 8 (p. 426). But the treatment of v. 9 on p. 423 implies that even his faith must journey on. I suggest that though v. 9 does contain an implicit allusion to the future in terms of the community's faith, Moloney fails to notice the role the verse plays in this scene primarily by summing up the *past* situation, i.e. by telling us why the Beloved Disciple came to faith for the first time at this point and not before.

12. It is generally agreed that the evangelist understands the Beloved Disciple to arrive at full faith at this point: cf. Brown, *John XIII–XXI*, p. 987; Lindars, *John*, p. 602; Schnackenburg, *Johannesevangelium*, III, p. 368; Moloney, 'John 20', p. 426. Another problem involved in building the 'race' into the Disciple's 'journey' of faith is that logically Mary Magdalene's running (albeit in the opposite direction) should likewise be incorporated into her 'journey of faith'. Yet I have the impression that for Moloney this is not the case.

disciple saw: the linen cloths lying there (*ta othonia keimena*). But he also sees from this position something more: 'the napkin (*soudarion*), which had been on his head, not lying with the linen cloths but rolled up in a place by itself'.[13] With respect to what one can see, the difference between being inside the tomb and remaining outside is this sight of the *soudarion*, which unlike the rest of the grave clothes cannot be seen from outside. When finally the Beloved Disciple enters the tomb (v. 8) 'he sees and he believes'. We are not told explicitly what he sees—the verb being left without an object perhaps because the evangelist wants to preserve, in a way anticipatory of v. 29, a more generalized phrase about 'seeing and believing'. But the whole build-up from the preceding statements suggests that he now sees what Peter saw from the same position: the linen cloths *and* the *soudarion* rolled up in a place by itself. It is the latter which has made all the difference.

In asking the question as to what brought the Beloved Disciple to faith at this point scholars tend to divide upon whether it was the mere presence of the abandoned grave clothes that ruled out purely natural explanations (grave robbery, etc.) or whether it had something to do with their position or form, in particular an indication that the risen Jesus passed through the cloths in a way that left them (miraculously) undisturbed. Brown critically reviews interpretations of the latter kind and rejects them on the grounds that all rely upon what is 'at most implied in John xx 19, namely that the risen body of Jesus had the power to pass through solid objects'.[14] He further notes that such interpretations also have difficulty with what seems to be by far the most acceptable translation of v. 7, namely the one suggesting that the *soudarion* was rolled up in a place by itself away from the other cloths. Brown's rejection of interpretations along these lines appears sound. But this does not mean that he is to be followed in abandoning all forms of the explanation that sees the position of the clothes as the relevant factor and in reverting simply to the theory that it was the mere presence of the clothes that led to faith. To do so would be to neglect the key distinction the evangelist has been making all along between the view of the clothes one has from outside the tomb and the fuller vision gained upon entry within. The theory holding the position of the clothes to be significant has validity provided one notes that its vital feature according to the

13. So the accepted translation; for the difficulties posed by alternatives, see the critical review given by Brown, *John XIII–XXI*, p. 986.

14. Brown, *John XIII-XXI*, pp. 1007-08.

thrust of the Johannine narrative is the separate location and state of the *soudarion*.[15]

We must now ask how the separate position of the *soudarion* could play such a decisive role in the arousal of faith. Mention of the *soudarion* calls to mind a detail from the episode of the raising of Lazarus in ch. 11. At the climax of this account (v. 44) we are told: 'The dead man came out, his hands and feet bound with bandages, and his face wrapped with a cloth (*soudarion*). Jesus said to them, "Unbind him, and let him go".' The connection between the raising of Lazarus and the resurrection of Jesus is by no means clear and most scholars simply note the possible link and pass on.[16] But the raising of Lazarus, as is generally agreed, plays a central role in this Gospel in that it sets in motion the events leading to the arrest, trial and execution of Jesus (cf. especially the High Priest's advice in 11.49-53).[17] More particularly, it presents Jesus as the one who deliberately put his own life at risk by coming to Judaea in order to give life to his 'friend'. The motif of the love of Jesus for Lazarus receives strong and reiterated stress from the evangelist—cf. vv. 3, 5 and 36. Lazarus who is given life through Jesus laying down his own life thus becomes the point of insertion for every believer who reads the Gospel and who can say with this 'beloved disciple', 'the Good Shepherd laid down his life in love in order to give life to me'.

In view, then, of this role played by Lazarus in the climactic events of the gospel, it is not unreasonable to expect that the parallelism between his death and raising and the death and resurrection of Jesus should be

15. In a final comment on this matter Brown argues that such a theory demands 'that Peter also should have come to believe...since he can hardly have missed the import' (of the position of the clothes) (*John XIII-XXI*, p. 1008) and Brown has already decided quite firmly that Peter did not come to faith. But this precisely begs the whole question. To have recourse as Brown does to Lk. 24.12, where it is clearly indicated that Peter remains unbelieving, represents in my opinion a wholly uncharacteristic lapse of exegetical judgment. How can the Lukan text decide an issue which the Johannine account leaves open—probably quite deliberately?

16. Cf. Brown, *John XIII-XXI*, pp. 986, 1008; Moloney, 'John 20', p. 426; Schnackenburg, *Johannesevangelium*, III, p. 367, devotes more consideration to the connection, but plays it down eventually on the grounds of the difference of vocabulary (*keiriai* in 11.44; *othonia* in 20.5-7) and detail (the *soudarion* on Lazarus's *face* in 11.44; said to have been on Jesus' *head* in 20.7).

17. Cf. C.H. Dodd, *The Interpretation of the Fourth Gospel* (Cambridge: Cambridge University Press, 1953), p. 367; Brown, *John XIII–XXI*, pp. 429-30.

running at this point. What the neatly folded and separately lying *soudarion* indicates is that whereas Lazarus was completely passive in his coming back to life, entirely reliant upon the command of Jesus and needing others to remove the facial cloth and so restore him to full human and social life, Jesus has actively raised himself. The neatly folded, separately placed facial cloth would appear to be the culminating indication of this totally self-possessed, majestic act of Jesus—an action aptly summed up in the statement of the Good Shepherd: 'No one takes it [my life] from me, but I lay it down of my own accord. I have the power to lay it down, and I have the power to take it again; this charge I have received from my Father' (10.18). Even without the Lazarus parallel the separately placed *soudarion* would thus serve to indicate the active rising of Jesus. But on the grounds suggested above an implicit allusion to the raising of Lazarus remains, in my opinion, highly likely.

In Johannine terms it is probably correct, in view of this pattern of associations stemming from chs. 10–11, to regard the separately lying *soudarion* as constituting a 'sign' for the Beloved Disciple. All the other resurrection witnesses (with the possible exception of Peter whose state of faith is uncertain, as we have seen) come to faith after the resurrection through a vision of the risen Lord. They see him and they believe. The Beloved Disciple does not see the risen Lord and yet he comes to faith on the basis of what he sees in the tomb, which for him is a genuine sign leading to full faith. 'Sign' faith is, of course, variously evaluated in John's Gospel.[18] But where such faith is negatively rated (e.g., 2.23-24; 3.2-3; 4.45-48; 6.14-15; 7.3-7) the problem is not so much that a sign initiates the process of faith as that the preoccupation with the sign proceeds from purely human categories and needs in a way that obscures rather than serves the divine revelation in Jesus. Such is not the case with the 'sign' faith of the Beloved Disciple. Along with the others, he had not understood the Scripture's witness that Jesus would rise from the dead (v. 9). So his faith, like theirs, had failed at the death of the Master. But greater love had quickened in him a keener sensitivity to signals of Jesus' risen life. Without seeing Jesus himself, he sees the sign

---

18. Cf. Dodd, *Interpretation*, pp. 141-43; R.E. Brown, *The Gospel according to John I-XXX* (AB, 29; New York: Doubleday, 1966), pp. 525-31, esp. 528-31; Schnackenburg, *The Gospel according to St John*, I (London/: Burns & Oates; New York: Herder & Herder, 1968), Excursus IV: 'The Johannine "Signs"', pp. 515-28; J.L. Martyn, *History and Theology in the Fourth Gospel* (Nashville: Abingdon Press, 2nd edn, 1979), pp. 93ff.

provided by the burial clothes and he believes.[19]

The phrase about 'seeing and believing' in v. 9 immediately evokes the culminating statement of the original Gospel (i.e. the Gospel less ch. 21) where Jesus pronounces a blessing upon those who come to faith without having seen: 'Because you [Thomas] have seen me you have believed. Blessed are those who have not seen and yet believe.' Is there any link in the evangelist's mind between the faith of the Beloved Disciple at the tomb and the faith of those subsequent generations who, unlike Thomas, Mary and the disciples gathered on the Sunday evening, must come to faith without a vision of the risen Lord? Brown notes that 'it has become fashionable...to see in his faith a dramatic anticipation of what Jesus will say to Thomas in xx.29b', but he contests this seeing that 'he believed on the basis of what he saw in the tomb, not on the basis of hearing, as would those envisaged in 29b'. Since 'he saw and he believed' he is clearly not one of those 'who have not seen and yet have believed'.[20] Moloney raises the same question and is inclined to see the Beloved Disciple as at least included under the macarism of v. 29b in the sense that he believes without having seen the risen Jesus.[21] The difficulties provided by v. 9, however, lead this scholar to draw, in a rather obscure fashion, a parallel between the Disciple's 'journey' of faith and that which the subsequent community has to make, founded on the experience of the resurrection witnesses and nourished further by reflection upon the Scriptures.[22]

Pace Brown and taking a somewhat different approach from that of Moloney, I should like to maintain that the evangelist does intend to forge a link between the faith of the Beloved Disciple and that of the later believers blessed in v. 29b. The point is not that of 'not seeing and

19. In ch. 21 (vv. 6-7) the abundant draught of fish will function in precisely the same way as a 'sign' for the Beloved Disciple. It leads him in his greater sensitivity to recognize the figure on the beach as the risen Lord and he communicates this to Peter.

20. *John XIII–XXI*, p. 1005.

21. 'John 20', p. 426.

22. On the difficulties provided by Moloney's interpretation of v. 9 see n. 11 above. Moloney, 'John 20', p. 426, raises the problems caused for him by v. 9 and then goes on: 'The solution to these problems is to be found by seeing that exactly the same thing happens in vv. 24-29, where Thomas' faith is met by a question concerning the grounds of faith and the beatitude of those who believe without seeing (vv. 28-29).' But what is it in v. 9 that 'exactly the same thing' refers to—since on Moloney's interpretation there is nothing 'exact' about v. 9?

yet believing', but rather of 'not seeing *Jesus* and yet believing'.[23] We should note the pronoun in the first part of Jesus' statement to Thomas: 'Because you have seen *me* you have believed'. The force of this is presumably to be carried on to the macarism that follows: 'Blessed are those who have not seen [me] and yet believe'. By leaving out the pronoun here the evangelist can reinforce the reminiscence of the 'he saw and he believed' in v. 8, where, as we have noted, the object of the 'seeing' is likewise omitted.

The Beloved Disciple does, of course, see something: he sees, as I have argued, the 'sign' constituted by the special arrangement of the burial clothes. What, one may ask, does the blessed community see? Are they not, as Brown maintains, in a totally different situation, since they do not see but on the contrary have to rely solely on what they have heard from the first witnesses and the later preaching?

To meet this difficulty and find the true basis of the congruence between the faith of the Beloved Disciple and that of the blessed community we have to look ahead to the evangelist's statement of purpose given in vv. 30-31. This culminating statement reverts to the language of 'signs'. It speaks of the 'many other signs' which Jesus did in the presence of his disciples, 'which are not written in this book', and goes on to assert that 'these are written that you may believe that Jesus is the Christ, the Son of God, and that believing you may have life in his name'.[24] That is, the testimony about Jesus provided for subsequent generations by this Gospel is precisely a testimony about his signs and it is testimony designed to promote faith through the recounting of these signs—a true and genuine 'sign' faith. The Gospel is written precisely so that the later generations who cannot have the unique privilege of seeing either the earthly or the risen Jesus can nonetheless join the pilgrimage of the first disciples—so that they can hear the opening invitation,

23. Cf. Lindars, *John*, p. 602.

24. The question of whether the evangelist has in mind here the faith of initial conversion or the on-going belief of the Christian cannot be decided solely on the basis of the preferred textual variant (the aorist subjunctive *pisteusēte* or the present subjunctive *pisteuēte* respectively) since the tense usage in this respect is not rigid; cf. Schnackenburg, *Johannesevangelium*, II, pp. 403-404. The interpretation given in this paper, where a parallel is drawn between the coming to faith of the Beloved Disciple and that of the later community, would favour the former alternative (initial faith)—but the idea of a growth in faith as one progressed through the Gospel is certainly not to be excluded and, again, the evangelist may have wished to leave both possibilities open.

'Come and see' (1.39), so that they can 'see' the 'greater things' promised in 1.50 and, all in all, come to see in the total career of Jesus the glory of the God whom no one has ever seen made visible in Jesus Christ (1.18). In this way, it seems to me, one can maintain that just as the Beloved Disciple saw a sign and so came to believe in the resurrection of Jesus without seeing Jesus himself, so the subsequent generations through the Gospel's witness to the signs of Jesus can come to faith in similar fashion without direct vision of him. In this lies the true point of connection between what is said of the Beloved Disciple in v. 8 and the macarism pronounced by the Lord in v. 29b.

The Structure and Scope of John 20 as a Whole

Looking more broadly now at the whole range of the resurrection story in ch. 20, we can see that it begins and ends with a similar kind of believing in the risen Jesus: the faith of the Beloved Disciple and that of the subsequent community. If the parallel I have argued for has any validity, it is right to see in the former a 'dramatic anticipation' of the latter and to view both as forming the outer frames, as it were, of the total narrative in terms of faith. What we have in between is the coming to faith of those who are granted visions of the risen Lord. As I have noted at the start, Moloney admirably describes this process in the case of Mary Magdalene and Thomas. The appearance to the disciples on the Sunday evening (vv. 19-23) is, however, given very short shrift. Moloney simply notes that the episode with Mary Magdalene is 'also followed by material which looks towards the Johannine community: the gift of the Spirit and the commission' and concludes somewhat prosaically, 'This moment in the story makes v. 9 and v. 29b possible, for without it, there would not have been a Johannine community'.[25]

In terms of Moloney's own analysis of the 'faith journeys' of the disciples much more can be made of this appearance to the disciples gathered together in the evening. The evangelist tells us nothing about their state of faith prior to the appearance of Jesus. To what extent they had believed Mary Magdalene's report we do not know. We are simply told that they had the doors locked through fear of the Jews. They are depicted as fearful, closed-in men. The appearance and greeting of Jesus and the showing of his hands and his side evokes in them recognition and joy: 'Then the disciples rejoiced when they saw the Lord' (v. 20).

25. 'John 20', p. 427.

This is simply 'recognition' faith, corresponding to the initial faith of Mary Magdalene after Jesus had called her by name (v. 16). But, as in her case, they are not simply to remain rejoicing in the restored presence of the Master they had known. They receive the promised gift of the Spirit, which is to equip them to carry on the reconciling mission that Jesus has from the Father. From being fearful men who sit behind closed doors clinging to a lost companionship now wonderfully restored, they are transformed into the community that is to proclaim 'We have seen the Lord' (cf. v. 25) and carry on the mission of Jesus now that he has returned to the Father. In this transformation we can surely detect a mature stage of faith corresponding to that which Moloney traces in the case of Mary and Thomas.

What is to be noted across these three central episodes of John 20 is the way in which the evangelist places stress on the announcements of having 'seen the Lord'. Mary makes this announcement to the disciples (v. 18); they in turn make it to Thomas (v. 25). His insistence upon a personal sight of the Lord and a share in the detailed inspection of Jesus' hands and side that they have been granted heightens the dramatic intensity concerning seeing and not seeing the risen Jesus before belief. It paves the way for the blessing pronounced in v. 29b upon those who believe without having personally seen the Lord. Everything seems to be building up to this climactic statement, anticipated in what is said of the Beloved Disciple in v. 8, which in a true sense delivers the entire Gospel into the hands of later generations.

In this way the neatness of construction which Moloney and other scholars have detected in so much of the Fourth Gospel has, I think, an even better claim for fulfilment in ch. 20 than his own analysis allows. The structure in terms of faith can be set out as follows:

Beloved Disciple	*Mary–Disciples–Thomas*	*Later Community*
'Sign' faith	'3-Stage' faith	'Sign' faith
(Believing, yet not seeing risen Jesus)	(Seeing Jesus and believing)	(Believing, yet not seeing risen Jesus).

The odd-man-out in all this is, of course, Peter. But perhaps we are now in a far better position to understand the evangelist's somewhat tongue-in-cheek approach to Peter in this chapter. The above analysis only serves to reinforce what has long been recognized about the first incident at the tomb, namely, that John wants the faith of the Beloved

Disciple to dominate the whole.[26] Peter is included in the incident perhaps because his central role in the historical tradition used by the evangelist in constructing his narrative was too well known to be eliminated (cf. Lk. 24.12), perhaps because the tradition of his being the prime resurrection witness (1 Cor. 15.4; Lk. 24.34) was too strong to be ignored. Moreover, his presence as 'competitor' for the Beloved Disciple in the race to the tomb does serve to bring out the greater love of this disciple and hence his greater readiness to see the 'sign' presented by the empty clothes. But the evangelist does not highlight Peter's faith because it is the faith of the Beloved Disciple that must have centre stage; that is something demanded by the whole construction of John 20. Nor is the relationship between the two as significant in this chapter as scholars have supposed.[27] I see no reason here to make distinctions, as Moloney does on the basis of ch. 21, between primacies of discipleship (Beloved Disciple) and authority (Peter).[28] There is nothing in this chapter about the authority of individual disciples. That is a later theological question—or at least a ch. 21 question, and it is a distraction to bring it in here. The evangelist neither denies Peter's primacy of faith nor explicitly affirms it. He certainly leaves room for it—and for this reason anti-Petrine interpretations have no foundation in this text. But Peter serves here as something of a foil for the faith of that 'other disciple' upon whom in John's design the central focus falls.

This in turn invites some final consideration of the role of the Beloved Disciple with respect to the faith of the later community. I do not wish to enter here into the question of his actual identity,[29] but simply to consider his role as it emerges from the internal evidence of the Gospel. Moloney speaks of him as 'the founding father, the inspiration and the

26. See n. 8 above.

27. Cf. esp. R. Bultmann, *The Gospel of John: A Commentary* (Oxford: Basil Blackwell, 1971), p. 685.

28. 'John 20', pp. 424-25.

29. On this matter see Brown, *John I–XII*, pp. xcii-xcviii; revised opinion in the same author's, *The Community of the Beloved Disciple* (New York: Paulist Press, 1979), pp. 30-34; Schnackenburg, *Johannesevangelium*, III, pp. 449-64. It is sometimes suggested that this disciple is to be identified with (the historical) Lazarus (cf. Brown, *John I–XII*, p. xcv). I would emphasize that the connection between Lazarus and the Beloved Disciple argued for in this paper is a literary and theological one only, confined to the structure of the Gospel; it does not imply any historical identification between the two.

model disciple for this community'.[30] While not denying the truth of all these roles sketched for him, my preference would be to describe him as the 'point of insertion' for the later generations into the pivotal events and experiences attested in the Gospel. One of the key concerns of this Gospel—perhaps even its central concern—is that of the 'absence' of Jesus for later generations. One has only to think of the 'going away' theme that dominates the Supper discourses (13.1, 3, 33, 36; 14.1-7, 12, 18-19, 25-31; 16.1-11, 16-22, 28; 17.11-13; cf. also 7.33-36; 8.21-22), the role of the Paraclete as 'the presence of Jesus when Jesus is absent'[31] and then this culminating concern in ch. 20 with the question of 'not seeing and yet believing'—and, one might add, the connected concern with not 'clinging' to Jesus but allowing him to go to the Father (v. 17). The Gospel of John seems to me to be composed very largely to give subsequent generations of believers access to the central events of Jesus' life, death, resurrection and return to the Father and to assure them that in this access they can have an encounter with Jesus every bit as valid and indeed more fruitful than that of those who actually saw him. It is above all through identification with the Beloved Disciple—with his being loved by Jesus and his return of love for Jesus—that later Christians can know that they are 'beloved' as he was, that Jesus laid down his life for them individually and personally and that they can experience the events of the Supper, death and resurrection with the closeness and intimacy to Jesus that the Gospel depicts of him.

True, these later believers cannot share the vision of Jesus that Mary, Thomas and the disciples gathered in the evening were granted. But they need not envy the first disciples or bemoan their lack of direct physical vision. They can believe in him through the 'signs' recorded in the Gospel, just as the Beloved Disciple came to believe through the sign given at the tomb. They can hear, too, the Lord pronounce them 'blessed' because a deeper, more creative faith is going to be drawn from their hearts. In this way the Gospel of John makes its own singular contribution to what is the central question of Christian theology: how the historical Jesus of Nazareth remains for all generations of mankind the abiding and saving revelation of God.

---

30. 'John 20', p. 426.
31. *John XIII–XXI*, p. 1141.

Additional Note

Since the completion of this paper in May 1983, there has appeared a study of Jn 20.1-10 by Dr Sandra M. Schneiders: 'The Face Veil: A Johannine Sign (Jn 20.1-10)', *BTB* 13.3 (1983), pp. 94-97. Dr Schneiders's study intersects with this present paper in its analysis of what the two disciples saw within the tomb (see pp. 95-96) and, as the title suggests, in regarding the position of the face veil as constituting a 'sign' for the Beloved Disciple. In interpreting the significance of the laid-aside veil, as well as in relating the episode to the remainder of John 20, Dr Schneiders takes a rather different tack. With respect to the face veil, she argues that its laid-aside condition evokes Jewish traditions, based upon Exod. 34.33-35, concerning Moses' ascent to God and so constitutes a 'sign' of Jesus' putting aside the veil of his flesh and ascent to the Father (p. 96). But the link with the Jewish tradition (in particular the proposed link between John's use of *soudarion* and the targumic Aramaic translation of the rare Hebrew word for 'veil' in Exod. 34.33-35) requires to my mind more convincing demonstration than is provided in the paper in question. Moreover, how is the claim that the laid-aside veil is a sign of Jesus' ascent to the Father to be reconciled with his statement to Mary Magdalene in the episode immediately following (20.17) that he has 'not yet ascended to the Father'? It seems preferable to relate the 'sign' in John 20 to the resurrection (cf. v. 9) rather than to the ascent of Jesus.

JSNT 49 (1993), pp. 21-44

THE BELOVED DISCIPLE AS IDEAL AUTHOR

Richard Bauckham

I

This article presupposes Martin Hengel's solution to 'the Johannine question' in his recent book.[1] For this solution Hengel has made a very impressive case, argued with a characteristic wealth of relevant learning and a characteristically sound historical judgment. In essence the solution is that John the Elder, to whom Papias refers in the famous fragment of his prologue (ap. Eusebius, *Hist. Eccl.* 3.39.4), was both the beloved disciple and the author of the Fourth Gospel, as well as the author of the three Johannine letters. This simple statement of Hengel's position would, to be fully accurate, require some minor qualifications, in respect both of the identity of John the Elder with the beloved disciple and of the extent of his authorship of the Fourth Gospel. We shall return to these qualifications later. But much of the cogency of Hengel's proposal lies in its essential simplicity, which, of course, runs quite counter to recent trends in Johannine studies, with their speculative reconstructions of the complex history of the Johannine community in relation to a variety of postulated Johannine authors and a variety of postulated stages of composition and redaction of the Gospel. Of course, simplicity is by no means self-evidently a virtue in historical reconstruction, since historical reality is often complex. In this case the simplicity of Hengel's solution is attractive because it adequately explains both the internal evidence of the Gospel and the external evidence about the Gospel,

---

1. M. Hengel, *The Johannine Question* (London: SCM Press; Philadelphia: Trinity Press International, 1989). Since Hengel's book provides abundant references to the relevant scholarly literature, such references will be kept to a minimum in the footnotes to this article.

whereas by contrast other solutions tend to set internal and external evidence against each other. The traditional attribution to John the son of Zebedee attempts to do justice to the external evidence, but at the price of imposing on the internal evidence an interpretation it can scarcely bear. More recent theories which tend to rely in principle on the internal evidence alone make the external evidence very difficult to explain.

The present article is one of a pair which take Hengel's position as their starting point. In the other[2] I have offered a detailed reassessment of the external evidence for the origin of the Gospel, demonstrating that the best external evidence supports Hengel's basic proposal much more strongly than he himself has realized. In the present article I am concerned with his treatment of the Fourth Gospel's own portrayal of the beloved disciple. It is in this area that criticism will be offered and a somewhat different interpretation, which will strengthen rather than detract from his overall proposal, will be advanced.

II

I noted above that my simple statement of Hengel's solution to the Johannine question requires some qualifications. First, with regard to the authorship of the Gospel, Hengel clearly regards it as substantially the work of John the Elder, but he allows that the form of the Gospel which we have (the only form that was ever 'published') is the result of a redaction by members of the Johannine school after John the Elder's death. The editors at least added the closing verses; Hengel leaves open the extent to which their editorial activity may have affected the rest of the Gospel.[3] This is relevant to the Gospel's portrayal of the beloved disciple, since Hengel tends to speak of major aspects of this portrayal as the work of the redactors and seems by no means decided how far John the Elder himself was responsible for the way the beloved disciple is portrayed.[4] Secondly, with regard to the identification of the beloved disciple, the sense in which the beloved disciple is intended to represent John the Elder himself is qualified in Hengel's argument by three, converging considerations.

---

2.   'Papias and Polycrates on the Origin of the Fourth Gospel', *JTS* 44 (1993), pp. 24-69.

3.   Hengel, *Johannine Question*, pp. 84, 94-96, 99-100, and especially 105-108.

4.   Hengel, *Johannine Question*, pp. 3, 78, 127-32.

a. He accepts the common view that the beloved disciple in the Gospel represents the ideal disciple.[5] This does not mean that the beloved disciple is not also a historical figure,[6] but it means that the portrayal of the figure has been idealized in the interests of portraying him as the ideal disciple.

b. Hengel emphasizes the enigmatic nature of the references to the beloved disciple, which leave his identity ambiguous: 'The editors—like the author—want the riddle to remain unsolved, the issue to be left open'.[7] But since he argues that the Gospel was 'published' (that is, circulated to other churches by its editors) with the title 'the Gospel according to John',[8] as well as with a clear identification of the beloved disciple as the author of the Gospel in 21.24, this ambiguity, at least on the part of the editors, cannot leave the identity of the beloved disciple entirely open.

c. Hengel thinks that in some respects the Gospel seems to hint at an identification of the beloved disciple with John the son of Zebedee, and thinks that certainly the redactors, perhaps even John the Elder himself, deliberately allowed the figure of the beloved disciple to suggest *both* John the Elder *and* John the son of Zebedee.[9] Hengel's discussion at this point is full of questions and conjectures, especially as to the respective intentions of John the Elder and the redactors, but it is clear at least that he thinks the ambiguity of the beloved disciple, for the first readers/ hearers, consisted in the possible reference to either of the two Johns, combined with the idealization of the figure.[10]

In my view, Hengel has quite unnecessarily complicated and compromised his proposal by allowing a relic of the old attribution to John the son of Zebedee back into his argument. In this context John the son

5.   Hengel, *Johannine Question*, pp. 78, 125.

6.   Hengel, *Johannine Question*, pp. 78-80.

7.   Hengel, *Johannine Question*, p. 128, cf. pp. 3, 77-78.

8.   Hengel, *Johannine Question*, pp. 74-76; cf. also, in more detail, M. Hengel, *Studies in the Gospel of Mark* (London: SCM Press, 1985), pp. 64-84, and the criticism of his view by H. Koester, *Ancient Christian Gospels: Their History and Development* (London: SCM Press; Philadelphia: Trinity Press International, 1990), pp. 26-27. But it is noteworthy that Koester's objection is to the view that the Gospels originally bore titles of the form, 'The Gospel according to...' (τὸ εὐαγγέλιον κατά...). He allows that Hengel may be correct in arguing that the Gospels must have circulated under the names of specific authors from the beginning.

9.   Hengel, *Johannine Question*, pp. 127-32.

10.   Hengel, *Johannine Question*, pp. 130-32.

of Zebedee is a phantom which needs to be finally and completely exor-
cized. Hengel is, in a way, obliged to reintroduce the son of Zebedee
into the Gospel by his conviction that the figure of the beloved disciple
is deliberately enigmatic and ambiguous. I shall argue that the beloved
disciple is not an ambiguous figure. In so far as there is anything
enigmatic about him, the enigma is dispelled at the end of the Gospel,
which functions clearly to identify him as John the Elder who wrote the
Gospel. This is not to deny an element of idealization, but the idealization
by no means produces ambiguity because it is not as the ideal *disciple*
that the beloved disciple is idealized, but as the ideal *author*. By this term
I mean that the beloved disciple is portrayed in the Gospel narrative in
such a way as to show that he is ideally qualified to be the author of the
Gospel.

III

It will be convenient first to dispose of the supposed deliberate hints that
the beloved disciple might be John the son of Zebedee. I need not repeat
Hengel's own argument that the beloved disciple is portrayed as a
Jerusalem disciple, not one of the twelve.[11] But in his argument that,
nevertheless, the reader is meant to have the option of thinking of John
the son of Zebedee, Hengel is too impressed *both* by the absence of the
sons of Zebedee from the Gospel apart from 21.2 *and* by their presence
in 21.2.

The argument about the absence of the sons of Zebedee assumes that
the author of the Fourth Gospel presupposes knowledge of the Synoptic
Gospels on the part of his readers, who would therefore remark the
absence of these disciples who were prominent in the Synoptics.[12] This
is a large assumption. It is likely enough that the author knew Mark, but
at this date Matthew's and Luke's Gospels need not have reached
Ephesus. But whichever Gospels were known to the author, it would be
a mistake to suppose that they were necessarily widely used and well
known in his community. Written Gospels from elsewhere would not
easily have supplanted or even competed with such a church's own oral
tradition, of which the author of the Fourth Gospel himself was the most

11. Hengel, *Johannine Question,* pp. 124-26, cf. 109-11; cf. also O. Cullmann,
The Johannine Circle (London: SCM Press, 1976), pp. 63-85; G.R. Beasley-Murray,
John (WBC, 36; Waco, TX: Word Books, 1987), pp. lxx-lxxv.

12. Hengel, *Johannine Question*, p. 129, cf. pp. 75, 91.

important exponent. It is possible that the portrayal of the beloved disciple in relation to Peter indicates the superiority of the Gospel over the Petrine Gospel of Mark.[13] But even this does not mean that the author is so constantly looking over his shoulder at Mark that his failure to mention James and John needs to be related to their prominence in Mark. It is probable that the Johannine tradition just happened to focus on other disciples. We should remember that the prominence of the sons of Zebedee in the Synoptics is largely due to Mark and to a lesser extent to special Lukan tradition; they never appear in special Matthaean tradition. We should also notice that none of the traditions in which the sons of Zebedee appear in the Synoptics occur in the Fourth Gospel. The latter's narrative of the call of the disciples, beginning as it does with those who were disciples of the Baptist, is a quite different tradition from Mark's. If it does not include the sons of Zebedee, nor does it include Thomas, a prominent disciple in the Fourth Gospel. Anyone tempted to identify the anonymous disciple of 1.34-39 as John the son of Zebedee ought to see at once that the presence of John the son of Zebedee without his brother James would be even more surprising here than the absence of John the son of Zebedee. Finally, we may notice that the one place in the Fourth Gospel where we could be justifiably surprised if the sons of Zebedee, as fishermen, did not appear, they do in fact appear (21.2).

This simple explanation for the single appearance of the sons of Zebedee in the Fourth Gospel should warn us also against finding their appearance in 21.2 significant for the identity of the beloved disciple. But in fact 21.2, far from allowing the possibility that the beloved disciple is John the son of Zebedee, actually excludes this possibility. The convention that the beloved disciple appears only anonymously in the Gospel is well enough established by this point for the reader not to expect it to be breached here, especially without any indication that it is and when there are no less than two genuinely anonymous disciples to cover the presence of the beloved disciple. To argue that 21.2 refers to four unnamed disciples, any of whom could be the beloved disciple, is specious. Everyone knew the names of the sons of Zebedee, who are quite sufficiently specified by the phrase οἱ τοῦ Ζεβεδαίου. If the beloved disciple could be one of them, he could also just as well be Thomas or Nathanael.

13. Hengel, *Johannine Question*, p. 125.

Thus 21.2 excludes the possibility that the beloved disciple is John the son of Zebedee, even as one possibility in a deliberately ambiguous portrayal. But this does not exhaust the interest of the curious way in which the beloved disciple is included in this list of disciples. There are seven disciples. The number seven is the number of completeness, and a list of seven can therefore be representative of all: the seven listed not being exhaustive, but standing for all. This is probably the significance of the seven churches in the book of Revelation: seven specific churches are selected to represent all churches. It is the significance of the seven signs in the Fourth Gospel itself: they are related as representative of all the many others which are not related (20.30). Thus the seven disciples who make the great catch of fish are representative of all the disciples of Jesus who are to be engaged in the mission of the church (and could not, of course, all appear in person in a story about fishing). From this point of view, it is significant that there are seven, not twelve or eleven (as in some other, though not all, post-resurrection commissionings of the disciples). These seven include some of the twelve, but also Nathanael, and therefore the beloved disciple can be included without the implication that he is one of the twelve.

It remains puzzling why there should be two anonymous disciples, rather than just one. There seem to be two possible explanations. One is that in drawing up his list, the Evangelist did not wish it to look as though he had deliberately excluded any of the disciples named in his Gospel (Andrew, Philip, Judas not Iscariot). The inclusive representativeness of the list is protected by leaving, as it were, an empty place. The other possibility, suggested by Cullman,[14] is that the two anonymous disciples are two members of the Johannine school: the beloved disciple and a colleague who had also been a personal disciple of Jesus and to whom, as a colleague of the beloved disciple, the latter's conventional anonymity is here extended. If we wonder what the point of such a reference would be, we might suppose that this other 'Johannine' disciple's eyewitness testimony made a contribution to the Gospel along with the beloved disciple's. We might suppose that the first person plural of eyewitness testimony in Jn 1.14 (and 1 Jn 1.1-3?) includes him (along with some others who had not been close enough to the inner circle of the disciples to appear in the Gospel's narrative). We might even wonder whether this second anonymous disciple is the problematic 'other disciple'

14. Cullmann, *Johannine Circle*, p. 76.

of 18.15-16, who (despite his association with Peter) is hardly introduced in such a way as to encourage the reader's identification of him with the beloved disciple.[15] The reader who thought that he must be the beloved disciple simply because, like the beloved disciple, he is anonymous, would find in 21.2 that the Gospel knows two anonymous disciples. For readers who knew this other 'Johannine' disciple, his close association with the high priest (18.15) would probably be sufficient to identify him.[16]

IV

The next stage of my argument must be to examine the Gospel's own statement of its authorship in 21.24, but before I do so it is necessary briefly to consider the relation of ch. 21, which in more than one respect is crucial for the understanding of the beloved disciple, to the rest of the Gospel. Against the general view that ch. 21, whether or not from the same hand as the rest of the Gospel, is in some sense an appendix to a Gospel originally intended to end at 20.31, Paul Minear, in a significant but neglected article, has made a convincing case for the view that ch. 21 was always an integral part of the design of the Gospel.[17]

Scholarship has been strangely mesmerized by the impression that 20.30-31 reads like the original conclusion to the Gospel. These verses are a conclusion of sorts, but there is no reason to regard them as the conclusion to *the Gospel*. They are the conclusion to the Gospel's account of the signs that manifested Jesus' glory and enable people to believe in him as messiah and Son of God (20.31). As such, they certainly signal the completion of the Gospel's main purpose, and so ch. 21 could be regarded as an epilogue. But an epilogue need not be an afterthought: it may be integral to the design of a work. This epilogue completes the double story of Peter and the beloved disciple, which

15. For a valuable survey of this issue, see F. Neirynck, 'The "Other Disciple" in Jn 18,15-16', in *idem*, *Evangelica* (BETL, 60; Leuven: Peeters/Leuven University Press, 1982), pp. 335-64.

16. If the beloved disciple is John the Elder, it is not difficult to suggest who the other 'Johannine' disciple must be. Aristion, whom Papias places alongside John the Elder as a disciple of the Lord, whom Papias himself had heard (*Ap. Const.* 7.46.8 associates Aristion with Smyrna) and, according to Eusebius, frequently mentioned in his writings (*H.E.* 3.39.7, 14), is the obvious candidate.

17. P.S. Minear, 'The Original Functions of John 21', *JBL* 102 (1983), pp. 85-98.

began in ch. 13, and thereby indicates the continuing history of the church between the resurrection appearances and the parousia (cf. 21.22). The story of the great catch of fish does not contradict the indication in 20.30-31 that the account of Jesus' signs is now completed. It is not a sign of the kind that the signs of chs. 2–20 are said to be, that is, signs that manifest Jesus' glory in order to enable belief in him. It has a quite different purpose: to symbolize programmatically the mission in which the disciples are now to engage. After ch. 20 no more needs to be said about Jesus himself: the central, christological purpose of the Gospel has been fulfilled. But more does need to be said about the disciples: the loose ends which the story of Peter and the beloved disciple up till this point has left must be taken up before the Gospel itself is complete. Minear has convincingly shown how 21.15-19 corresponds closely to earlier material in the Gospel, not in such a way as to indicate a secondary addition to the Gospel, but in such a way as to show that this conclusion to the Gospel's story of Peter must have been presupposed all along.[18] I may add, as of particular interest to my purpose, that the otherwise unnecessarily full way in which the beloved disciple is described in 21.10 (after he has already appeared in 21.7) must form a deliberate *inclusio* with 13.23-25, indicating that the double story of Peter and the beloved disciple which began there ends here. Of course, the view that ch. 21 is integral to the Gospel cannot tell us whether or not the last three or two verses of the chapter are an editorial addition. The story of Peter and the beloved disciple could, certainly, have ended satisfactorily at 21.22. But it could not have ended satisfactorily at 21.19.

The basic significance of 21.24-25 ought to be clear, even though it has been continually debated. A single editor speaks for himself in the first person singular of v. 25 and on behalf of the Johannine school in the first person plural of v. 24. He writes evidently with the concurrence and approval of other members of the school, but there is actually no justification in these verses for even Hengel's constant references to redactor*s* of the Gospel. We know of only one editor, who acted on behalf of the school. More significantly, however, this editor distinguishes both himself and the school from the *author* of the Gospel (v. 24), who is identified as the beloved disciple to whom the preceding three verses refer. The meaning of γράψας cannot plausibly be so

---

18. See also, on the relation of 13.36-38 and 21.15-19, R. Bauckham, 'The Martyrdom of Peter in Early Christian Literature', *ANRW*, II.26.1 (ed. W. Haase; Berlin: de Gruyter, 1992), pp. 539-95.

extended as to make the beloved disciple less than the author.[19] Of course, it could mean 'had it written by a secretary' (the most that 19.19-22 as a parallel could legitimate), and a secretary could be given more or less freedom by an author. But an author employing a secretary is still an author. It is a long way from authorship in this sense to the idea of the beloved disciple as merely the source or guarantor of the tradition which the Gospel incorporates. Jn 21.24 designates the beloved disciple as the *author* of the Gospel.

Moreover, we learn from 21.23 that the Johannine school certainly thought they knew very well who the beloved disciple was. The common interpretation of this verse in the light of the expectation that the parousia would come before the generation of those who had known Jesus died out (cf. Mk 9.1; 13.30) is compelling. We know that for this reason the passing of the first generation of Christian leaders caused a problem (2 Pet. 3.4), although all the evidence suggests that it was a quite temporary problem of the late first century, the period when the first generation seemed to have almost passed away. As many of those who were well known as personal disciples of Jesus, such as Peter (Jn 21.18-19), died, attention would have focused on any still known to be alive. That the beloved disciple, as a rare, perhaps finally unique, survivor should at the end of his life have been rumoured to be the subject of a personalized version of Mk 9.1 is easily credible. The rumour would certainly be of no interest if the beloved disciple were regarded as an unknown disciple. It is explicable only if the beloved disciple were a well-known figure. The rumour, of course, must have circulated before the death of the person it referred to.

The rumour could have been based on 21.22 in an earlier version of the Gospel which ended at 21.22 or it could have been based on an alleged saying of Jesus which already circulated before the completion of the Gospel and of which 21.22 gives a version. In either case, the conclusion is inescapable that, in the light of 21.23, 21.24 designates as the author of the Gospel that specific individual who was generally regarded, in the Johannine churches, as the disciple to whom the saying in 21.22 refers. Thus these verses allow no ambiguity, for the first readers/hearers of this final form of the Gospel, as to the identity of the

19. G. Schrenk ('γράφω', *TDNT*, I, p. 743) offers no evidence at all for such a usage, while F.R.M. Hitchcock ('The Use of γράφειν', *JTS* 31 [1930], pp. 271-75) shows that the kind of evidence which is sometimes alleged does not meet the need.

author or of the beloved disciple. They presuppose that the identity of the disciple to whom the saying in 21.22 refers is well known and they claim that he wrote the Gospel. Hengel's argument for deliberate ambiguity about the identity of the beloved disciple in the final redaction of the Gospel is at all plausible only because he seems to be thinking of the Gospel as intended to circulate far beyond the circle in which the beloved disciple was well known. But this plausibility depends on two gratuitous assumptions: (a) that the Gospel was primarily intended for churches beyond the circle of the Johannine churches; and (b) that as the Gospel circulated further afield, the common knowledge of the Johannine churches as to the identity of the beloved disciple would not be expected to spread with it.[20] Both assumptions are highly questionable.

Thus the identity of the beloved disciple becomes unambiguous at least at the end of the Gospel in its finally redacted form. But the closing verses of the Gospel also raise for us the question of the extent of the final redaction. That the editor distinguishes both himself and the Johannine school from the author would be consistent with a degree of editing of the author's work. For our purposes, it is relevant to ask whether the portrayal of the beloved disciple may not be due to the redaction, rather than to the author. This is possible, though it would mean that there was rather extensive redaction. However, we should note that, in the light of 21.24, such a portrayal of the beloved disciple by the redactor would be precisely his portrayal of *the author* of the Gospel. He would be inserting references to the author into the author's own work. My argument, to be presented below, that the beloved disciple is portrayed as the ideal author would thus be quite consistent with this attribution of the references to the beloved disciple to the redactor.

However, there is one consideration which suggests at least that not all the references to the beloved disciple within the Gospel are due to the redactor. This is the relation between 21.24 and 19.35 (although the latter is not, of course, a reference to the beloved disciple *as* the beloved disciple). From the close verbal relationship between these verses, it is

20. The evidence we have suggests that, as the Gospel circulated, the identity of its author as another John, not the son of Zebedee, was in most places very soon forgotten and the assumption that the John in question must be the son of Zebedee was made. But this is no reason for supposing that this effect was intended by the redactor of the Gospel.

clear that the writer of 21.24 modelled his words on 19.35. It is also clear how he understood 19.35. Although modern exegetes debate the identity of both ὁ ἑωρακώς and ἐκεῖνος, the writer of 21.24 clearly took both to be the author of the Gospel. But whereas in 19.35 the author himself vouches for the truth of what he says (ἐκεῖνος οἶδεν), in 21.24 the Johannine school vouches for the truth of his witness (οἴδαμεν). The difference is most easily understood if 19.35 really comes from the hand of the author. The witness's own knowledge that he tells the truth is a remarkably weak way of substantiating his witness (cf. 8.13-18), but it is the only claim a single author can make. The Johannine school's claim that the author speaks the truth carries more weight. The redactor would surely have written οἴδαμεν in 19.35 as he did in 21.24.

This is not quite a compelling argument. It could be said that the nature of the witness in 19.35 is such that no-one else could verify it, though this raises the question of the sense in which members of the Johannine school could claim in 21.24 to verify the truth of the Gospel as a whole. They could not themselves have been eyewitnesses of the events, for the rumour of 21.23 must presuppose that the beloved disciple was then one of the very last disciples of Jesus still alive. They could have known other eyewitnesses in the past.

Of course, even if we could be sure that 19.35 is from the hand of the author, not that of the redactor, it would not necessarily follow that the same is true of the passages in which the beloved disciple is so called. However, we shall argue below that, despite its quite different character, 19.35 in fact presupposes and coheres with the other passages in which the beloved disciple appears.

We cannot be certain whether the figure of the beloved disciple is due to the author or the redactor. However, we can be fairly confident that in either case the figure of the beloved disciple represents the author and that in either case it correctly represents the author as a personal disciple of Jesus and eyewitness of some of the events of the Gospel story. The redactor who added 21.24-25, along with the Johannine school on whose behalf he wrote, was in a position to know this. These verses must have been added along with v. 23 and therefore soon after the death of the beloved disciple, if v. 23 presupposes this, or even before, if it does not. The Gospel could never have ended with v. 23. So banal and anticlimactic an ending to a work of such artistry is inconceivable. It could have ended at v. 22, which would be a highly effective ending, or, if the figure of the beloved disciple is entirely due to the redactor, we cannot tell how the author ended his work. But in either case v. 23 must have been written along with v. 24. So v. 24, like v. 23, must date from the time when the claim that the beloved disciple would not die either was still believed and needed correcting or had only recently been disappointed by the beloved disciple's death and needed explaining.

To sum up, in 21.24 the redactor of the Gospel, speaking for the Johannine school, identifies as the author of the Gospel a figure well known to his first readers/hearers as the disciple of Jesus to whom the saying in 21.22 referred. He does so, at the latest, soon after the death of this person whom he considers both the beloved disciple and the author of the Gospel. In such a context he cannot have been mistaken either about the author of the Gospel or about the author's identity with the beloved disciple. If the beloved disciple already appeared in the author's work, the redactor could not have been mistaken in supposing that the author portrayed himself as the beloved disciple. If the figure of the beloved disciple is due to the redactor, he cannot have been mistaken in supposing that the author had been a personal disciple of Jesus who witnessed significant events in the Gospel story. He cannot have been mistaken, and so the only alternative to accepting his claim that the beloved disciple authentically represents the author of the Gospel would be to regard the Gospel as pseudepigraphal.[21] In other words, soon after the beloved disciple's death someone else (whom we must then call the author, not the redactor) wrote the Gospel and represented the beloved disciple as its author. My reasons for preferring to accept the Gospel's claim to authorship are largely Hengel's and need not be repeated here. But it should be noted that, even if the Gospel were pseudepigraphal, my argument that it identifies its author unambiguously is unaffected. Whether the beloved disciple was genuinely or only fictionally the author, he was a specific individual well known to the first readers/ hearers, and for these first readers/hearers the Gospel in its final form pointed unambiguously to that individual as its author.

Having established that the Gospel identifies its author unambiguously, we turn to the way in which the Gospel portrays the beloved disciple as its author.

---

21. One scholar who accepts that the Gospel is pseudepigraphal (though on the basis of 1.14) is J. Ashton, *Understanding the Fourth Gospel* (Oxford: Clarendon Press, 1991), pp. 437-39.

V

It is a rather popular notion, taken up by Hengel, that the beloved disciple is portrayed as the ideal disciple.[22] If this means that he represents, as a model for others, the ideal of discipleship, it is certainly misleading. The beloved disciple may sometimes function in this way, just as other disciples (such as Nathanael and Mary Magdalene) in the Fourth Gospel do, but such a function cannot satisfactorily account for most of what is said about him. Even if we confine ourselves to the passages in which the beloved disciple is so called, the only undisputed references to him, we find an emphasis on an exclusive privilege which is precisely not representative. In 13.23-26, the beloved disciple has the place of special intimacy next to Jesus at the supper, which it is not possible for more than one disciple to occupy, and he is therefore uniquely placed to enquire and be enlightened as to Jesus' meaning and purpose. In 20.1-10 his understanding faith in the resurrection is enabled by his observing the empty tomb and the grave clothes: it relates to the role of eyewitness which he shares with Peter but not with later disciples. The passage most easily susceptible to an interpretation of the beloved disciple as ideal disciple is 19.26-27, where he is certainly portrayed as the only one of Jesus' male disciples who is faithful enough to be with him at the cross. The scene may well represent the new relationships established by Jesus' death and resurrection (cf. 20.17), but even here the representativeness of the beloved disciple cannot replace his unique and particular privilege. The point is not simply that any faithful disciple becomes the son of Jesus' mother, though to an extent this is true. The beloved disciple uniquely takes the mother of Jesus into his own home.

Most difficult of all, for the thesis that the beloved disciple is the ideal disciple, is his last appearance (21.20-23). The story of the Gospel undoubtedly ends on a note of discipleship, with Jesus' words, 'Follow me!', in v. 19 repeated, as the last words of Jesus in the Gospel, in v. 22. But the words are spoken to Peter and there is no indication here that the beloved disciple is the model of discipleship, either for Peter or for the readers/hearers. The beloved disciple's discipleship is indicated in v. 20 (ἀκολουθοῦντα), but the course it will now take should be of no

---

22. See now K. Quast, *Peter and the Beloved Disciple: Figures for a Community in Crisis* (JSNTSup, 32, Sheffield: JSOT Press, 1989), who combines this idea with the view that the beloved disciple represents the Johannine community.

concern to Peter, or, it is implied, to the readers/hearers. Whereas the attention of the readers/hearers is drawn to Peter's future discipleship, as shepherd of Jesus' sheep who will in the end give his life for them, it is pointedly deflected from that of the beloved disciple. Where, if the beloved disciple represents the ideal disciple, we should expect the Gospel to leave the reader with an emphatic indication of this role, we find exactly the opposite. Since the portrayal of the beloved disciple throughout the Gospel is so closely connected with that of Peter and since the *inclusio* between 13.23-25 and 21.20 deliberately draws attention to the fact that 21.20-22 concludes the story of the two disciples which began in 13.23-25, any interpretation of the role of the beloved disciple in the Gospel must justify itself by a convincing and consistent explanation of this final scene.

In interpretations of the beloved disciple as the ideal disciple he is usually contrasted with the figure of Peter, understood as a less than ideal disciple. The beloved disciple's relationship to Peter, whose portrayal in the Gospel is much more complex and detailed than that of the beloved disciple, is certainly important for understanding the role of the latter. It must be highly significant that in almost all cases where the beloved disciple is portrayed in relation to Peter, the beloved disciple in some sense takes precedence (13.23-26; 20.1-10; 21.7; also 1.35-42; 18.15-16, if the anonymous disciple in these cases is the beloved disciple, as I think he must be in 1.35-39 but need not be in 18.15-16),[23] while in 19.26-27 (also 19.35, which in my view must refer to the beloved disciple) Peter's absence similarly gives the beloved disciple a kind of superiority to Peter. However, precisely the consistency of this feature up to and including 21.7 must make it also very significant that in the beloved disciple's final appearance it is not found. Jn. 21.20 offers a subtly ambivalent picture. On the one hand there seems to be the implication that the beloved disciple is already doing (ἀκολουθοῦντα), as he has done throughout the Gospel, what Peter is now commanded to do (ἀκολούθει μοι), but on the other hand there is the impression that the beloved disciple now lags behind. An adequate interpretation of the relationship between the beloved disciple and Peter must also take account of this.

There is an important sense in which, up to and including 21.7, the beloved disciple is represented as superior to Peter. But the sense in

23. Here I judge the probabilities differently from Hengel (*Johannine Question*, pp. 78-79).

which this is true only becomes apparent when we see that Peter and the beloved disciple represent two different *kinds* of discipleship: active service and perceptive witness. Peter is portrayed as the disciple who is eager to follow and to serve Jesus (13.6-9, 36-37; 18.10-11, 15). He will not let Jesus serve him until he realizes that he cannot be a disciple otherwise and then his eagerness exceeds Jesus' intention (13.6-9). He is ready to follow Jesus into mortal danger and to lay down his own life to save Jesus from death (13.37). But just as he does not understand that Jesus must wash his feet, so he does not understand that Jesus the good shepherd must lay down his life for him (cf. 13.37 with 10.11, 15; this lack of understanding appears similarly in 18.10-11). Only after Jesus' death (13.36: 'afterward'; cf. 13.7) will he be able to follow Jesus to death (13.36). So Peter's love for Jesus, though eager and extravagant, is expressed in ignorant self-confidence that ends in failure when he denies Jesus (13.38; 18.15-27). It is after the resurrection (when Peter's characteristic of active eagerness reappears: 20.3-6; 21.7-8) that Jesus not merely restores Peter to discipleship but enables Peter to become for the first time a disciple who understands what discipleship means for him and can at last truly follow Jesus to death. To Peter's threefold denial of Jesus corresponds the threefold pledge of love which Jesus now draws from him (21.15-17; note the charcoal fire which links 21.9 with 18.18). To this new Peter, who now loves Jesus as the good shepherd who has given his life for his sheep, can now be given the commission to follow Jesus (21.19, 22; cf. 13.36) as the chief under-shepherd of Jesus' sheep, who is to care for the sheep and, following Jesus, give his own life for them (21.18-19; cf. 12.33; 13.32). In this role Peter's eagerness for service is redeemed, but his self-will is replaced (21.18) by true discipleship. Thus the point of the Gospel's portrayal of Peter—which can really only be appreciated when ch. 21 is understood as integral to the Gospel—is not to denigrate Peter, but to show him as the disciple who through failure and grace is enabled by Jesus to become the chief pastor of the church. Although the Gospel does acknowledge a minor role for Peter as witness to the events of the Gospel story (20.6-7), it gives him primarily the role of shepherd. This is not at all the role of the beloved disciple, who therefore becomes at the end irrelevant to Peter's own call to discipleship (21.20-22).

The beloved disciple is given a superiority to Peter only in respects which qualify him for his own role of perceptive witness to Jesus. This understanding of his role also explains the way in which the beloved disciple is portrayed much more adequately than the idea that he is the ideal disciple does. This portrayal can be analysed as having three elements. In the first place, there is the beloved disciple's special intimacy with Jesus, which is stressed already in 1.35-40. The anonymous disciple here is almost certainly the beloved disciple, who cannot, of course, on first acquaintance be called, as he is later, 'the disciple Jesus loved'. Of course, to the first-time reader/hearer of the Gospel the anonymous disciple of these verses is enigmatic, but the curiously precise specification of the hour of the day may already be intended to give a hint of eyewitness testimony. Certainly, the reader/hearer is bound to notice the anonymity of this disciple, since all other disciples in 1.35-51 are named and the reader/hearer would naturally expect one of the first two of Jesus' disciples to be a disciple already well known to those acquainted with the Gospel tradition. Thus the reader/hearer who subsequently encounters the anonymous disciple Jesus loved in 13.23 would have no difficulty in retrospectively identifying him with the anonymous disciple of 1.35-40. But what is important about the little that is already said of this disciple in 1.35-40 is that it stresses the opportunity he and Andrew had to get to know Jesus, a point which is not made about the disciples who are recruited subsequently. Although the beloved disciple then disappears from the narrative until ch. 13, the point has been made that he was able to get to know Jesus before any other disciple except Andrew. When he reappears in 13.23-26 it is his intimacy with Jesus that is stressed, so that he alone is in a position to ask Jesus a delicate question and to hear and observe the way Jesus answers it. His specially close relationship with Jesus again emerges in 19.26-27.

Secondly, the beloved disciple is present at key points in the story of Jesus. Again, his initial appearance at 1.35 is more significant than is usually noticed. It makes the beloved disciple a witness of John's testimony to Jesus, as well as to the beginning of Jesus' ministry, and it is certainly not accidental that the beloved disciple on his first appearance in the Gospel hears John the Baptist's testimony to Jesus as the sacrificial lamb of God (1.35, cf. v. 29). When the beloved disciple's own witness is explicitly highlighted at 19.35, it is his eyewitness testimony to the fulfilment of precisely these words of John the Baptist: he sees the flow of blood and water, along with the fact that no bone is broken, as showing Jesus to be the true passover lamb (19.31-37). The fact that the beloved disciple is present at the cross makes him superior to Peter not simply as a disciple, but precisely as that disciple—the only male disciple—who witnesses the key salvific event of the whole Gospel story, the hour of Jesus' exaltation, towards which the whole story from John the Baptist's testimony onwards has pointed.

If the disciple of 18.15-16 is the beloved disciple, this passage also portrays him as present at a key event: Jesus' trial before Annas, along with Peter's denials. If his entry only into the courtyard of the building makes him more obviously a witness to Peter's denials than to the trial, nevertheless his relationship to the high priest may well be intended to indicate access to information (cf. also the implications of 18.10, 26). Since it is the disciple's relationship to the high priest, rather than his relationship to Jesus, that matters for his role as witness in this context, this may account for the fact he is not here introduced as the disciple Jesus loved. (Alternatively, as I suggested above, the disciple in question may be another of the Johannine school on whose witness the Gospel has drawn at this point.)

Thirdly, the beloved disciple is portrayed as a *perceptive* witness, with spiritual insight into the meaning of the events of the Gospel story. However, despite his special intimacy with Jesus, it is not at all clear that this quality emerges before the resurrection. In 13.25-30 the beloved disciple witnesses, more fully than the other disciples, the way in which Jesus designates the betrayer and thus shows his awareness and willing acceptance of the fate that he must undergo as a divine destiny. The beloved disciple is given the material for a key insight into the meaning of the events that lead to Jesus' death, but it is not said that he himself at the time *understands* any better than the rest of the disciples (13.28). His breakthrough to understanding seems to come in 20.8-9. The narrative of the two disciples at the tomb skilfully correlates the two. The beloved disciple arrives first, but Peter goes in first. Peter has the priority as a witness to the evidence, but the beloved disciple has the superiority in perceiving its significance. This point is usually misunderstood by those who see the beloved disciple as the ideal disciple. He is not here portrayed as the model for later Christians who believe in the resurrection without seeing (20.29), since it is expressly said that 'he saw and believed' (20.8). The point is that, like Peter, he provides the eyewitness testimony that later Christians need in order to believe without seeing, but, unlike Peter, he already perceives the significance of what they both see. The same priority in spiritual recognition of the truth of Jesus is attributed to the beloved disciple in 21.7.

These three features of the portrayal of the beloved disciple qualify him to be the ideal witness to Jesus, his story and its meaning. These qualities are displayed to a large extent by way of contrast with Peter, but the point is not a general superiority to Peter. The beloved disciple is better qualified to be the author of a Gospel, but he is not better qualified to be the chief under-shepherd of Jesus' sheep, which is Peter's mode of discipleship. It is worth noticing that, whereas in Peter's case the Gospel emphasizes his love for Jesus, in the beloved disciple's case it emphasizes Jesus' love for him. The former emphasis is appropriate for the active role of discipleship as participation in Jesus' activity of serving and sacrificing: it corresponds to Jesus' love for his disciples. The latter emphasis is appropriate for the more receptive role of discipleship as witness and corresponds to Jesus' enjoyment of his Father's love (cf. the correspondence between 13.23 and 1.18). The different, complementary roles of the two disciples shows that it is not rivalry between different branches of early Christianity (the so-called great church and the Johannine churches) that is at stake in their relationship. The Gospel acknowledges Peter's leading role in the whole church, to which its own community belongs, while claiming for the beloved disciple a role of witnessing to the truth of Jesus which is equally significant for the whole church.

Finally, on the relation between Peter and the beloved disciple, we should note that the point of their portrayal, in comparison and contrast with each other, is neither the way each relates to the other nor the way each relates to others within the narrative. Peter is not shown as 'shepherd' to other disciples within the narrative, nor does the beloved disciple act as a witness to others within the narrative. Except at 21.7, his relation to Peter is not that of mediator to Peter of his superior insight into the truth of Jesus. Rather he is represented as the disciple who was so related to Jesus and the events of Jesus' story that he can bear witness *to the readers/hearers of the Gospel*. The point of the double story of the two disciples is to show how each, through his own, different way of following Jesus, relates to the church after the resurrection. Just as Peter's role in the story enables him to become the chief under-shepherd of Jesus' sheep, not within the narrative but later, so the beloved disciple's role in the story enables him to witness to others not within the narrative but later. Although both can serve from time to time in the narrative as representative disciples, models for all Christians, the overwhelming emphasis is on the special roles which their personal discipleship of Jesus enables them to play in the church. In the beloved disciple's case, this is his witness as author of the Gospel.

VI

In the last section, we saw how the beloved disciple is portrayed as qualified to be the ideal witness. That this amounts to his being the ideal author of the Gospel will become clearer if we focus again on 19.35. We have already seen that, in the light of 21.24 in the final form of the Gospel, 19.35 explicitly portrays the beloved disciple as author of the Gospel. But we need also to note the important connection between 19.35 and 20.30-31, which the writer of 21.24-25 also recognized in echoing both of these passages. Only in these two passages are the readers/hearers of the Gospel directly addressed in the second person. Moreover, the same words are addressed to them: ἵνα καὶ ὑμεῖς πιστεύητε (19.35); ἵνα πιστεύητε (20.31). Second person address to readers/hearers draws attention to the writer who addresses them, in a way that third person narrative usually does not. In these two passages the author addresses his readers/hearers as author, in a way that is paralleled only by the unique authorial first person plural of 1.14.

Moreover, there is an important material correspondence between the two passages. Jn 20.30-31 speaks of the written narrative of chs. 2–20 which it concludes: the narrative of Jesus' signs which the author has written so that his readers/hearers may believe. The seventh of these signs, the climactic and pre-eminently important one (cf. 2.18-19), which alone enables believing perception of Jesus' full significance, seems to be his death and resurrection. It is not the resurrection alone, which for Johannine thought is significant only in very close relation to the cross as the event of Jesus' salvific exaltation and glorification. Arguably the seventh sign itself is actually the more specific event of the flow of blood and water (19.34) which shows both the reality of Jesus' death and its significance as the sacrifice that gives life. At any rate, this is the supreme revelatory moment of the seventh sign, and it is the author's witness to this moment that 19.35 declares. Jn 20.30-31 does not use the vocabulary of witness: the author does not claim his own eyewitness testimony to the other signs. But at the most important moment of the whole narrative of the signs the author addresses his readers/hearers as witness (19.35).

We should also notice that 20.30 says of the signs that are not recorded that Jesus did them 'in the presence of the disciples' (ἐνώπιον τῶν μαθητῶν). Of course, this means that the signs which are recorded were also done in the presence of the disciples. This again highlights the significance of the beloved disciple as author. Only he and the women disciples were present at the cross (19.25-26). Thus in the light of the connection of 19.35 with 20.30-31, as well as in the light of the redactor's comment in 21.24, there can be no doubt that the witness of 19.35 is indeed the beloved disciple.

However, this verse is quite different in character from all the other appearances of the beloved disciple in the Gospel (including 1.35-40 and 18.15-16, and excepting only 21.24), and this difference of character is again appreciable in the light of its connection with 20.30-31. Unlike all other references to the beloved disciple, 19.35 does not give him a role *in the narrative*. It assumes that the witness is there observing the events, and so it presupposes the presence of the beloved disciple as a character in the narrative in 19.26-27, without which the readers/hearers could not tell who the witness is. But 19.35 itself speaks of the beloved disciple's activity of bearing witness to what he then saw, an activity which takes place not within the story the Gospel tells, but beyond it. More precisely, we could say that it is the beloved disciple's activity as author of the Gospel telling this part of the story of the Gospel. Perhaps μεμαρτύρηκεν also includes the lifetime of bearing witness which preceded and was summed up in the writing of the Gospel, but it must mean primarily, as the activity of witnessing which is relevant to the readers/hearers, the writing of the Gospel. (The perfect tense μεμαρτύρηκεν is used appropriately, as in 20.31: γέγραπται; contrast 3.11, 32, which in other respects resemble the beginning of 19.35.) That the witnessing includes perceptive witness to the spiritual significance of the events is clear from καὶ ὑμεῖς ('you *also*'), which implies the prior belief of the witness himself, as also from the pregnant ἀληθῆ. But it is not said that he saw the full meaning of the events at the time. It is his witness to them in writing that conveys their significance for faith.

Thus whereas the other references to the beloved disciple before 21.24 show him, by his role in the Gospel narrative, to be qualified to be the ideal author of the Gospel, in 19.35 he appears actually as the ideal author and addresses his witness directly to the readers/hearers.

VII

The idea of the beloved disciple as the ideal author makes the way he finally appears at the end of the narrative (2.20-22) explicable, just as the idea of him as the ideal disciple makes it inexplicable. The roles of Peter and the beloved disciple in the mission of the church (symbolized in

21.3-11) are different, and the way their respective roles relate to the story told in the Gospel differs. Of Peter there is a further story to be told, concluding with the death by which he will glorify God (21.19). But of the beloved disciple there is nothing more to be said, since his role is to witness to Jesus, his story and its meaning. What the beloved disciple has to do after the events of ch. 20 is precisely to tell the story which the Gospel tells up to and including ch. 20. If he has done so orally for a lifetime, at the end of his life he does so finally as author of the Gospel. His role in the mission of the church is fulfilled with the writing of the Gospel and, strictly speaking, is fulfilled at the end of ch. 20, which concludes his witness to Jesus (and therefore looks rather too like a conclusion to the book). His role as witness to Jesus is given a place in ch. 21, at v. 7, in order to indicate its place in the mission of the church, but also to allow Peter's story then to take over the epilogue.

The beloved disciple's personal future is of no relevance to Peter (21.20-22). But it should also be of no concern to the readers/hearers. If the author himself ended his Gospel at 21.22, it was a masterly conclusion. The beloved disciple's personal fate, once the Gospel is written, is a matter for Jesus and himself alone. Like Peter, the readers/hearers are deflected from curiosity about the beloved disciple's own future and left with the summons to follow the Jesus to whom he has witnessed in the Gospel.

It might have been thought that whereas it was appropriate to Peter's mode of discipleship for him to lay down his life for the sheep, as Jesus had done, it would be appropriate for the beloved disciple's mode of discipleship for him to remain until the parousia. As the specially privileged witness to Jesus, his survival to the parousia would ensure the continuance of his witness to Jesus until Jesus' coming. But by the time he writes 21.20-22, this thought is no longer necessary. He has now written the Gospel in which he sums up and completes his witness. His witness can now remain until the parousia, whether or not he personally does. So in the end the speculation about the beloved disciple's future is used as a way of emphatically saying nothing more about the beloved disciple. Although modern readers also speculate that v. 23 presupposes the beloved disciple's death, the Gospel itself, even in its final form, actually tells us neither whether he has died or remains. This is irrelevant to his witness as author. The beloved disciple has appeared in the Gospel's narrative only as its ideal author, and of his activity after the events he narrates it tells us only that he wrote the Gospel.

Thus 21.20-23 brilliantly succeeds in leaving no doubt of the beloved disciple's identity (he is that disciple who, it was widely supposed, would not die) while at the same time telling us nothing whatever about him that the Gospel has not already told. The Gospel thus allows us to know him only as its ideal author. If the disciple who was expected not to die was in fact John the Elder, then it is curiously appropriate that, as scholars critical of the attribution of the Gospel to him have so often complained, we know almost nothing about John the Elder.

VIII

The notion of the beloved disciple as ideal author is not intended to suggest that his role in the Gospel's narrative is counter-factual. Naturally, we should assess neither this nor any other aspect of the Gospel's narrative by modern concepts of history. The historicity of the beloved disciple's role in the Gospel narrative must be assessed in the same way as the historicity of the Gospel in general, taking account of the Gospel's own characteristic conjunction of realistically told story and richly symbolic significance. But we can at least remark here that a *purely* ideal author could easily have been given a much more extensive role in the Gospel. He could have witnessed all the signs. Although the beloved disciple's presence in the Gospel narrative is at some of the most significant points, it is also very limited in extent. Precisely those features of his role which have convinced Hengel and many others that he is not depicted as a Galilean disciple who accompanied Jesus throughout his ministry suggest that the portrayal of the beloved disciple in the Gospel is restricted by the remembered career of the historical disciple he represents. The term 'ideal author' is not meant to prejudge the degree of historicity in the portrayal of the beloved disciple. It simply means that what is said about him portrays him as the ideal author of the Gospel.

Yet we still have not asked why the ideal author should be portrayed as anonymous. This question has not often been asked in the right way, because it has usually been understood as: why is the identity of the beloved disciple concealed from the readers/hearers? Here we presuppose that in the oral context of the first readers/hearers the identity of the beloved disciple was well known. If there was any doubt it would be finally dispelled by 21.22-23. The correct question is not why the beloved disciple's identity is concealed, but why the beloved disciple, whose identity was well known to the first readers/hearers, is *portrayed* anonymously in the Gospel.

Probably the best answer is that anonymity is a literary device which serves to mark out the beloved disciple, who is also the author, from the other disciples in the narrative in which he appears with them. His anonymity makes him not just one named disciple among others or even the disciple closest to Jesus but, so to speak, different in kind. It gives the reader/hearer the sense that this disciple is in a different category from the others.[24] Of course, use of the first-person singular (as in, for example, the *Gospel of Peter*) also readily distinguishes the author from other characters in the narrative. But it has the additional effect of disrupting the pastness of the narrative. The author's 'I' makes the reader/hearer aware of him as the one now telling the story, and so the character in the story is at the same time acting in the narrative and addressing the reader/hearer. As we have seen, the author of the Fourth Gospel deliberately achieves this effect within the narrative only once, at 19.35, not by using the first person but by using the second person. At this point, in a parenthesis, the author wishes to speak of what he is doing in telling the story. At the point in the narrative at which his eyewitness testimony is most important, he deliberately obtrudes his authorial presence into the pastness of the narrative. But the other appearances of the beloved disciple do not have this effect. They are not appearances of the author *as author* addressing his readers/hearers, but only of the author as a character in the narrative, whose role in the story qualifies him to become the author. Anonymity distinguishes him without disrupting the third-person narration of the past. The literary device has in fact functioned in this way for all those readers—the vast majority of the Gospel's readers—to whom the identity of the beloved disciple never seemed a mystery. But for modern critics to whom the identity of the beloved disciple has become a problem, this function of his anonymity in the narrative has not been able to operate and so has not been recognized. Once we see that the identity of the beloved disciple was not intended to be concealed or even ambiguous, we can again recognize that his anonymity is that of the ideal author within his narrative.

---

24. This understanding of the anonymity of the beloved disciple needs minor qualification if the suggestion I made above, that the anonymous disciple of 18.15-16 is not the beloved disciple but another 'Johannine' disciple, is adopted. This would mean that the literary device of anonymity marks out not only the author himself, but also another personal source of the Gospel narrative, who could perhaps be regarded as, in a minor way, a co-author.

JSNT 15 (1982), pp. 51-80

THE CROSS AS AN EXPIATORY SACRIFICE IN THE FOURTH GOSPEL

Bruce H. Grigsby

Introduction

Even to the casual reader of the Fourth Gospel, everything related to the mission of Jesus appears subsumed under the Evangelist's[1] idea of revelation—especially the climax of this mission, Jesus' death.[2] Far from being a scandal or offense, the Johannine cross appears to have a 'positive' thrust.[3] As Johannes Beutler suggests, the Evangelist has apparently reworked the traditional passion material in the larger context of the Johannine 'Offenbarungstheologie'.[4] The Johannine Jesus is not

---

1.   It is presupposed that the Gospel reflects the mind and method of interpretation of the Beloved Disciple at every stage of editing—including the last. As such, the Fourth Gospel in its final form will be treated as thoroughly 'Johannine'.

2.   R. Bultmann thus writes, 'John has subsumed the death of Jesus under his idea of Revelation—in his death Jesus himself is acting as Revealer' (*Theology of the New Testament* [trans. K. Grobel; 2 vols.; London: SCM Press, 1952–1955], II, p. 53). Terence Forestell has recently arrived at the same conclusion: 'The literary treatment of the cross in the gospel as a whole, and especially in the passion narrative, points to the fact that the Evangelist evaluates the death of Jesus in the light of his characteristic understanding of Jesus' mission as one of revelation' (*The Word of the Cross* [Rome: Biblical Institute Press, 1974], p. 17).

3.   As Grant Osborne has recently pointed out, John has removed the details which suggest the horror of the crucifixion: the wine mixed with myrrh, the cry of dereliction and the Elijah account, the darkness, and the taunts of the bystanders ('Redactional Trajectories in the Crucifixion Narrative', *EvQ* 51 [1979], p. 92). Throughout the Johannine passion narrative, as Lindars has observed, 'there is a pervading calm like an Italian primitive painting' (*The Gospel of John* [NCB; London: Oliphants, 1972], p. 573).

4.   'Die Heilsbedeutung des Todes Jesu im Johannesevangelium nach Joh 13.1-20', in *Der Tod Jesu* (Freiburg: Herder, 1976), p. 203.

'crucified'; rather he is 'lifted up' and 'glorified'. Above all else, the Johannine cross is meant to be 'seen',[5] and as such, it might fairly be described as a kind of 'divine marquee', shining[6] with a heavenly message for all.

Investigations into the Fourth Gospel's understanding of the death of Christ have been quick to isolate and emphasize this distinctive, revelatory outlook. At the turn of the century, both G.B. Stevens[7] and E.F. Scott[8] concluded that the Evangelist's understanding of the cross as a place of revelation permeated his passion theology to the degree that traditional notions of expiation and atonement were excluded. Scott observed:

> His appearance in the flesh constituted his sacrifice. The death at the close could not add anything that was essential...In the true Johannine doctrine there is no logical place for the view of the death of Christ as an atonement.[9]

After a brief lapse, Bultmann popularized this somewhat extreme approach around 1950. He writes in part:

> While for Paul the incarnation is secondary to his death in importance, one might say that the reverse is true in John...In John, Jesus' death has no pre-eminent importance for salvation, but is the accomplishment of the work which began with the incarnation. Thus Jesus' death takes on a double aspect in John: it is the completion of his obedience, but it is also Jesus' release from his commission, and he can return to the glory he had in pre-existence.[10]

---

5.   The Johannine cross is presented as an event to be *seen*. This is suggested in the prologue—ἐθεασάμεθα τὴν δόξην αὐτοῦ (1.14)—implied in the comparison of the cross and bronze serpent (3.14), and emphasized at the crucifixion sight itself (19.35, 37).

6.   There is a close correlation between δόξα/ὑψόω themes and the Johannine treatment of φῶς in the Fourth Gospel. Accordingly, it does not seem to be speculative to discuss the Johannine cross as a 'sign'. Nor is it too far afield to describe the Johannine cross as the place where the 'Light of the World' is lifted up or displayed.

7.   *The Theology of the New Testament* (New York: Charles Scribner's Sons, 1899), pp. 224-33.

8.   *The Fourth Gospel, its Purpose and Theology* (Edinburgh: T. & T. Clark, 1906), pp. 207-12.

9.   Scott, *Fourth Gospel*, pp. 208, 225.

10.   *Theology of New Testament*, II, pp. 52-53.

More recently, Terence Forestell has adopted this approach to the Fourth Gospel's understanding of the cross. His work, which incorporates ingenious if not altogether convincing bits of exegesis, is epitomized in the following statements:

> The theology of the cross is not a theology of sacrifice and expiation but a theology of revelation;...the death of Jesus upon the cross is given a peculiar Johannine treatment; it is presented as the culmination of the revelatory work of Jesus and not as a vicarious work of satisfaction nor as an expiatory sacrifice for the sins of men.[11]

Forestell is not alone among modern scholars in his evaluation of Johannine passion theology. Among others,[12] Ulrich Müller,[13] Johannes Beutler,[14] and Siegfried Schulz[15] stand out as noteworthy supporters.

However, alongside the obvious revelatory themes just noted, the casual reader of the Fourth Gospel must also recognize that the Evangelist conceived of an expiatory[16] rationale, however 'johannized',

11. *Word of the Cross*, pp. 113, 120.

12. For example, Ernst Käsemann writes (*The Testament of Jesus* [trans. G. Krodel; London: SCM Press, 1968], p. 7): 'One is tempted to regard it [Passion] as being a mere postscript which had to be included because John could not ignore this tradition nor yet could he fit it organically into his work'. Friedrich Büchsel concludes that the Johannine cross stands poles apart from the Pauline cross—both in vocabulary and thought ('Die Stelle des Johannesevangeliums in einer Theologie des Neuen Testaments', *TBl* 16 [1937], p. 304).

13. See especially his article, 'Die Bedeutung des Kreuzestodes Jesu im Johannesevangelium', *KD* 21 (1975), pp. 49-71. He writes at one point (p. 69): 'Das Johannesevangelium,...erkennt zwar die Realität des Kreuzes Jesu an, ignoriert aber seine bleibende theologische Bedeutung'.

14. 'Die Heilsbedeutung des Todes Jesu im Johannesevangelium', pp. 188-205. He writes (p. 203): 'Auch wo das Johannesevangelium in traditionellen Wendungen vom Tod Jesu und seiner Heilsbedeutung spricht, sind diese doch eingebettet in die grösseren Zusammenhänge der johanneischen Offenbarungstheologie, die Jesus als den vom Vater gekommenen und aus dieser Welt zum Vater heimkehrenden Offenbarer darstellt...'

15. *Das Evangelium nach Johannes* (Göttingen: Vandenhoeck & Ruprecht, 13th edn, 1975), pp. 237-38: 'Der vierte Evangelist kennt zwar die theologische Aussage vom Sühntod Jesu, aber er entwickelt keine ausgesprochene Kreuzestheologie. Sie ist keineswegs ein beherrschender Zug johanneischer Verkündigung... Der Kreuzestod wird nicht mit Hilfe der Sühne bzw. des Sühnopfermotives theologisch zur Sprache gebracht, sondern als "Weggang" des Erlösers aus der Welt der Fremde verkundigt.'

16. The term 'expiatory' as used in this article refers primarily to those aspects of

behind Christ's death. Salvation in the Fourth Gospel is presented not only as the bestowal of eternal life, but also as a state of existence wherein sin is eliminated and judgment is escaped; and though an expiatory rationale between Christ's death and sin's removal is not as explicitly spelled out as in the Pauline literature, there are sufficient hints throughout the Gospel to suppose that the Evangelist endorsed such a rationale.

Three such 'hints' will now be examined:[17] (1) the casting of Jesus in the role of the Paschal Victim; (2) the relating of Jesus to the Isaac figure as reconstrued in Rabbinic speculation on Gen. 22.1-14; and (3) the introduction to the crucifixion narrative of the description of the effluence of blood and water from the side of Christ. These three

the ceremonial, ritualistic rites within the Levitical cultus which were incorporated by New Testament authors into their respective understandings of Christ's death—which does not, of course, exclude from consideration 'expiatory' elements in the later Isaianic (vicarious suffering), Maccabaean (atoning value of martyr's death) and Rabbinic ('Akedah' speculation) material. Thus the term is being used synonymously with the adjective, 'cultic'.

Whether this Old Testament expiatory rationale discerned by the New Testament authors primarily focused on the *appeasement* ('propitiation') of God's wrath or the *taking away* ('expiation') of sin is outside the scope of this article. Demonstrating the validity of either semantic category (as both C.H. Dodd and Leon Morris have so ably accomplished for their respective preferences) is an exhausting exercise, depending heavily on one's lexical expertise with both the כפר and ἱλάσκομαι word groups.

17.   There are indications in the Fourth Gospel that the Evangelist placed Christ in the role of a Messianic High Priest, which might be considered a fourth 'hint'. It is apparent that the idea of Christ as the High Priest in the Fourth Gospel, though far from explicit, is nonetheless 'une excellente inférence théologique' (Joseph Coppens, 'Le Messianisme sacerdotal dans le NT', in *La Venue Messie* [ed. E. Massaux; Louvain: Desclée de Brouwer, 1962], p. 109). This motif most clearly emerges in two passages: 17.19 and 19.23. In 17.19 Christ refers to his impending death as an act of self-sanctification, resulting in the believer's sanctification as well. In 19.23 the Evangelist, in contrast with the synoptic accounts, mentions that Jesus' discarded tunic was 'seamless, woven in one piece'. If this detail is not a later addition, or taken from a source independent of the synoptics, then it represents yet another bit of Johannine creativity. A likely theological motive appears to be the presentation of Christ as a High Priest. For the Evangelist, a seamless garment 'rappelait la robe du grand Prêtre' (F.-M. Braun, *Jean le Théologien* [4 vols.; Paris: Gabalda, 1959–1972], II, p. 99). Cf. further A. Feuillet, 'La Sacerdoce du Christ et de ses envoyés, les apôtres, d'après Isaïe 53 et d'après le quatrième évangile', *NVet* 49 (1974), pp. 102-12.

Johannine features, taken together, ought to caution any interpreter against understanding the death of Christ in the Fourth Gospel as an exclusively revelatory event.[18] There appears to be ample room in the Evangelist's passion theology for both revelatory *and* expiatory themes.

Christ the Paschal Victim

This theme emerges at several points in the Fourth Gospel. Despite the skepticism of Dodd,[19] it appears to be a leading idea of the Evangelist. Acknowledging the prominence of this thematic development, one may reasonably conclude with Schnackenburg that the Evangelist necessarily envisioned some form of expiatory rationale between Christ's death and sin's removal.[20] This is especially true since the expiatory power of the Paschal sacrifice, though not at all certain at the inception of the Passover,[21] was a commonly accepted feature by the time of the Fourth Gospel's composition.[22]

18. A recent observation of James McPolin is to the point here: 'A more feasible explanation could be that John combines a variety of perspectives among which one must also include that of the cross as removing sin, even if this is not as dominant as the revelatory aspect of Jesus' death' ('Studies in the Fourth Gospel—Some Contemporary Trends', *IBS* 2 [1980], p. 7).

19. This is voiced most strongly in *The Interpretation of the Fourth Gospel* (Cambridge: Cambridge University Press, 1953), pp. 230-40. Recently his skepticism has been shared by van den Bussche in his commentary on the Fourth Gospel (*Jean* [Paris: Desclée de Brouwer, 1967], p. 538). After surveying the important research in this area of Johannine thought, Robert Kysar sounds a note of caution: 'These efforts towards clarifying the intention of the Evangelist to provoke paschal similarities in the account of Jesus seem on the one hand most convincing but on the other most excessive' (*The Fourth Evangelist and his Gospel* [Minneapolis: Augsburg, 1975], p. 140).

20. 'As soon as Jesus was regarded as the paschal lamb of the New Testament, the thought of his expiatory death was necessarily involved' (Rudolf Schnackenburg, *The Gospel according to St John* [3 vols.; trans. K. Smyth; New York: Herder & Herder, 1968–81], I, pp. 299-300).

21. The blood of the original Paschal Lamb is normally described as *apotropaic* (a means of protection from evil spirits) rather than *kathartic*. The origins of such apotropaic rites are obscure. G.B. Gray (*Sacrifice in the Old Testament: Its Theory and Practice* [Oxford: Clarendon Press, 1925], p. 363) conjectures that the Israelites drew upon the 'door' rituals of surrounding cultures. In these rituals, blood was smeared on the outside of a closed door to reinforce it against an evil spirit. Either blood, salt, plants, or even the outline of an outstretched hand, was used in this regard to repel spirits.

22. By New Testament times, the blood of the Paschal Lamb was clearly regarded

Before proceeding to the direct exegetical evidence for the theme of Christ the Paschal Victim in the Fourth Gospel, brief mention should be made of more indirect indications in this direction. For example, Aileen Guilding has attempted to interpret the Fourth Gospel as a form of Christian Haggadah, read in the synagogue in conjunction with the corresponding Jewish *sedarim* and *haphtaroth*.[23] Her results, though not widely nor wholly accepted,[24] have at least contributed positively to the ongoing question of John 6 and its *Sitz im Leben* as a Christian Passover Haggadah.[25] If Guilding is right about John 6, and indeed Peder Borgen

as expiatory. In fact, by the time of the close of the Old Testament, 'all sacrifices were believed to have atoning value' (C.R. North, *A Theological Word Book of the Bible* [ed. A. Richardson; New York: Macmillan, 1950], p. 206). 'Everything in any way connected with sacrifice acquired an expiatory power' (Johannes Pedersen, *Israel: Its Life and Culture* [trans. A.I. Fausbøll; 3 vols.; London: Oxford University Press, 1926–47], III, p. 364). Rabbinic thought fully endorsed this infusion of expiatory significance to all sacrifices. Cf. especially *Exod. R.* 15.12: 'I mercifully take pity on you by means of the Paschal Blood and the blood of circumcision, and I propitiate your souls'. See further Str-B (IV, p. 40) and G. Dalman (*Jesus-Jeshua* trans. P. Levertoff; New York: KTAV, 1971], p. 167).

23. *The Fourth Gospel and Jewish Worship* (Oxford: Clarendon Press, 1960), pp. 48, 62.

24. Cf. especially the telling critique of Leon Morris (*The New Testament and Jewish Lectionaries* [London: Tyndale, 1964]) with regard to her 'exact' lining-up of corresponding *sedarim* and *haphtaroth*.

25. Notice especially 6.4 (ἦν δὲ ἐγγὺς τὸ πάσχα), the idea of manna from heaven (manna is prominently mentioned in the liturgy of the Passover meal), and extensive parallels with Jewish Passover texts used as synagogical readings. Work in this direction was pioneered shortly before Guilding's work reached the press. In 1956, David Daube (*The New Testament and Rabbinic Judaism* [London: Athlone, 1956], pp. 36-51) argued well for the thesis that John 6 might originally have been designed as a form of Christian, Passover haggadah. In 1958, G. Ziener suggested that the Fourth Gospel can be placed within the framework of a Passover celebration, although he dealt generally with the book of 'signs' rather than specifically ch. 6 ('Johannesevangelium und urchristliche Passafeier', *BZ* 2 [1958], pp. 263-74). In the same year, Wilhelm Wilkens suggested that the original form of the Fourth Gospel— i.e., the first layer of editing in his 'redactional' scheme—was that of a 'passover gospel' (*Die Entstehungsgeschichte des vierten Evangeliums* [Zollikon: Evangelischer Verlag, 1958]). In 1959, Bertil Gärtner produced a work on the 'Passover' setting of John 6, where he argues that John 6 was originally in the form of a Christian, Passover haggadah (*John 6 and the Jewish Passover* [Lund: Gleerup, 1959], pp. 29-38). More recently, Raymond Brown has found this approach to John 6 very satisfactory. He notes that 'the mention of Passover certainly fits the whole theological

after her,[26] then John 6 (especially vv. 35-38) was probably read by Christians each Passover season in conjunction with appropriate Jewish synagogical readings for Passover. Thus, the mystery of Christ's death in John 6, which results in life for the world, would have been expounded each year against the backdrop of Passover texts—some of which, at least, concerned the expiatory death of the Paschal Lamb.[27]

Other indirect indicators of the Evangelist's concern for Paschal themes might be gleaned from W. Wilkens's thesis that the Fourth Gospel evolved from, and still reflects, an original 'Passover' framework;[28] from Wayne Meeks's proposal that Moses served as a Model for the Evangelist's prophet-king Christology;[29] from the role of the Johannine Christ as a 'new' Moses, accomplishing a 'new' Exodus;[30] and, not incidentally, from the nineteen references to the Passover in the Fourth Gospel.[31] These indirect indicators serve to set the stage for the Evangelist's more direct presentation of Christ as the Paschal Lamb which will now be considered.

outlook of the chapter. Its presence is not an isolated act of editorship [as Bultmann alleges, *Gospel of John, ad loc.*]; and there is nothing to contradict the possibility that the scene was originally connected with Passover' (*The Gospel according to John* [AB, 29, 29A; New York: Doubleday, 1966, 1970], I, p. 245).

26. *Bread from Heaven* (NovTSup, 10; Leiden: Brill, 1965).

27. Miss Guilding suggests the following three year cycle of *sedarim* used at Passover season: year 1—Genesis 1–8; year 2—Exodus 11–16; year 3—Numbers 6–14.

28. See above, n. 25.

29. *The Prophet-King* (NovTSup, 14; Leiden: Brill, 1967). Meeks has basically isolated a rather complex set of Jewish and Samaritan 'Moses' traditions centered in Galilee at the time of Christ. He has persuasively related these traditions to the bulk of Johannine material which seems to present Jesus as a type of prophet-king.

30. Cf. especially Braun's treatment of Christ as the 'new' Moses of the 'new' Exodus (*Théologien*, III.1, pp. 161-65). F.F. Bruce attests to the prominence of this motif in all the Gospels ('Our God and Saviour', in *The Saviour God* [ed. S.G.F. Brandon; Manchester: Manchester University Press, 1963], p. 64): 'The presentation of the redemptive work of Christ in terms of the Exodus motif in so many strands of the New Testament teaching shows how primitive was the Christian use of this motif—going back, quite probably, to the period of Jesus' ministry... The coincidence of Jesus' death with the Passover season no doubt helped the interpretation of his work as a new Exodus.' It should also be noted that the performance of signs by Jesus and their purpose seem to recall the theology of 'signs' as performed by Moses. So Karl Rengstorf (*TDNT*, VII, pp. 256-57).

31. The term πάσχα occurs ten times, while the term ἑορτή, with reference to the Passover, occurs nine times.

There are four different places in the Fourth Gospel where the Evangelist indicates to his readership that Christ is fulfilling the role of *the* Paschal Lamb:[32] 1.29; 19.14; 19.29; and 19.36. These passages will be considered in turn.

(1) 1.29. There are good reasons to believe that the Evangelist[33] intended the Baptist's statement in 1.29—'Behold the Lamb of God who takes away the sin of the world'—to refer to the Paschal Lamb rather than the Suffering Servant of Isaiah 53. First, as Raymond Brown points out,[34] Christ is addressed as a Lamb directly. Isaiah 53 can only offer statements that *compare* the Servant with a lamb. Secondly, the Evangelist appears to follow up this initial connection between Christ and the Paschal Lamb at later points in the Gospel—6.45-46; 19.14, 29, 36. Thirdly, it should be noted that the book of Revelation, a work with many Christological affinities to the Fourth Gospel, presents Christ as a slain lamb (5.6), whose blood serves cultically as a ransom (5.9).

However, as there exist equally good reasons for seeing the Suffering Servant behind the title in 1.29,[35] it seems best to accept both options.[36]

32. 19.34 might be another direct reference to Christ as the Paschal Lamb according to J.M. Ford's article ('"Mingled Blood" from the Side of Christ', *NTS* 15 [1969], pp. 337-38). She cites Rabbinic passages which state that the blood of the Paschal Lamb needed to be mixed (cf. 19.34) so that it might not congeal. She also cites the frequent Rabbinic description of the 'spurting forth' (קלח) of the Paschal Lamb's blood—a phenomenon she finds euphemistically expressed in the Evangelist's description εὐθὺς ἐξῆλθεν αἷμα.

33. Whether the Baptist intended the title to refer to the Paschal Lamb is another matter. There is no serious objection to the thesis that the 'Johannine' Baptist knew Christ at his baptism as either the Suffering Servant or the true Paschal Lamb. Barrett ('Lamb of God', *NTS* 1 [1955], pp. 210-18), as with Braun (*Théologien*, II, p. 83), concludes that the Baptist originally understood his utterance in terms of an apocalyptic Lamb. For Barrett, this apocalyptic Lamb was a standard pre-Christian, Messianic title. Barrett then argues, again as does Braun, that the Evangelist intended the title to refer primarily to the Paschal Lamb. In contrast, Dodd (*Interpretation*, pp. 330-35) contends that the Evangelist continued the Baptist's apocalyptic understanding of this title.

34. *Gospel according to John*, I, p. 63.

35. Although J. Morgenstern's peremptory verdict of 'beyond all doubt' ('The Suffering Servant—A New Solution', *VT* 11 [1961], p. 425) on the relationship between 1.29 and Isaiah 53 appears unduly dogmatic, the evidence encourages such finality. Lexically, ἀμνός ('lamb') could derive from the terms שׂה and πρόβατον in Isa. 53.7, especially if an original Aramaic טליא ('lamb' *or* 'servant') paved the way (pioneered by C.J. Ball, 'Had the Fourth Gospel an Aramaic Archetype?', *ExpTim* 21

That the Evangelist would have juxtaposed the Servant and the Paschal Lamb in his Christology is not unprecedented either in the New Testament[37] or early Christian thought.[38]

(2) 19.14. The time of Christ's death is recorded in 19.14 as twelve noon (sixth hour). The day of the week is Friday,[39] the day of the month is Nisan 14,[40] and the year is either AD 30 or 33.[41] These chronological

[1909], pp. 91-93, and C.F. Burney, *The Aramaic Origin of the Fourth Gospel* [Oxford: Clarendon Press, 1922], pp. 107-108). In addition, a rather convincing case can be built for the Baptist's ability and desire—at least within the Johannine tradition—to find Jesus' Messianic identity within the Servant Songs. For most copious defense of Jn 1.29/Suffering Servant identity, see Eric May's dissertation, *Ecce Agnus Dei: A Philological and Exegetical Approach to John 1.29, 36* (Washington: Catholic University of America Press, 1947). For the most articulate critique of this theory, see the commentaries of both Dodd and Barrett on Jn 1.29.

36. So Feliks Gryglewicz, 'Das Lamm Gottes', *NTS* 13 [1967], p. 137 and Forestell, *Word of the Cross*, p. 163. Brown observes ('Three quotations from John the Baptist in the Gospel of John', *CBQ* 22 [1960], p. 295), 'We suggest,…the literal or gospel sense of the text, while not excluding the apocalyptic lamb, concerns chiefly the Paschal Lamb and/or the Suffering Servant'.

37. Cf. especially 1 Pet. 2.22-25, which develops the ideas of Isa. 53.1-12 in a distinctly Paschal setting.

38. This is best illustrated in a passage from Justin (*Trypho* 3): ἦν γὰρ τὸ πάσχα ὁ χριστὸς ὁ τυθεὶς ὕστερον ὡς καὶ Ἡσαΐας ἔφη αὐτὸς ὡς πσόβατον… (Isa. 53.7).

39. 19.31, 42. See Bultmann (*Gospel of John*, p. 664 n. 5) for discussion of παρασκευή and its frequent meaning of 'Friday'.

40. The phrase, παρασκευὴ τοῦ πάσχα, refers to the day before the Passover, i.e., Nisan 14. This is confirmed in 18.28 where the crucifixion appears to antedate the Passover meal in the Johannine passion chronology.

41. Although there have been advocates for every year between 21 and 36 (cf. Harold Hoehner's list in *Chronological Aspects of the Life of Christ* [Grand Rapids: Zondervan, 1977], pp. 96-97), 30 and 33 are the only two viable options. Years before 26 are eliminated because that was Pilate's inaugural year as procurator. Other possibilities, namely 26, 28, 29, 32, 34, and 35, are eliminated because astronomical calculations have determined that neither Nisan 14 nor 15 occurred on a Friday during those years (cf. detailed discussion of Joachim Jeremias, *The Eucharistic Words of Jesus* [Oxford: Basil Blackwell, 1955], pp. 36-41). Both 27 and 31 are tenuous on astronomical grounds. Conceivably, Nisan 14 occurred on a Friday in 27, but only if the sighting of the new moon's first, faint disc (normally spotted some 30 hours *after* actual appearance of new moon) was delayed a day by clouds or atmospheric conditions. 31 is an option only if the year 31 was a leap year. Finally, the year 36 is eliminated because it runs into serious harmonization problems with the Luke-Acts chronology. Thus, the years 30 and 33 emerge as the most likely options.

details differ from the synoptic sequence with regard to the hour of the day[42] and the day of the month.[43] In both instances the Johannine account offers a time sequence which emphasizes Christ's role as the Paschal Lamb.[44] Indeed, 'if the Johannine narrative is read by itself in light of Jewish Paschal custom all is straightforward'.[45]

It appears to some that the Evangelist has intentionally altered sound historical tradition to serve his own theological interests.[46] 'This may not be good history', as Barrett observes,[47] 'but it does seem to be Johannine theology'. And, as he elsewhere argues, 'it can hardly be due to anything other than theological interest, and this in turn can hardly be other than the conviction that Jesus himself was the true Paschal Lamb offered at the appointed hour in the afternoon of Nisan 14'.[48] For Barnabas Lindars, this 'theological' understanding of 19.14 is hard to avoid: 'it is difficult to eradicate the impression that the death of Jesus on the eve of the Passover is a purely Johannine invention, dictated by

42. In Jn 19.14, the crucifixion begins about noon (sixth hour), in the synoptics at 9 a.m. (third hour).

43. In the Fourth Gospel, Christ appears to be crucified on Friday, Nisan 14, but in the synoptics on Friday, Nisan 15.

44. The Paschal Lambs were slaughtered in the temple precincts on the afternoon of Nisan 14. Thus the reader of 19.14 was pointed towards the role of Christ as the Paschal Lamb. In addition, there is reason to believe that the lambs were begun to be slaughtered at noon (sixth hour as in the Fourth Gospel) on Nisan 14. This was because the Paschal Lamb was slain as early as possible (noon being the earliest, Exod. 12.6) when Passover eve happened to fall on Sabbath eve; i.e., Friday the 14th (*m. Pes.* 5.1-3). For discussion of Rabbinic evidence, consult Bonsirven ('Hora Talmudica: La notion chronologique de Jean 19.14, aurait-elle un sens symbolique?', *Bib* 33 [1952], pp. 511-15) and Str-B (II, p. 836). Brown (*Gospel according to John*, II, p. 833) suggests that the lambs were slaughtered at noon in Jesus' day (original injunction in Exod. 12.6 called for evening sacrifice) because of the sheer number that needed to be slaughtered. Thus, by casuistry, the Rabbis interpreted the 'evening' of Exod. 12.6 to begin at noon when the sun began its decline.

45. Gray, *Sacrifice*, p. 389.

46. Studies of the four Evangelists' redactional activities in the crucifixion narrative have indicated that the Fourth Evangelist was relatively 'busy' in his composition. Grant Osborne remarks that 'even more than Luke, John is orchestrating a theological masterpiece in his crucifixion narrative' ('Redactional Trajectories in the Crucifixion Narrative', p. 91). For Osborne, the Paschal imagery is 'obvious' (p. 95).

47. *The Gospel according to St John* (London: SCM Press, 2nd edn, 1978), p. 51.

48. 'Lamb of God', p. 211.

his theological interests, regardless of the traditions which he was actually handling'.[49]

The above analysis assumes that the synoptics were historical and the Fourth Gospel theological with regard to 'fixing' Christ's death in time. However, this assumption is far from certain. Apart from assuming the converse—that is, the Fourth Gospel is historical and the synoptics are theological[50]—it is possible to assume that both traditions are historical. Although 'it seems impossible to reconcile the dates',[51] various reconciliatory schemes have been proposed in an effort to harmonize the conflicting traditions.

First, Torrey[52]—tentatively endorsed by Jeremias[53]—has suggested that the phrase in 19.14b, παρασκευὴ τοῦ πάσχα, reproduces the Aramaic ערובתא דיפסחא rather than the Hebrew ערב הפסח. Thus a fuller Greek rendering produces the construction: παρασκευὴ τοῦ σαββάτου ἐν πάσχα ('preparation of the Sabbath of Passover Week').[54] Thus the Fourth Gospel does not demand a Nisan 14 date for

49. *Gospel of John*, ad loc. Cf. also his *New Testament Apologetic* (London: SCM Press, 1961), p. 96. Günter Reim also detects 'theological activity' in 19.14: 'Stammt der Zeitpunkt der Kreuzigung Jesu aus theologischen Erwängungen des Evangelisten, was ich für wahrscheinlich halte, so hat auch Johannes Jesus als das Passahlamm angesehen' (*Studien zum alttestamentlichen Hintergrund des Johannesevangeliums* [SNTSMS, 22; Cambridge: Cambridge University Press, 1974], p. 177).

50. Sydney Temple (*The Core of the Fourth Gospel* [Oxford: Mowbrays, 1975], p. 47) suggests that Jesus did die on Friday, Nisan 14. Thus the Fourth Gospel, according to Temple, is historical and the synoptics are theological, having been altered to make the Last Supper a Passover meal. Dodd concurs (*Interpretation*, pp. 424-25): 'It seems highly probable that the Evangelist is following a pre-Johannine tradition in the date he assigns to the crucifixion, and not shaping the narrative to suit his theological preconceptions'. Thus, for Temple and Dodd, the Talmudic tradition which dates the death of Jesus on Nisan 14 (*b. Sanh.* 43a) represents an independent and accurate tradition without Johannine influence.

51. Barrett, *Gospel according to St John*, p. 48.

52. 'The date of the Crucifixion according to the Fourth Gospel', *JBL* 50 (1931), pp. 232-51. Cf. also his article, 'In the Fourth Gospel the Last Supper was the Paschal Meal', *JQR* 42 (1952), pp. 237-50. His understanding of this phrase has been recently supported by Fritz Chenderlin, 'A Distributed Observance of the Passover—A Preliminary Test of the Hypothesis', *Bib* 57 (1976), pp. 1-24.

53. *Eucharistic Words*, p. 80. He regards this as 'undoubtedly an Aramaism', although he leans toward the option ערובת פסחא rather than Torrey's proposed ערובתא דיפסחא.

54. Bultmann has shown that the term παρασκευή, from the Aramaic ערוב פסחא,

the Friday crucifixion. In Torrey's scheme, the Friday of Passover week in the Fourth Gospel is both the 'preparation of the Sabbath' and Passover—that is, Nisan 15. Accordingly, harmonization with the synoptics' Nisan 15 crucifixion date is possible.[55]

A second attempt to reconcile Jn 19.14 with the synoptic dating involves regarding the Last Supper as only a pseudo-Passover meal.[56] Thus there is no need to view the date of the synoptic crucifixion as Friday, Nisan 15, which was required if Thursday evening's meal (Nisan 15 began at 6 p.m. Thursday) was a true Passover meal. The date of the synoptic crucifixion may then be moved back a day to the 14th, in line with the Fourth Gospel. Bertil Gärtner, who takes this approach, writes, 'the Last Supper, chronologically speaking, was not a Passover meal, but, viewed from a theological angle, contained elements drawn from among the concepts and the liturgical practice of the Passover'.[57] Both Gärtner[58] and Théodore Preiss[59] point out that the Paschal Lamb, supposedly the central focus of any Passover meal, is not specifically mentioned in any Last Supper account; rather Jesus links his death to the bread and wine.[60]

came to mean any day before a feast (rest day), but especially the day before the Sabbath—Friday (*Gospel of John*, p. 664 n. 5).

55. Str-B (II, p. 836) find Torrey's Greek paraphrase untenable: 'Diese Deutung scheitert daran, dass παρασκευὴ τοῦ πάσχα Wiedergabe des hebräischen פסח ערב ist; und wie dieses niemals vertauscht werden konnte mit einem ערב שבת בפסח, so konnte ein Mann, der an jüdische Vorstellungs- und Ausdrucks- weise gewöhnt war—und ein solcher war doch der Apostel Johannes—nimmer den Ausdruck παρασκευὴ τοῦ πάσχα im Sinne von παρασκευὴ τοῦ σαββάτου ἐν πάσχα verwenden.'

56. What kind of meal was it then? G.H. Box has suggested that it was a Jewish *Kiddush* meal. This was a ceremony around a meal which pronounced a blessing on the eve of a Sabbath or feast day ('The Jewish Antecedents of the Eucharist', *JTS* 3 [1902], pp. 357-69). Hans Lietzmann has suggested that it was a *Haburah* meal. This was an intimate meal shared by a group of like-minded friends, especially at a wedding or funeral (*Mass and Lord's Supper* [trans. D.H.G. Reeve; London: SCM Press, 1954], pp. 170-71). Cf. Jeremias, *Eucharistic Words*, pp. 16-26, for a telling critique of both of these proposals.

57. *Jewish Passover*, p. 45. See also Brown ('The Problem of Historicity in John', *CBQ* 24 [1962], p. 5) who suggests that the Last Supper was not a Passover meal *per se* but a meal with Passover characteristics.

58. *Jewish Passover*, p. 45.

59. 'Aramäisches in Joh 8.30-36', *TZ* 3 (1947), p. 80.

60. However, Jeremias has amassed some impressive evidence in contending that

A third reconciliatory attempt comes from Mlle. Jaubert.[61] She suggests that Jesus and the disciples followed a 364-day, Jewish solar calendar, in use in the Qumran community. This calendar, dating from the Babylonian captivity, always had Passover occur on a Tuesday/Wednesday. Therefore, she reasons, the synoptics record a legitimate Passover meal on Tuesday evening, Nisan 12, of that year. With this reckoning, two and a half days could have elapsed before Christ's death on Friday, Nisan 14. However, the Fourth Evangelist, using the traditional Jewish calendar, recorded the Friday of Christ's death as the day *before* the Passover. Harmonization is thus possible.[62]

A fourth attempt to chronologically line up the four Gospels comes from the work of Harold Hoehner.[63] After a lengthy summary of previous reconciliatory attempts, he opts for a solution based upon discrepancies in beginning the Jewish day. After citing evidence for both a sunrise to sunrise and a sunset to sunset reckoning of a day,[64] Hoehner postulates that the synoptics, Jesus, disciples, and Pharisees followed the Galilean reckoning of sunrise to sunrise. On the other hand, the Evangelist and the Sadducees adhered to the Judaean reckoning of

the Last Supper was a Passover meal—in all four Gospels (*Eucharistic Words*, pp. 41-62). For arguments supporting the view that the Johannine Last Supper was a Paschal Meal, cf. Jeremias (*ibid.*, p. 81), Torrey ('In the Fourth Gospel the Last Supper was the Paschal Meal', pp. 237-50), and Hoehner (*Chronological Aspects*, pp. 76-77).

61. 'Jésus et le Calendrier de Qumran', *NTS* 7 (1960), pp. 1-30; *The Date of the Last Supper* (trans. I. Rafferty; New York: Albo, 1965); 'Le Mercredi où Jésus fut livré' (1968), pp. 145-64. She is followed and endorsed by Eugen Ruckstuhl (*Chronology of the Last Days of Jesus* [trans. V.J. Drapela; New York: Doubleday, 1965).

62. For a critique of Jaubert, cf. especially Josef Blinzler, 'Qumran-Kalender und Passionchronologie', *ZNW* 49 (1958), pp. 238-51; George Ogg, 'Review of Mlle. Jaubert, *La Date de la Cène*', *NovT* 3 (1959), pp. 149-60; Norman Walker, 'Pauses in the Passion Story and their Significance for Chronology', *NovT* 6 (1963), pp. 16-19; Jeremias, *Eucharistic Words*, pp. 24-25; and K.A. Strand, 'John as Quartodeciman: A Reappraisal', *JBL* 84 (1965), pp. 251-58.

63. See his section, 'The problem of harmonization', *Chronological Aspects*, pp. 81-93.

64. Hoehner establishes the simultaneous existence of these two methods in Old Testament texts. However, his attempt to establish their existence in the first Christian centuries is not as successful. The texts which he cites (from the Mishna and Josephus) are ambiguous, capable of being used against his thesis as well (*Chronological Aspects*, p. 86).

sunset to sunset. Thus the synoptic account is simply 'advanced' twelve hours before the Johannine account, having begun its day that much earlier. In this way, the Paschal Lambs were slaughtered on two consecutive days in the temple—on Thursday afternoon, Nisan 14, according to synoptic reckoning and on Friday afternoon, Nisan 14, according to Johannine reckoning. More importantly, the discrepancy in dating Christ's death is easily explained. The synoptics reckon it as Friday afternoon, Nisan 15—their 15th having begun at 6 a.m.—and the Fourth Evangelist as Friday afternoon, Nisan 14—his 15th not commencing until 6 p.m.

In conclusion, the Evangelist appears determined to present Jesus as the true Paschal Lamb in 19.14. This is especially true if he has intentionally departed from sound historical tradition for his chronological referents. And even if one of the various attempts to reconcile the Fourth Gospel with the synoptics is accepted, the theological impact of 19.14 might be slightly minimized, but not nullified.[65]

(3) 19.29. The incident where the sponge was lifted to Jesus' mouth on the hyssop stem appears to be a third passage where Jesus is presented as a Paschal Lamb. Hyssop is certainly related to cultic sprinkling elsewhere[66] and was the agent which applied the blood of the Passover Lamb to the door (Exod. 12.22). Thus, with Raymond Brown, 'the mention of hyssop may well be symbolically evocative of Jesus' dying as the Paschal Lamb of the new covenant'.[67]

However, such symbolism is far from clear, as the analogy is far from precise. Bultmann's skepticism is understandable: '…it is scarcely believable that Jesus should be designated as the Passover Lamb through the statement that a sponge with vinegar was stuck on a hyssop stem'.[68] Yet two factors must be kept in mind before dismissing the possibility that 19.29 represents a piece of theological symbolism.

First, there is good reason to believe that the reading ὑσσώπῳ, undoubtedly original,[69] is a deliberate departure from the Markan tradition

65. Temple (*Core of the Fourth Gospel*, p. 47) and Dodd (*Interpretation*, pp. 424-25; *Historical Tradition*, pp. 109-11) both argue that the historicity of Jn 19.14—which they support—eliminates the need to find a Paschal theology in the Johannine passion narrative.

66. Lev. 14.6-7; Num. 19.6; Ps. 50.9; Heb. 9.19; Barnabas 8.1, 6.

67. *Gospel according to John*, II, p. 930.

68. *Gospel of John*, p. 674, n. 2.

69. Externally, the reading ὑσσώπῳ is attested by every major Greek MS except Θ…thus the 'A' rating by the UBS textual committee. Internally, it is

wherein a 'reed' (κάλαμος) lifts the sponge.[70] The hyssop stem was admirably *unsuited* for lifting a heavy, wet sponge. It entirely lacked the necessary stiffness.[71] Thus the Evangelist has introduced a term which 'is prompted not by tradition, but by the motif of the Passover'.[72]

Secondly, precise analogies are not the hallmark of Johannine symbolism. One need only look at 3.14-15, 7.37-39, or 19.36 to appreciate that the Evangelist can evoke Old Testament themes in highly imaginative ways. As Brown so aptly observes, 'it is difficult to apply rigorous logic to Johannine symbolism'.[73] It should also be noted that Paschal allusions are already present in the Fourth Gospel (1.29; 19.14, 36). Thus the presence of such an allusion in 19.29, though admittedly vague, is not uncharacteristic of the Evangelist.

In conclusion, 19.29 ought to be regarded as a possible Paschal allusion,[74] as theological motives appear to be behind the Evangelist's substitution of ὑσσώπῳ for κάλαμος. The analogy with Exod. 12.22, though far from precise, is nonetheless tolerable by Johannine standards.

(4) 19.36. In this passage, the Evangelist notes that the refusal of the soldiers to break Christ's legs (v. 33) has fulfilled an Old Testament Scripture: ἐγένετο γὰρ ταῦτα ἵνα ἡ γραφὴ πληρωθῇ, Ὀστοῦν οὐ συντριβήσεται αὐτοῦ. Whether or not this verse is intended to evoke a Paschal allusion depends on the origin of the Old Testament quotation.

also to be preferred as the *lectio difficilior*. The alternative reading, ὑσσῷ ('javelin'), either resulted from haplography—YCCWΠEPIΘENTEC written for YCCWΠWΠEPIΘENTEC—or a scribal desire to replace the enigmatic term 'hyssop' with the contextually more suitable 'javelin' or 'spear' (cf. term 'perticae' in Latin MSS).

70. So Barrett, *Gospel according to St John*, p. 553. Perhaps the hyssop was attached to a reed. *M. Par.* 12.1 suggests such a procedure (using scarlet thread and a 'spindle reed') if the hyssop used for cultic sprinkling is so stubby that the priest's fingertips are in jeopardy of contacting the sacrificial blood or water.

71. In the Old Testament, hyssop is referred to as 'the humblest of shrubs' (1 Kgs 4.33). It was very brittle and often grew from cracks in stone walls. Although the term can refer to several species, it most likely was *Origanum Maru* of the labial family (Brown, *Gospel according to John*, II, p. 909). A more common name would be wild Marjoram (see Dalman, *Arbeit und Sitte in Pälastina* [Gütersloh: Bertelsmann, 1928], p. 371), which is related to mint and thyme.

72. Lindars, *New Testament Apologetic*, p. 101.

73. *Gospel according to John*, II, p. 930.

74. Cf. V.C. Pfitzner's statement ('The Coronation of the King—Passion Narrative and Passion Theology in the Gospel of St John', *LThJ* 10 [1976], p. 6): '…it remains just possible that John wishes to make a paschal allusion in 19.29'.

If 19.36 draws upon Exod. 12.10, 46 and Num. 9.12, then a Paschal allusion is fairly certain. The bones of the Paschal Lamb were not broken and, by analogy, neither were Christ's bones broken in his sacrificial death. However, if 19.36 draws upon Ps. 33.21 (LXX)—κύριος φυλάσσει πάντα τὰ ὀστᾶ αὐτῶν ἓν ἐξαὐτῶν οὐ συντριβήσεται—then a Paschal allusion need not be present.

Three considerations make it probable that the Evangelist intended to recall Exod. 12.10, 46 and/or Num. 9.12, rather than Ps. 33.21 (LXX)[75] or both Ps. 33.21 and Exod. 12.10, 46.[76] First, linguistic considerations: With regard to the LXX, Jn 19.36 is virtually identical with Num. 9.12 (codex Alexandrinus),[77] and very similar to Exod. 12.10.[78] With regard

75. The connection between this verse and Jn 19.36 is well argued by Dodd (*Interpretation*, pp. 230-38), Forestell (*Word of the Cross*, p. 90 n. 32), Bultmann (*Gospel of John*, p. 677 n. 1), van den Bussche (*Jean*, p. 536), and Vergote ('L'Exaltation du Christ en croix selon la quatrième évangile', *ETL* 28 [1952], p. 18). All of these cite the common passive form συντριβήσεται and the fact that the Evangelist has a penchant for the Psalms in his passion narrative. Despite the foregoing support, Ps. 34(33).20(21) is not all that similar, linguistically, to Jn 19.36. The Psalm has the plural 'bones' rather than the singular, and the term is not the subject of the passive verb as it is in the Fourth Gospel. Accordingly, Reim finds it surprising that anyone could prefer the Psalm passage to Num. 9.12—where excellent verbal parallels are provided in the LXX (Codex A) *and* the MT. He exclaims (*Alttestamentlichen Hintergrund*, p. 52): 'Es ist mir nicht einsichtig, weshalb eine unbekannte Psalmstelle, die sprachlich am weitesten vom Johanneszitat entfernt ist, den bekannten Pentateuchstellen [by which he means primarily Num. 9.12], von denen zwei dem Johannes-Zitat sprachlich sehr nahe stehen, vorgezogen werden sollte'.

76. Barrett originally saw a dual Old Testament reference in 19.36 ('The Old Testament in the Fourth Gospel', *JTS* 48 [1947], p. 157): 'It is so difficult to make up one's mind between these sources for the Old Testament reference [Ps. 34.20 and Exod. 12.10] that it is not unnatural to consider whether the Evangelist would have rigorously excluded either'. However, a recent remark in his commentary (introduced in 2nd edn of 1978) indicates that he prefers the Paschal reference (*Gospel according to St John*, p. 558): 'It may be that John's source referred to the Psalm but that he, with his paschal interests, preferred the Passover reference'. Lindars also finds both sources behind 19.36 (*New Testament Apologetic*, p. 96), but regards the Paschal reference indicative of the Evangelist's ultimate design for the text.

77. It reads: οὐ καταλείφουσιν ἀπ' αὐτοῦ εἰς τὸ πρωὶ καὶ ὀστοῦν οὐ συντρίφεται ἀπ' αὐτοῦ. Cf. Dalman (*Jesus–Jeshua*, p. 92) and E. Freed (*Old Testament Quotations in the Gospel of John* [NovTSup, 11; Leiden: Brill, 1965], p. 113) who both relate this form of Num. 9.12 to Jn 19.36.

78. οὐκ ἀπολείφετε ἀπ' αὐτοῦ ἕως πρωὶ καὶ ὀστοῦν οὐ συντρίφετε ἀπ'

to the MT, 19.36 closely follows the Hebrew of Num. 9.12.[79] In fact, of all Old Testament texts (LXX and MT), Günter Reim concludes that, linguistically, Num. 9.12 (MT) stands by far the closest to Jn 19.36.[80]

Secondly, contextual considerations: As argued above, with regard to 19.14, the death of Christ took place in the Fourth Gospel on Friday, Nisan 14. In light of this, '"on ne lui brisera pas un os" doit être interprété et compris comme la prescription rituelle juive qui défend de briser les os de l'agneau pascal'.[81] The soldiers' action, or better, refusal to act in v. 33, becomes perfectly understandable from the Evangelist's perspective. In addition, the apparent haste in removing Jesus' body from the cross (19.31, 38) also becomes understandable. The slain Paschal Lamb must not remain until the next day, which began at 6 p.m. that evening.

Thirdly, liturgical considerations: If Guilding's thesis is accepted that the Fourth Gospel was originally read in the synagogue in tandem with the appropriate Jewish lectionaries,[82] then 19.36 was designed as part of a Passover Haggadah. Guilding concludes that 19.31–20.29 was one of four Christian, Passover Haggadoth or synagogical readings in the Fourth Gospel.[83] As such, it was read in connection with Jewish lectionary readings for Nisan. These readings included Exod. 12.46 (read in second of three year cycle) and Num. 9.12 (read in final year of cycle) which suggests that 19.36 might have drawn upon the same Old Testament texts.

Conclusion. The cumulative effect of the four above-mentioned passages and the numerous less specific indicators of Passover allusions in the Fourth Gospel is impressive. The Evangelist was apparently concerned with presenting Jesus as the perfect Paschal Victim, the complete antitype of the old sacrificial order. J.K. Howard's conclusion to this effect captures the 'paschal' spirit of the Fourth Gospel:

αὐτοῦ τὰ δὲ καταλειπόμενα ἀπ᾽ αὐτοῦ ἕως πρωὶ ἐν πυρὶ κατακαύσετε.

79. The עצם corresponds nicely to the singular ὀστοῦν of 19.36 (contra Ps. 33.21 LXX which has plural). The phrase לא ישברו 'kann mit οὐ συντριβήσεται wiedergegeben werden' (Reim, *Alttestamentlichen Hintergrund*, p. 52). And the αὐτοῦ of 19.36 is a very acceptable translation of the בו in the MT.

80. See his analysis on pp. 51-54 (*Alttestamentlichen Hintergrund*).

81. B. Hemelsoet, 'L'ensévelissement selon Saint Jean', *Studies in John* (ed. W.C. van Unnik; NovTSup, 24; Leiden: Brill, 1970), p. 58.

82. *Jewish Worship*, pp. 48-60.

83. *Jewish Worship*, p. 48. She lists the first three haggadoth as chs. 2c–3a; 6; and 12–13.

We see that from the moment of the Baptist's cry there is a steady march of events in which Passover symbolism plays a large part, leading up to its eventual culmination upon Golgotha's hill and the sacrifice of Him who was the fulfillment of all the Old Testament types, the Real and Perfect Passover, now remembered and recalled in the Christian Eucharist.[84]

Christ the Isaac Figure

A second Johannine theme which demonstrates that the Fourth Evangelist understood Christ's death as a cultic event which cleansed or expiated sin is the 'Akedah' motif of Genesis 22.[85] By relating Christ to the 'Akedah' motif, the Evangelist has assigned to Christ's death the same expiatory force which Isaac's death contained in contemporary Rabbinic thought. Before looking at the development of this theme in the Fourth Gospel, a brief look at the state of the 'Akedah' tradition in the first Christian century is in order.

During the first Christian century,[86] the 'Akedah' motif was intrinsically bound up with the Paschal sacrifice.[87] Isaac was seen as the

---

84. 'Passover and Eucharist in the Fourth Gospel', *SJT* 20 (1967), p. 337.

85. This term comes from the Hebrew verb עָקַד, 'to bind'—found only in Gen. 22.9; and the Aramaic noun עֲקֵדָא 'binding'—found in *Targ. Gen.* 22.14. It has come to refer to all Rabbinic speculation which has grown around the Isaac story in Gen. 22, although technically, it ought to be limited to only the haggadic presentation of Isaac's vicariously atoning sacrifice in Gen. 22.

86. Despite the weighty and articulate objections of some, a consensus of contemporary scholarship regards the 'Akedah' motif as pre-Christian; i.e., an antecedent of New Testament soteriology. Cf. especially its alleged development in the indisputably pre-Christian sources (*Jubilees* and Philo) and the earliest Palestinian Targum recension (*Neofiti I*). Leading those who would question or reject this conventional view on dating the 'Akedah' are B.D. Chilton and P.R. Davies. For them, at least, '...there is no pre-Christian Aqedah'. Rather, they 'consider the hypothesis that the Aqedah's matrix is to be found in developments after 70 CE, in which the mission of the Church is a crucial factor, to be the most plausible explanation of the rabbinic evidence' ('The Aqedah: A Revised Tradition History', *CBQ* 40 [1978], p. 517).

87. Cf. esp. *Targ. Neof.* Gen. 22 (A. Díez Macho's edition) and Jub. 18.26 (second century BC). Vermes writes (*Scripture and Tradition in Judaism* [SPB, 4; Leiden: Brill, 2nd edn, 1973], p. 215): 'there is evidence that the association of the Akedah with Passover was established well before the beginning of the Christian era'. In Jubilees 18 and *Exod. R.* 15.7-12, the Akedah is chronologically located on Nisan 15. N. Hillyer notes that not only was the Akedah placed on Nisan 15, but also Isaac's birth and natural death ('Servant of God', *EvQ* 41 [1969], p. 152; cf. also H.J. Schoeps, *Paul* [trans. H. Knight; London: Lutterworth Press, 1961], p. 147).

sacrifice *par excellence*, who willingly offered himself[88] in death[89] as a burnt offering on Nisan 15.[90] His blood, not the Paschal Lamb's, was regarded by Yahweh on the first Passover night,[91] and he expiated the sins of Israel on the altar.[92] It is not surprising that the 'Akedah' tradition is regarded by some as the definitive material which shaped the New Testament doctrine of Christ's sacrificial death.[93]

Now where does this 'Akedah' tradition show itself in the Fourth Gospel? Apparently in three distinct passages with differing degrees of clarity and force.[94] They will be looked at consecutively.

88. Cf. Sifre on Deut. 32 where Isaac binds himself on the altar.

89. Cf. *Gen. R.* 55.5, and in the New Testament, Heb. 11.17 (Abraham 'offered up' Isaac) and Jas 2.21 ('Was not Abraham our father justified by works, when he offered up Isaac his son on the altar?'). According to *Gen. R.* 56.8, Isaac was 37 years old at the time.

90. So *Jub.* 18.2-16. Cf. Hillyer ('Servant of God', p. 152 n. 64) and Vermes (*Scripture and Tradition*, pp. 215-17).

91. *Mek.* Exod. 14.15, Besh. 4 (Lauterbach edn, I, p. 222).

92. See *Targ. Neof.* Gen. 22.14 (Díez Macho, ed., *ad loc.*, n. 10), and *Cant. R.* 1.14 §1. The latter reads: '"My beloved is unto me as a cluster of henna". "Cluster" refers to Isaac, who was bound on the altar like "a cluster of henna" (*kopher*): because he atones (*mekapper*) for the iniquities of Israel.'

93. See especially the conclusions of Israel Levi ('Le Sacrifice d'Isaac et le Mort de Jesus', *REJ* 64 [1912], pp. 161-84) and, more recently, J.E. Wood ('Isaac Typology in the New Testament', *NTS* 14 [1968], pp. 583-89), R.J. Daly ('The Soteriological Significance of the Sacrifice of Isaac', *CBQ* 39 [1977], pp. 45-75), and M. Wilcox ('"Upon the Tree"—Deut. 21–22–23 in the New Testament', *JBL* 96 [1977], pp. 97-99). In this regard, H.J. Schoeps writes ('The Sacrifice of Isaac in Paul's Theology', *JBL* 65 [1946], p. 391): 'When Paul says in 1 Cor. 5.7 that "Christ our Passover is sacrificed for us"...it seems probable to me that he is under the influence of Jewish conceptions related to the Akedah... Just as Paul patently identified the servant of the Lord with Christ, so he built the doctrine of the expiatory power of the sacrificial death of Christ on the binding of Isaac.'

94. In addition to these three cf. 8.56. Here the Evangelist asserts that Abraham saw Christ's day and rejoiced. Could not the Evangelist, influenced by Rabbinic tradition, be thinking here of Abraham's vision of the cross, which was precipitated by the 'binding' of his son? So Braun, citing especially the Targumic exegesis of Gen. 22.1-18 in *Neofiti I* and *Targum Pseudo-Jonathan* ('Le sacrifice d'Isaac dans le quatrième évangile d'après le Targum', *NRT* 101 [1979], pp. 482-84).

Cf. also 6.1-2. It is possible, according to C.T. Ruddick ('Feeding and Sacrifice: The Old Testament Background of the Fourth Gospel', *ExpTim* 79 [1968], pp. 340-41), that the peculiar Johannine twist given to this tradition is explained by the Evangelist's use of Gen. 22. He observes that the superfluous question to Philip

(1) 1.29. Certainly the main Old Testament allusion behind the 'Lamb of God' title in 1.29 is *not* the Isaac figure of the 'Akedah' tradition. Rather, the title recalls the Suffering Servant of Deutero-Isaiah, the Paschal Lamb, or the apocalyptic, horned bell-wether. However, because the Evangelist connects the title with the expiatory function of 'taking away' the world's sin, one is justified in seeing some degree of influence by the 'Akedah' tradition. For in this tradition, as shown above, Isaac's sacrificial death was both expiatory and anticipatory of the Paschal sacrifice. In a very real sense, Rabbinic thought recast Isaac as the 'Lamb of God' who takes away sin. Thus it is not surprising that such men as Braun,[95] Vermes,[96] and Lindars[97] postulate a close connection between Jn 1.29 and the Rabbinic treatment of Genesis 22.

(2) 3.16. It is entirely possible that the Fourth Evangelist, in tune with this popular view of Genesis 22, relied on the 'Akedah' motif for the ideas behind 3.16. In fact, Vermes concludes that 'the fullest Johannine expression of the Christian Akedah appears in Jn 3.16',[98] with the sacrifice of the new Isaac.[99] The similar features are striking. Braun lists the three main ones:

> La correspondance est 1) dans le fait qu'un fils unique a été livré a la mort par son père; 2) que ce fils est celui dont dépendaient les promesses de l'alliance (Gen. 17.19); 3) que l'extension de cette Alliance à toutes les nations de la terre provient du sacrifice de l'unique.[100]

in 6.5, the theme of 'testing' in v. 6, the reference to a mountain in v. 3, the presence of a lad to furnish food in v. 9, and a reference to the Passover in v. 4 are all unique features of the Johannine account of this tradition. He suggests the Evangelist 'either consciously or not' relied on Gen. 22.1-14 for these features.

95. *Théologien*, III.1, pp. 160-65.

96. *Scripture and Tradition*, pp. 224-25.

97. *New Testament Apologetic*, pp. 139, 146 n. 2. See further Richardson (*Theology of the New Testament*, p. 228) and Gerhard Delling (*Der Kreuzestod Jesu in der urchristlichen Verküdigung* [Göttingen: Vandenhoeck & Ruprecht, 1972], p. 98).

98. *Scripture and Tradition*, p. 225.

99. That 3.16 refers to Christ's death rather than his incarnation of 'sending' is widely accepted. Loisy writes (*Le Quatrieme Evangile* [Paris: Gabalda, 2nd edn, 1921], p. 167): 'Apres ce qui a été insinué du crucifiement, le don ne saurait se rapporter en general à la mission du Christ; il concerne sa mort'. Braun concurs (*Théologien*, III.1, p. 157): 'il n'est pas douteux que le don du Fils unique devrait s'entendre, non de l'Incarnation, ni de la mission du Christ en general, mais de son elevation, sur la Croix'.

100. *Théologien*, III.1, p. 157.

(3) 19.17. In this verse Jesus is described by the Evangelist, in contrast with the synoptic account, as bearing his own cross to Golgotha. As Stephen Smalley cautiously ventures, 'this may be an allusion to the sacrifice of Isaac, who himself carried the wood upon which he was to be offered'.[101] Admittedly, Isaac typology is far from clear in this verse; however, in view of its emergence at other points in the Gospel, such typology remains an interesting explanation of the Evangelist's apparent departure from synoptic tradition at 19.17.

Conclusion. The 'Akedah' theology of Genesis 22, if indeed of pre-Christian origin, has left its mark on the Fourth Gospel. As the Evangelist placed Christ in the role of the new Paschal Lamb, the anti-type of the old sacrificial order, so he has placed Christ in the role of the new Isaac. In fact, these two roles had become intrinsically bound up with one another by the first Christian century. By showing an interest in the Isaac of popular Jewish speculation, the Evangelist has again shown an interest in *how* the death of Christ was redemptive. The Isaac figure removed Israel's sins through his cultic, expiatory death. The death of Christ, in his role as the new Isaac, was understood along similar lines by the Evangelist. As Braun remarks, a cultic understanding of Christ's death is reasonably expected of the Evangelist, given that he integrated the 'Akedah' theology into his Gospel:

> Dans ces conditions, il serait paradoxal de penser qu'en se rattachant à Gen 22 par l'intermédiare de la tradition juive, qui attribuait à l'Aqéda d'Isaac une valeur sacrificielle, Jean se serait montré réfractaire à la notion du *sacrifice* de la Croix, telle qu'elle était professée dans la communauté primitive, et en particulier par le théologien de l'épître aux Hébreux.[102]

Christ the Cleansing Fountain

Unique to the Johannine crucifixion narrative is the effluence of blood and water from the pierced side of Christ (19.34).[103] The cultic

101. *John*, p. 226. Brown makes a similar analysis (*Gospel according to John*, II, p. 917): 'Another possible theological reason for the Johannine stress that Jesus carried his own cross may have been a desire to introduce the typology of Isaac who carried the wood for his own sacrifice. This interpretation was frequent among the Church Fathers.' Interestingly, according to a post-Christian Rabbinic tradition (Gen. R. 6.3), Isaac is compared to a condemned man bearing his own cross.

102. *Théologien*, III.1, p. 160.

103. Would the phenomenon described in 19.34 have been physiologically possible? One should first consult the various attempts to establish the credibility of this account before passing judgment. For example, medical men have tried to

overtones of this incident are difficult to ignore. Certainly, the description of outpoured blood indicates the Evangelist's awareness of an expiatory rationale between Christ's death and the removal of sin.[104] Yet the recording of outpoured water can be construed as an equally 'cultic' feature, underscoring further the Evangelist's cultic understanding of Christ's death.

The water which flows from Christ's side in 19.34 appears to thematically culminate the Evangelist's development of the 'living water' theme.[105] The water made available by the death of Christ is the 'living

demonstrate that a ruptured heart causes blood to flow into the pericardium, where it coagulates into a red clot (blood) and limpid serum (water). Then, when pierced, the pericardium would produce a visibly discernible flow of blood and water. It is then argued that Jesus had a ruptured heart prior to the lance thrust. This could have been caused by sorrow (cf. Ps. 69.20 where a 'broken heart' is predicted of Jesus as well as his being offered vinegar to drink [Jn 19.29]), great mental agony, or shock. For details of this approach, with minor variations, cf. W.B. Primrose ('A Surgeon Looks at the Crucifixion', *HibJ* 47 [1949], pp. 385-88), *ISBE* (s.v. 'Blood and Water'), and especially Raymond Schmittlein (*Circonstances et cause de la mort du Christ* [Bade: Editions Art et Science, 1950]), who has based his findings on wartime studies of cadavers which underwent traumatic shock.

104. Although sacramental referents are not as clear in 19.34 as in 6.51c-58, they are apparent nonetheless. As in 1 Jn 5.6-8 where the 'blood' and 'water' associated with Jesus' earthly life *presently* 'bear witness' to the Johannine community, so too appears to be the thought in 19.34. The 'blood' and 'water' which flowed from the cross continue their testimony in the sacramental activity of baptism and the eucharistic meal. So Bultmann (*Gospel of John*, p. 678): 'it can scarcely be other than that in the death of Jesus on the cross the sacraments of Baptism and the Lord's Supper have their foundation'; De la Potterie ('Naître de l'eau et naître de l'Esprit', *Sciences Ecclésiastiques* 14 [1962], p. 440): 'ils symbolisent l'efficacité salutaire du sacrifice du Christ, efficacité qui devient operanté dans l'église, par les deux grands sacrements du baptême et de l'Eucharistie'; and Schulz (*Das Evangelium nach Johannes*, p. 240): 'Der Sinn ist zweifellos der, dass im Kreuzestod Jesu die beiden Sakramente des Abendmahls und der Taufe ihren letzen und eigentlichen Grund haben'.

105. That the Evangelist predicted in 7.37-39 that living water would flow from Christ on the cross is enhanced by accepting the so-called 'Western' punctuation of 7.38 (full stop after ὁ πιστεύων εἰς ἐμέ in v. 38 and no punctuation after πινέτω in v. 37; the implication is that Jesus is the source of living water *not* the believer) and the place of Jesus' 'glorification' in v. 39 as the cross. Such an event, eschatological in scope for the Evangelist, was probably interpreted from the perspective of certain prophetic, Old Testament texts. These texts concerned either the wilderness account of water from the rock, given eschatological significance as in Isaiah 43–48, or the effluence of eschatological, life-giving waters from the new temple (Jesus = new

water' promised to the Samaritan woman, the 'living water' dramatically offered to the throngs of religious pilgrims at the climax of the Feast of Tabernacles, the 'true drink' given by the new Moses. Indeed it is the outpouring of the Spirit which was withheld until this moment of 'glorification' (7.39; cf. 19.30).

This interrelating of the 'living water' motif with the outpoured water from the crucified Christ is yet another indicator of the Evangelist's interest in the cultic aspect of Christ's death. In the Old Testament—especially the passages which appear to most directly shape the Evangelist's presentation of this theme[106]—Rabbinic literature,[107] and Qumran's Manual of Discipline,[108] 'living water' functions as a cleansing agent which washes away the stains of sin. The Evangelist, although emphasizing the 'life-giving' properties of 'living water', apparently incorporates this pre-Christian, cultic dimension of the symbol into his development of the 'living water' theme.

This appreciation of 'living water' as a cleansing agent is most clearly

temple in John) as in Zechariah 13–14. Thus it is not out of line to regard the Evangelist's account of the crucifixion in 19.34 as a fulfillment of such prophetic texts. In this way, 19.34 might be regarded as a consummation of all that the Evangelist has previously said about living water. As Herbert Klos observes (*Die Sakramente im Johannesevangelium* [Stuttgart: Katholisches Bibelwerk, 1970], p. 76), 'Nun Wird in 19.34 das das "Bild" von 7.38b "konkretisiert"'.

106. The effluence of water from the cross is taken to be a fulfillment of the eschatological outpouring of 'living water' from the new Jerusalem (i.e., out of the new temple—Christ; Zech. 14.8; Ezra 47.1-12; cf. Rev. 22.1, 17) and/or the eschatological outpouring of water from the wilderness rock (Exod. 17.3-7; Isa. 43.14-21; 44.3; cf. 1 Cor. 10.4-6). In Zech. 13.1, the 'living water' of the new Jerusalem is described as a 'fountain for sin and impurity' which will be opened up in the 'last days'. In Ezra 47.1-12, the cleansing function of the outpoured, eschatological water is not as explicit; however, it is clearly spelled out in 35.25-27, 33. Here these same eschatological waters serve to cleanse the faithful remnant from all filthiness. It is no surprise, then, that 'living waters' (מים חיים: ὕδωρ ζῶν) find a place in the Levitical Cultus as a primary cleansing agent (Num. 19.9, 17).

107. See especially *m. Par.* 6-9, which elaborates on the Living Water of Num. 19 and its expiatory power in the Cultus.

108. 1QS 4.20-21 (Dupont-Sommer, *Essene Writings from Qumran, ad loc.*): 'Then [time of final judgment] God will cleanse by his truth all the works of every man... and purify him of all wicked deeds by the Spirit of Holiness; and he will cause the Spirit of Truth to gush forth upon him like lustral water (= "living water" of Num. 19.9, 17].' Cf. also 1QH 3.21. In 1QH 7.6; 9.32; and 16.12, entry into the community was marked by a complete transformation and purification, effected by the Spirit (symbolized often by 'water' in 1QH).

seen in the Evangelist's depiction of the footwashing account as a symbolic episode, prophetically anticipating Christ's humiliation on the cross.[109] Taken as such, the cleansing water applied to Peter's feet appears to anticipate the cleansing water from Christ's side, especially if the short text of v. 10 is accepted.[110] As the water of 13.10 'washes' (λούω)[111] sin and renders Peter completely 'clean' (καθαρός)[112] he has no need to 'wash' (νίπτω) further—so the water of 19.34 potentially fulfills the same cultic functions for all men. Raymond Brown's summary to this effect is worth reproducing:

> The simplest explanation of the footwashing, then, remains that Jesus performed this servile task to prophesy symbolically that he was about

109. 13.1-20 appears to be far more than an exhortation to imitate Christ's humility in washing the disciples' feet despite the vigorous protestations of J. Michl ('Der Sinn der Fusswaschung', *Bib* 40 [1959], pp. 697-708). Understanding the account as symbolic of Christ's passion is gathering a consensus of leading Johannine scholars. Cf. especially Klos (*Die Sakramente*, pp. 89-91), Müller (*Das Heilsgeschehen*, pp. 68-69), J.D.G. Dunn ('The Washing of the Disciples' Feet in John 13.1-20', *ZNW* 61 [1970], pp. 247-52), Beutler ('Die Heilsbedeutung des Todes Jesu', p. 195), W.K. Grossouw ('A Note on John 13.1-3', *NovT* 8 [1966], p. 129), Braun (*Théologien*, III.1, p. 187), Brown (*Gospel according to John*, II, p. 568), Hunter (*Gospel according to John, ad loc.*) and P. Boismard ('Le Lavement des Pieds', *RB* 71 [1964], pp. 8-10).

110. With the short text, 'he who has bathed (λούω) has no need to bathe further (νίπτω)', v. 10 becomes somewhat of a proverbial saying rather than a direct response to Peter's enthusiastic request of v. 9. Jesus is saying in effect, 'Peter, there is no need to wash twice. "The one who has washed" (ὁ λελουμένος; this refers back to the washing of v. 8, not to some prior, initial "bath") has no need to be "washed" (νίπτω) again—as you just requested (v. 9). My washing, such as you just underwent (v. 8), is complete and removes all of your sins, since it represents the once for all cleansing of my death on the cross.'

The short text reads: ὁ λελουμένος οὐχ ἔχει χρείαν νίψασθαι. Eternally, it is supported in ℵ, it^aur, c, the Vulgate (Wordsworth edition), Tertullian and Origen. Internally, its support is stronger. Simply put, the short reading is 'more intelligible in the context' (Barrett, *Gospel according to John, ad loc.*). Or as Dunn puts it ('Washing of Disciples' Feet', p. 250): 'The inner logic of John's thought thus indicates that the shorter text in v. 10 must be original'. The long reading demands that the washing of v. 8 is some sort of secondary washing, subordinate to an initial 'bath' (baptism?).

111. This term is typical of early Christian baptismal texts where the waters of baptism cleanse the believer's sins (Acts 22.16; Tit. 3.5).

112. To be 'clean' in Johannine thought is to be free from the impurities caused by sin.

to be humiliated in death. Peter's questioning, provoked by the action, enabled Jesus to explain the salvific necessity of his death; it would bring men their heritage with him and it would cleanse them of sin.[113]

Conclusion

Apparently, the traditional concept of an expiatory rationale between sin's removal and Christ's death has exerted its influence on the Fourth Evangelist. Through the use of 'Akedah', Paschal, and 'living water' themes, the Evangelist has clearly endorsed the cultic rationale wherein sin is cleansed by either the outpoured blood of the sacrificial victim or the cultic washing with 'living water'. To disregard this influence, to maximize the difference between Paul and the Evangelist at this point as Bultmann has done,[114] must be seen as a radical approach. Thus Braun observes with a slight trace of agitation:

> Lorsque Bultmann soutient la gageure de limiter la fonction du Christ johannique à la Révélation, quand il pose en fait que la notion de la mort expiatrice de Jésus ne cadre pas avec la théologie du quatrième évangile, on est deconcerté par un exclusivisme aussi radical.[115]

To be sure, the exact relationship between Christ's death and the elimination of sin is not explicit. However, as Braun observes, 'Rien ne permet de supposer que le théologien du verbe incarné ait repugné à la necessité de l'acte redempteur'.[116] And as Joseph Lachowski cautions, 'Although there is not to be found any word in the Fourth Gospel

---

113. *Gospel according to John*, II, p. 568. See also the observation of Hunter (*Gospel according to John, ad loc.*): 'The deeper meaning is that there is no place in his fellowship for those who have not been cleansed by his atoning death'.

114. So also Schulz (*Das Evangelium nach Johannes*, pp. 238-39): 'Für die Seinen und Freunde hat der Kreuzestod Jesu keine besondere Heilsbedeutung [referring to Fourth Gospel], jedenfalls nicht im Sinn der vor- und paulinischen Sühntodaussagen...Mann kann und darf keineswegs diese eigenständigen Lösungen miteinander harmonisieren und z. B. paulinische Kreuzestheologie in die des Johannes oder der Synoptiker eintragen.'

115. *Théologien*, III.1, p. 181. Klaus Haacker has also brought attention to the tenuous nature of Bultmann's conclusion in this area (*Die Stiftung des Heils* [Stuttgart: Calwer Verlag, 1972], p. 173]: 'Die Geschlossenheit, mit der Bultmann seine Interpretation [referring to Bultmann's subjection of the Fourth Gospel to the all-encompassing "Offenbarungstheologie"] durchführt, muss jeden faszinieren, der einen Nerv für systematisches Denken hat. Als historische Exegese jedoch bedarf seine Auslegen einer grundlegenden Korrektur.'

116. *Théologien*, III.1, p. 182.

which translated would spell out "Redemption", the reality expressed by this word cannot be called into question'.[117] One can reasonably claim, as James Denney has done, that the death of the Johannine Jesus 'really fills the place it does everywhere in the New Testament, and has the same decisive importance'.[118]

117. Lachowski, *The Concept of Redemption*, p. 130.
118. *The Death of Christ* (ed. R.V.G. Tasker; London: Tyndale Press, 1951), p. 145.

JSNT 47 (1992), pp. 35-48

NARRATIVE CRITICISM, HISTORICAL CRITICISM,
AND THE GOSPEL OF JOHN

M.C. de Boer

1. *Introduction*

In his review of scholarship on the Gospel of John, published in 1986, Jürgen Becker pointed to the 'conflict of methods' in Johannine studies.[1] He meant the conflict between traditional, historical-critical approaches and the new literary criticism which is characterized by a deep reserve toward certain kinds of historical-critical exercises, especially source and redaction criticism (old-style literary criticism).

In Johannine studies the new emphasis upon the Gospel as literature— more particularly, as 'story' or as 'narrative'—is commonly associated with the name of R. Alan Culpepper, whose book *Anatomy of the Fourth Gospel*, subtitled *A Study in Literary Design*, set the new agenda in 1983.[2] The basic concerns and aims of this narrative-critical approach, however, were signalled, somewhat ironically perhaps, by a historical critic, M. de Jonge of Leiden, in a 1977 collection of his essays on the Gospel of John, *Jesus, Stranger from Heaven and Son of God*, which was published in the United States.[3] De Jonge's remarks have frequently been cited, both by Culpepper[4] and by Johannine scholars who do not necessarily adopt a narrative-critical methodology.[5] Culpepper's work

---

1. 'Das Johannesevangelium im Streit der Methoden (1980–1984)', *TRu* 51 (1986), pp. 1-78, esp. pp. 7-21.

2. Philadelphia: Fortress Press, 1983.

3. Missoula, MT: Scholars Press, 1977. See also B. Olsson, *Structure and Meaning in the Fourth Gospel: A Text-Linguistic Analysis of John 2.1-11 and 4.1-42* (ConBNT, 6; Lund: Gleerup, 1974).

4. *Anatomy*, p. 5 n. 6.

5. G. Nicholson, *Death as Departure: The Johannine Descent–Ascent Schema*

and other literary-critical exercises[6] thus reflect in some respects
the change of emphasis that 'was already under way in Johannine
scholarship.[7]

2. *Narrative Criticism and Historical Criticism*

In his book, de Jonge proceeds with 'the assumption that the Fourth
Gospel is a meaningful whole'. The exegete's basic task is to interpret
the given text as a literary unity.[8] De Jonge acknowledges that this
approach is partly motivated by scepticism about being able to distinguish redactional layers from one or more possible sources and by doubt
about being able to glean any historical information from the Gospel:
'some writings', he says, 'particularly a Gospel, may be used only with
great circumspection as historical sources'.[9] But his basic concern seems
to emerge out of a perceived abuse of source- and redaction-critical
approaches to the Gospel. These approaches, he implies, have frag-
mented the text, or story, of the Gospel and focused interpretative
efforts on clearly hypothetical literary strata rather than on the Gospel as
a (more or less) finished literary product. Though it may be true that
'the present text cannot be explained without some knowledge of its history', de Jonge writes, 'one can never be content with simply describing
that history and restrict oneself to the "original" meaning and function
of its constituent parts'.[10] In his own approach, then, 'both supposedly
redactional and supposedly traditional elements are treated as integral
parts of a new literary entity'. He buttresses this point with the comment

(SBLDS, 63: Chico, CA: Scholars Press, 1983), pp. 15-16; M.M. Thompson, *The
Humanity of Jesus in the Fourth Gospel* (Philadelphia: Fortress Press, 1988), p. 10.

6.   Cf. R. Kysar, *John's Story of Jesus* (Philadelphia: Fortress Press, 1984);
P.D. Duke, *Irony in the Fourth Gospel* (Atlanta: John Knox, 1985); G.R. O'Day,
Revelation in the Fourth Gospel: Narrative Mode and Theological Claim
(Philadelphia: Fortress Press, 1986); J.L. Staley, *The Print's First Kiss: A Rhetorical
Investigation of the Implied Reader in the Fourth Gospel* (SBLDS, 82; Atlanta:
Scholars Press, 1988).

7.   And, of course, elsewhere. For the wider picture, see S.D. Moore, *Literary
Criticism and the Gospels: The Theoretical Challenge* (New Haven: Yale University
Press, 1989), esp. pp. 3-7. According to Moore, 'Culpepper's book is the most
comprehensive account to date of the narrative mechanics of a Gospel' (p. 50).

8.   *Jesus*, pp. vii-viii, 199.

9.   *Jesus*, pp. 198-99.

10.   *Jesus*, p. viii.

that the Gospel must be studied as a whole, since it actually 'functioned' in this way 'among people [that is, the original, historical readers] who did *not* take its prehistory into account'.[11]

Narrative criticism, however, takes a step further this focus on the final, given form of the Gospel text as an assumed, coherent literary whole. For this method is intrinsically and rigorously *a*historical— although it does sometimes seem as if its practitioners are motivated by an expressly *anti*historical bias and agenda. Culpepper, after all, begins his monograph with a rather stinging attack on historical criticism, on what he labels the 'stratification' of Gospel text and the 'dissection and differentiation of elements within the gospel', whereby scholars can study 'the history of the material, the process by which the gospel was composed, and developments within the Johannine community...'[12] Culpepper writes that the subject of *his* study is the 'gospel as it stands rather than its sources, historical background, or [for that matter, theological] themes'.[13]

Narrative critics such as Culpepper concern themselves with the story the Gospel tells and, more particularly, with the ways in which that story is told—in Culpepper's words, with 'what it is, and how it works'.[14] For

---

11. *Jesus*, p. 198 (emphasis original). Cf. C.H. Dodd, *The Interpretation of the Fourth Gospel* (Cambridge: Cambridge University Press, 1953), pp. 289-91; C.K. Barrett, *The Gospel according to St John* (Philadelphia: Westminster Press, 2nd edn, 1978), pp. 15-26. De Jonge's approach here approximates what Moore discusses under the heading of 'composition criticism' (*Literary Criticism*, pp. 3-7), an approach that represents an extension of redaction criticism.

12. *Anatomy*, p. 3. This page contains numerous intertextual echoes of the title and opening paragraphs of the well-known article by J.L. Martyn, 'Glimpses into the History of the Johannine Community', in *The Gospel of John in Christian History* (New York: Paulist Press, 1979), pp. 90-121, first published in M. de Jonge (ed.), *L'évangile de Jean: Source, rédaction, théologie* (BETL, 44; Leuven: Leuven University Press, 1977), pp. 149-75.

13. *Anatomy*, p. 5. Culpepper's narrative criticism, in contrast to redaction criticism or composition criticism (see n. 11), is thus also *a*theological as well as *a*historical. On this problem, see the extended discussion of Moore, *Literary Criticism*, pp. 3-7, 56-68. Culpepper understandably wants to overcome a reading (or a raiding) of the Gospel for theological propositions and themes that is oblivious to its narrative dynamics and integrity. But Moore points out that 'narrative criticism is admirably equipped to...undertake a complementary investigation of a gospel's theology' (p. 57), particularly if the latter is understood to refer to a Gospel's 'ideological point of view' (p. 56; emphasis removed).

14. *Anatomy*, p. 5.

this reason, narrative critics devote their interpretative efforts to the Gospel's 'literary design', to such matters as plot, narrative point of view, the portrayal of the characters, the uses and effects of symbolism, irony and misunderstanding, and other literary devices and strategies.

By definition the method cannot allow its practitioners to go beyond or outside of the text. The author and the readers can be only those 'implied' by the 'world of the story' itself. The 'implied author' is not the real author but the image or picture of the author created by the story and the way it is told. The implied author, therefore, is a mere 'construct' of the narrative, as J.D. Kingsbury puts it.[15] The same can be said about the 'implied reader': 'In the narrative-critical model of readership', Kingsbury writes, 'the primary reader is neither the contemporary of the historical Jesus nor the intended reader of the late first century nor the interested reader of the twentieth century but the implied reader'.[16] The implied reader is a construct of the text. Narrative critics of the Fourth Gospel seek to describe *how* the implied author of John tells a story to the implied reader. The role of the latter is to fulfill or to achieve what may perhaps be called the 'implied intentions' of the implied author.[17]

In his recent book on narrative criticism,[18] Mark Powell points out that this focus on the world of the text (or better: on the world of the story the text tells) differentiates narrative criticism from reader-response criticism, at least in part.[19] When Culpepper writes that 'the experience of reading the text is more important than understanding the process of its composition',[20] he gives voice to the emphasis of reader-response criticism. Culpepper's own concern as a narrative critic proper is to understand 'the gospel as a narrative text, what it is, how it works', as we noted above. Narrative criticism explores the ways in which an implied author determines an implied reader's response (through the

15. 'Reflections on the "Reader" of Matthew's Gospel', *NTS* 34 (1988), p. 455.

16. 'Reflections', p. 455.

17. See J.D. Kingsbury, *Matthew as Story* (Philadelphia: Fortress Press, 2nd edn, 1988), p. 38; M.A. Powell, *What is Narrative Criticism?* (Minneapolis: Fortress Press, 1990), pp. 20, 96-97. Kingsbury and Powell, however, speak of the intention *of the text*. See further on this matter in n. 23 below.

18. See previous note.

19. See also Moore, *Literary Criticism*, esp. p. xxi. Moore's study contains two parts, the first devoted to narrative criticism, the second to reader-response criticism.

20. *Anatomy*, p. 5.

medium of the text) 'rather than on ways in which the [actual] reader determines meaning'.[21] The latter is the province of reader-response criticism (also known as reception theory). Narrative criticism overlaps with reader-response criticism in that the ultimate 'goal of narrative criticism' (that is, of narrative-critical exercises) is to enable the critic, or any reader today, 'to read the text as the implied reader' is expected to.[22] Narrative criticism, however, overlaps with the aims of historical criticism in that it respects the text and allows it to function critically over against any actual reader and what such a reader may bring to the text: 'Narrative criticism', like historical criticism, 'is a text-centered approach which holds that the text sets parameters on interpretation'.[23]

The basic 'communications model' of author–text–reader is the same for the two methodologies:[24]

21. Powell, *Narrative Criticism*, p. 18.

22. Powell, *Narrative Criticism*, p. 20.

23. Powell, *Narrative Criticism*, p. 95. Powell, however, differentiates narrative criticism from historical criticism by claiming that the 'objective criteria' by which narrative criticism seeks to evaluate its interpretations of the text are 'defined in terms of the intention of *the text* rather than the intention of *the author*' (p. 96; emphasis original). But this sets up a false antithesis, as Powell concedes in his next sentence: 'The text, of course, includes what we have called the implied author and so takes into consideration authorial intent insofar as this has been incorporated into the text itself'. Historical criticism, to be sure, is concerned with the (real) author's intention but, in a manner quite analogous to that of narrative criticism, *only insofar as this intention comes to expression in the text, or texts, under scrutiny*. As E. Schüssler Fiorenza writes (in this case, about the author of Revelation): 'The author's interests and intentions in writing the work are not something that *lie behind* the text, but they manifest themselves *in* the form-content configuration and social function of the book' (*The Book of Revelation: Justice and Judgment* [Philadelphia: Fortress Press, 1985], p. 21; emphasis added).

24. Adapted from Powell, *Narrative Criticism*, p. 19, who has adapted it from Roman Jakobson (pp. 8-9). The 'author' and 'reader' of both models can of course also be pluralities. Powell thinks this communications model does not apply to historical criticism which, he says, regards a Gospel text 'as the end product of a process of development' and not as 'the middle component in an act of communication', as narrative criticism does (p. 9). Historical criticism, however, does not *require* an evolutionary view of a Gospel or any other biblical document. Furthermore, the 'end product' (or even a prior edition) can be regarded as 'the middle component in an act of communication' from a real author to a real reader (in the past).

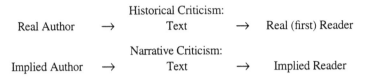

For both methodologies, then, the text stands at the center and is allowed to control interpretation. What sets them apart is the different approaches to authors and readers. Historical criticism presupposes real authors and real (first) readers who existed extrinsic to the text.[25] Narrative criticism does not; authors and readers exist only 'in the text'.[26]

Precisely for this reason, however, the narrative-critical method can also be used by those who have a historical-critical agenda. As Kingsbury writes,

> one of the principal contributions narrative criticism can make to Gospel studies is perhaps elementary but crucial: to alert the interpreter both to the literary existence of the 'world of the story' and to the importance of scrutinizing it. Once one fully understands the 'world of the story', one can then move to a reconstruction of the 'world of the evangelist' [and the 'world of the intended reader'].[27]

25. N.B.: Historical criticism concerns itself not only with the author but also with the (real, historical) reader. See C.M. Tuckett, *Reading the New Testament: Methods of Interpretation* (Philadelphia: Fortress Press, 1987), p. 41: 'in order to understand what the authors were saying, we have to try to place ourselves as far as possible in the position of the people for whom the texts were written'. Similarly, J.L. Martyn attributes to Walter Bauer the following hermeneutical rule which he himself adopts as fundamental: '*On the way* toward ascertaining the intention of an early Christian author, the interpreter is *first* to ask how the original readers of the author's document understood what he had said in it' ('How I Changed My Mind', paper read to the Annual Meeting of the Society of Biblical Literature, New Orleans, November 18, 1990; emphasis original). The principle originates at the dawn of historical criticism: Johann Jakob Wettstein (*Novum Testamentum Graecum* [1751–1752]) wrote: 'If you wish to get a thorough and complete understanding of the books of the New Testament, put yourself in the place of those to whom they were first delivered by the apostles as a legacy'. Earlier still Matthias Flacius Illyricus (*Clavis Scripturae* [1567]) maintained that an interpreter must learn 'how the readers understood' the texts. Quoted from W.G. Kümmel, *The New Testament: The History of the Investigation of its Problems* (Nashville: Abingdon Press, 1972), pp. 50, 29, respectively.

26. Powell, *Narrative Criticism*, p. 18.

27. Kingsbury, 'Reflections', p. 459.

The world of the story, says Kingsbury, may well prove to be an 'index' of the Evangelist's world and that of the original, intended readers.[28] Kingsbury concludes that 'it is not too much to say that as preparation for the task of historical reconstruction, thorough familiarity' with the world of the text and thus with the implied author and reader 'would seem to commend itself as well-nigh indispensable'.[29] The method itself, of course, is ahistorical, but its results (with suitable safeguards against anachronistic and inappropriate application) can be fruitfully applied in historical-critical endeavors and exercises, particularly when, as in the case of de Jonge, the focus remains on the finished form of the document. A pertinent example of such fruitful application in fact is the last chapter of Culpepper's *Anatomy*, entitled 'The Implied Reader',[30] where Culpepper steps outside the proper bounds of narrative criticism and explores what the Gospel story's implied readers may disclose about its intended historical readers.

3. *The Question of the Finished Form of the Text*

But what of the claim that the focus of exegetical efforts, as well as all other interpretative efforts, ought to be the final or canonical form of the text? As I observed previously, it is not just those who adopt a narrative-critical methodology who make this claim. This is the view of de Jonge and numerous others in recent years who eschew, intentionally and happily—perhaps too happily—the extensive scholarly literature that attempts to come to grips with the composition history of the Gospel. They thus neatly evade the implications of such historical reconstructions for exegesis.[31]

---

28. Kingsbury, 'Reflections', p. 459. Cf. Powell, *Narrative Criticism*, p. 97. Powell notes that the term 'index' is 'helpful because it connotes an indirect or general indication of something without implying specificity or certainty' (p. 122 n. 28). In short, the implied author or reader cannot be simply equated with the real author or reader; critical evaluation of the relationship is essential.

29. Kingsbury, 'Reflections', p. 459.

30. *Anatomy*, pp. 203-27.

31. See, for example, Delbert Burkett, *The Son of the [sic] Man in the Gospel of John* (JSNTSup, 56; Sheffield: JSOT Press, 1991), p. 14: 'Given the lack of consensus in this area...[t]he Gospel as it stands will be the object of investigation'. Similarly, J. Lieu, *The Second and Third Epistles of John: History and Background* (Studies of the New Testament and its World; Edinburgh: T. & T. Clark, 1986); M.M. Thompson, *The Humanity of Jesus in the Fourth Gospel* (Philadelphia:

However, it may be said that historical-critical exercises, including source- and redaction-critical reconstructions, when properly understood and applied, are not antithetical to the aim of understanding the final form of the text but may actually serve to achieve precisely that aim. This is evidently the view of Raymond Brown in his monumental commentary on the Gospel.[32] Brown posits a long and complex history of the Gospel's composition and yet also explicitly makes it his task to comment on the final, canonical form of the text. His theory of composition is not done for its own sake but as an aid to the task of understanding and commenting on the final, finished form of the document.[33]

It is unfortunate that, as de Jonge suggests, some interpreters mistakenly identify source- and redaction-critical *exercises* with the totality of the exegetical task. That is a false assumption and, when repeated by narrative critics or by others who eschew probing the origins of the Gospel and the history of its community, a misleading caricature.[34] The caricature often entails the familiar complaint that historical criticism regards the text merely as a 'window' on a world that lies 'behind' the text.[35] Powell claims (wrongly, I think) that, for historical critics, the 'interpretive key...lies in background information' and 'not within the text itself'.[36] Undoubtedly, the Gospel has been read as a 'window' on Johannine Christianity, its particular history and its circumstances.[37] And there is no reason why an ancient text cannot be read with such an aim in view. But such exercises can also have as their ultimate aim to discern precisely how the Gospel (in its final form) functioned as a 'mirror' (to use a favorite term of literary critics) for Johannine Christians in their very particular circumstances. Furthermore, it may perhaps also be said that the Gospel is not in any event really a 'window' on Johannine

Fortress Press, 1988). See my reviews of these last two books in *JBL* 108 (1989), pp. 546-49 and *CBQ* 52 (1990), pp. 366-68, respectively.

32. *The Gospel according to John* (AB, 29, 29A; Garden City, NY: Doubleday, 1966, 1970).

33. Brown also, incidentally, pays considerable attention to the literary artistry of the Gospel, including such literary devices as symbolism, irony and misunderstanding.

34. Powell's extremely helpful book (*Narrative Criticism*) contains numerous misconceptions about historical criticism. For examples, see nn. 23 and 24 above. See further below.

35. See Culpepper, *Anatomy*, pp. 3-4.

36. Powell, *Narrative Criticism*, p. 5.

37. The composition history of the Gospel and the history of Johannine Christianity are closely related areas of inquiry. See, e.g., Martyn, 'Glimpses', pp. 90-91.

history, as if those bent on historical reconstruction simply look *through* it at a world it does not itself contain or attest. The history of Johannine Christianity and of the Gospel's composition is not brought *to* the text by critics bent on its fragmentation or on its marginalization for the actual interpretative task. This history is in fact imbedded, or encoded, within the text itself and any imaginative reconstruction of this history must find its impetus and its foundation and certainly its confirmation in the evidence provided by that text[38]—the *extant, finished* form of that text.[39]

4. *The Question of Coherence*

Another facet to the concern for the final form of the Gospel on the part of narrative critics and others is the assumption that the final form is a coherent unity or whole. Thus M.M. Thompson, appealing to both Culpepper and de Jonge, writes: 'In exegeting John, one must offer a synthetic interpretation of the whole Gospel as a coherent text'.[40] Can any avowedly *critical* method, however, really presuppose coherence, whether thematic or literary, as an unquestionable principle?[41] Many a novelist has thought his or her novel to be thematically coherent and narratively cohesive, but many a reviewer has thought otherwise.[42] The

38. See the classic works of J.L. Martyn, *History and Theology in the Fourth Gospel* (Nashville: Abingdon Press, 2nd edn, 1979) and R.E. Brown, *The Community of the Beloved Disciple* (New York: Paulist Press, 1979). Martyn's reading of John 9 in its extant final form as a two-level drama is extremely illuminating both of the Johannine *Sitz im Leben* and of the literary artistry of the story itself (see *History and Theology*, pp. 24 n. 8, 112 n. 171). Brown follows Martyn's two-level reading of the Gospel and insists that his reconstruction of Johannine history and of the various groups in the Johannine setting is derived from a close reading of the finished Gospel and is not dependent on a prior reconstruction of the Gospel's literary history (*Community*, pp. 20-21)—though, in my opinion, his reconstruction would have gained in precision and in plausibility had he brought it into conversation with his theory about the origin and composition of the Gospel outlined in his commentary.

39. Of course, historical-critical methodology allows and even encourages attempts to find *further* confirmation outside of the text (from other sources both documentary and archaeological roughly contemporaneous with the Gospel) as a way of reducing the possibility of eisegesis. The same requirement, however, willy-nilly imposes itself on narrative-critical exercises, as we shall see below.

40. *Humanity of Jesus*, p. 10.

41. Cf. Becker, 'Streit', pp. 20-21.

42. I prefer to use the terms 'coherent'/'incoherent' in connection with the

critical interpreter must, like a discerning reviewer of a novel, go wherever the evidence—the data given in the extant, canonical form of the text—may lead.[43] The data may well lead to the conclusion, a narrative-critical one, that the text is a unified, coherent whole, but then again they may lead to the opposite conclusion, or at least a different one. Coherence or unity, no more than incoherence or fragmentation, cannot be a methodological presupposition that stands beyond critical testing in the public arena and empirical validation from the text itself, *whatever method is used*.[44]

A strong case has often been made that the Fourth Gospel is not conceptually coherent nor narratively cohesive, even if it is stylistically uniform. The literary discrepancies and disjunctions, which historical critics are wont to label 'aporias', have been deemed too numerous and pervasive to be explained (away) simply in terms of a narrative purpose. Indeed, Culpepper himself concedes as much, for he argues that ch. 21 looks like an appendix and is thus probably a later addition to the Gospel from the hand of an editor.[45] At a stroke Culpepper undercuts the integrity of the narrative-critical methodology he adopts, a method that supposedly assumes the integrity of the whole document, as well as his opening polemic against those who undertake to reconstruct the composition history of the text by source- and redaction-critical means. He in effect concedes some level of narrative incohesion and a history of composition to explain it.[46]

---

thematic or conceptual content of the Gospel (e.g. realized and future salvation), while reserving the terms 'cohesive'/'incohesive' for its narrative flow and structure (e.g. the geography of Jn 5–7). A Gospel may be a cohesive narrative while also being conceptually incoherent, or vice versa. The two sets of terms and their points of reference do not necessarily overlap, though they may of course do so. On the relationship between literary-contextual discrepancies and conceptual inconsistencies, see the nuanced discussion of J.V. Brownson, 'The First Farewell: A Redaction-Critical Reconstruction of the First Edition of the Farewell Discourse in the Gospel of John' (unpublished dissertation, Princeton Theological Seminary, Princeton, NJ, 1989), pp. 25-44. Moore's discussion of the form/content conundrum is provocative although it also remains too theoretical (*Literary Criticism*, pp. 64-68).

43. Cf. Brownson, 'First Farewell', pp. 45-59.

44. See further the fascinating discussion in Moore, *Literary Criticism*, pp. 52-53, on Gérard Genette's reading of Marcel Proust's *A la recherche du temps perdu*.

45. *Anatomy*, pp. 45, 47.

46. See further the remarks of Becker, 'Streit', pp. 20-21.

De Jonge and others (including Brown in his commentary[47]) are probably right, however, when they claim that it is impossible to bring about word-for-word reconstructions of any putative sources and/or prior editions of the Gospel. But, as John Ashton has recently pointed out, the inability to effect word-for-word reconstructions hardly vitiates the relevance for the interpretative task of the conclusion, actually shared by de Jonge and Culpepper and others who follow them, that the Gospel shows clear evidence of previously written traditions and of a long process of composition: 'the difficulty of the enterprise does not diminish the significance of the data that make it necessary'.[48] Ashton remarks that these reconstructions, despite the variety in the proposals, remain 'the right *kind* of solution'.[49] Word-for-word reconstructions may not be possible; more modest ones, capable of eliciting wide consent, outlining the basic content, characteristics, emphases and purposes of putative sources or prior editions may well be. The evidence for such modest efforts is, it seems, plain enough to any discerning reader who is willing to put presuppositions and predilections at risk. If that were not so, de Jonge and Culpepper and others would presumably not be able to acknowledge, as they do, the probability that the Gospel is the product of a long and complex history of composition. Their acknowledgment undercuts their working assumption that the extant Gospel is a thematically coherent and narratively cohesive unity.

For these reasons, among others, one could take issue with de Jonge's provocative claim, quoted earlier, that the Gospel 'functioned as a whole among people who did *not* take its prehistory into account'. This claim, approvingly quoted by Culpepper, is unlikely to be true if, as de Jonge and Culpepper acknowledge, the Gospel is the literary product of a single community with a distinctive history and reached its final form only after a long process of writing and rewriting. Robert Fortna, in his recent redaction-critical study, *The Fourth Gospel and its Predecessor*, must then be right when he points out that the original readers would

47. *John*, p. xxiv.

48. J. Ashton, *Understanding the Fourth Gospel* (Oxford: Oxford University Press, 1991), p. 80. He attributes this insight to J. Wellhausen in 1907 (p. 35) and writes: 'The data on which Wellhausen and his successors base their case are incontrovertibly there and hard to reconcile with any theory of unified composition' (p. 80).

49. Ashton, *Understanding*, p. 246 (emphasis original). Furthermore, in my opinion, there is less variety in the proposals than appears at first sight, particularly when peculiarly idiosyncratic or methodologically flawed proposals are left out of account.

have been familiar with any putative sources or previous editions of the Gospel.[50] (One could add that they, or several of their number, would also have had a hand in composing those sources and/or editions.) Fortna reasons that 'the original historical reader...would in fact have appropriated it [the Gospel] in a way closely analogous to the modern method of the redaction critic, comparing old with new'. Thus 'the redaction-critical method closely *parallels the way the original readers would have perceived and understood the text*'.[51]

If anything, historical-critical investigation of the Gospel's composition history has firmly established that the Gospel of John is 'an imperfectly edited whole', as Brown says.[52] For this reason, it is hermeneutically perilous to assume or to maintain its thematic coherence and its narrative cohesion. The reader implied by the text is then likely to be nothing more than 'an idealized abstraction',[53] bearing little or no relation to real, historical readers[54] nor providing much guidance for real readers today.

5. *Conclusion*

Culpepper's own recent work shows that historical and literary approaches need not be mutually exclusive.[55] Even in his *Anatomy*, he

50. *The Fourth Gospel and its Predecessor* (Philadelphia: Fortress Press, 1988), pp. 8-9. This redaction-critical exercise is meant to complement his source-critical study *The Gospel of Signs: A Reconstruction of the Narrative Source Underlying the Fourth Gospel* (SNTSMS, 11; Cambridge: Cambridge University Press, 1970).

51. *Predecessor*, pp. 9, 8, respectively. Emphasis original.

52. Review article in *TS* 21 (1960), p. 639.

53. Powell, *Narrative Criticism*, p. 21.

54. For example, the Gospel's implied reader seems to be both familiar and unfamiliar with Judaism and its traditions. To his credit, Culpepper's critical probing of this confusing picture of the implied reader compels him to write that the 'difficulty posed by the tension between presumption of familiarity with Jewish festivals, especially in the discourses, and explanatory comments which make the gospel intelligible to readers unfamiliar with Judaism probably indicates that by the time the composition of the Fourth Gospel was completed a broader readership was envisioned than was originally intended', namely, a readership that included 'gentile Christians who knew little about Judaism' (*Anatomy*, p. 225). In short, Culpepper here resolves (rightly, I think) a problem raised by narrative-critical analysis by resorting to a possible, even likely, historical-critical explanation. See Moore, *Literary Criticism*, p. 94.

55. See R.A. Culpepper, 'John', in B.W. Anderson (ed.), *The Books of the Bible* (New York: Charles Scribner's Sons, 1989), I, pp. 203-28; and R.A. Culpepper,

called for a 'dialogue' between the narrative and historical approaches.[56] Culpepper rightly acknowledges that the Gospel of John, like other New Testament, documents, are ancient texts and that they presuppose the ideological conceptions, social mores, literary conventions, and, of course, the very language of the ancient Hellenistic world. Johannine symbolism, he observes, cannot be comprehended apart from philological, archaeological, historical and sociological study.[57]

Mutatis mutandis, it can also be said that this symbolism cannot be understood apart from attention to Johannine history, the history of the community and the composition history of its major document, the Gospel of John. Within the methodological constraints of narrative criticism itself, in fact, the possibility has to be left open that in the Gospel's literary world the *implied* author presupposes knowledge both of a communal history and of a composition history on the part of the *implied* reader. Reconstructive efforts thus also have their place within the logic of narrative criticism itself, even if narrative criticism, unlike historical criticism, intrinsically declines to make historical judgments about the real first readers or about 'what actually happened'.

Narrative criticism provides a methodology that encourages close attention in a new and fresh way to what the text says and how it actually goes about saying it. For that historical critics, and certainly exegetes, can be grateful indeed. There is no reason, it seems, why

'L'application de la narratologie à l'étude de l'évangile de Jean', in J.-D. Kaestli *et al.* (eds.), *La communauté Johannique et son histoire* (Le Monde de la Bible; Geneva: Labor et Fides, 1990), pp. 97-120.

56. *Anatomy*, p. 5. See further the recently published monograph by M.W.G Stibbe, *John as Storyteller: Narrative Criticism and the Fourth Gospel* (SNTMS, 73; Cambridge: Cambridge University Press, 1992).

57. 'L'application', p. 100; cf. Powell, *Narrative Criticism*, pp. 29, 86, 97. This acknowledgment shows that historical criticism is not simply a method but a manner of approach that uses diverse and ever-changing methods. This manner of approach fundamentally respects the undeniable fact that the various books of the Bible were written and first heard by flesh-and-blood human beings in quite specific historical and cultural contexts different from our own. Thus, the rejection or abuse of any particular historical-critical method (say, source criticism) does not necessarily vitiate historical inquiry as an indispensable, even morally obligatory, step in the interpretative process. See further M. de Jonge, 'De historisch-kritische methode', in A.F.J. Klijn (ed.), *Inleiding tot de studie van het Nieuwe Testament* (Kampen: Kok, 2nd edn, n.d.), pp. 71-85; E. Krentz, *The Historical-Critical Method* (Philadelphia: Fortress Press, 1975); Tuckett, *Reading the New Testament*.

narrative criticism cannot be another useful tool in the repertoire of the historical critic. For the historical critic, however, the real work of interpretation has only begun when the work of the narrative critic is finished.[58]

---

58. I do not mean to imply that reconstructive historical-critical exercises, or other forms of historical inquiry, constitute the totality of the interpretative agenda. See further my essay, 'John 4.27: Women (and Men) in the Gospel and the Community of John', in G.J. Brooke (ed.), *Women in the Biblical Tradition* (Lampeter: Edwin Mellen, 1992), pp. 208-30.

JSNT 43 (1991), pp. 41-69

JOHN AND THE GNOSTICS:
THE SIGNIFICANCE OF THE APOCRYPHON OF JOHN FOR THE DEBATE
ABOUT THE ORIGINS OF THE JOHANNINE LITERATURE

Alastair H.B. Logan

I

Irenaeus, bishop of Lyons in the 180s, but originally from Asia Minor, is perhaps the first mainstream Christian writer to defend the orthodoxy of the Fourth Gospel over against its extensive use by Valentinians and other Gnostics.[1] He includes a summary of the attempt by the Ptolemaean school of Valentinianism to derive their theogony from the Prologue as an awful warning of the perils of eisegesis.[2] And he sets his defence in the context of the public tradition of orthodox teaching transmitted from the apostles themselves by the succession of Catholic bishops, notably in Rome, but also found in such representatives as Polycarp of Smyrna, disciple of apostles, converter of heretics and

---

1. *Adv. Haer.* 3.11.1 (Harvey, II, 40); 11.7 (II, 46). Tatian had been the first to include it in a four-gospel harmony, but had done so as an Encratite heretic. Theophilus of Antioch, *Ad Autolycum* 2.22, of about 177, had simply cited Jn 1.1 with reference to the holy Scriptures and the Spirit-inspired writers including John. On Valentinian use of John, see W. von Loewenich, *Das Johannisverständnis im zweiten Jahrhundert* (Giessen: Töpelmann, 1932); J.N. Sanders, *The Fourth Gospel in the Early Church* (Cambridge: Cambridge University Press, 1943); F.-M. Braun, *Jean le théologien et son évangile dans l'église ancienne* (Paris: Gabalda, 1959); M.F. Wiles, *The Spiritual Gospel* (Cambridge: Cambridge University Press, 1960); B. Lindars, *The Gospel of John* (NCB; London: Marshall, Morgan & Scott, 1972), pp. 28-29; D.M. Smith, *Johannine Christianity* (Columbia, SC: University of South Carolina Press, 1984), p. 5.

2. *Adv. Haer.* 1.8.5 (Harvey, I, 75-80).

teacher of Irenaeus himself when young.[3] The heretics conversely were of recent vintage and had been refuted by people like Polycarp. Irenaeus then relates—at second hand—Polycarp's story of how the apostle John fled from the baths at Ephesus on seeing Cerinthus inside lest the whole place collapse at the presence of such a notorious enemy of the truth![4]

Cerinthus had already featured along with the Valentinians and other representatives of 'the falsely so-called knowledge' in the genealogy of heresy going back to Simon Magus which concludes Irenaeus's first book.[5] Indeed a major plank in his defence of the orthodoxy of the Fourth Gospel is his claim that it was written precisely to answer the dualist and docetic errors of Cerinthus—Irenaeus assumes that its author was John, the son of Zebedee, who was also the seer of the book of Revelation, living on to a great age in Ephesus.[6] And he goes on to claim that none of the heretics could assent to Jn 1.14: 'The Word became flesh'.[7]

While scholars have noted but generally discounted the claim about Cerinthus,[8] they have not, apart from R.M. Grant, made anything of the fact that Irenaeus couples Cerinthus's views with what he calls a much older error, that of the Nicolaitans, whom he associates with Cerinthus in a very brief note in the catalogue in Book I, but here qualifies as an off-shoot (*vulsio*) of the Gnostics.[9] His description of their heretical views

3.   3.3.4 (Harvey, II, 12-13).

4.   3.3.4 (Harvey, II, 12-13).

5.   1.22-31, esp. 26.

6.   Cf. 3.1.1 (Harvey, II, 6); 4.20.11 (Harvey, II, 222); 5.30.3 (Harvey, II, 410); etc.

7.   3.11.3 (Harvey, II, 42).

8.   See on this R. Schnackenburg, *The Gospel according to St John*, I (New York: Burns & Oates, 1968), pp. 169-70. The scholars supporting the thesis that Cerinthus was the main target mostly appeal to 1 John, whose assertions, Schnackenburg contends, do not exactly suit Cerinthus's doctrines as reproduced by Irenaeus's catalogue (1.26.1: Harvey, I, 211-12). In the most detailed discussion, R.M. Grant ('The Origin of the Fourth Gospel', *JBL* 69 [1950], pp. 305-22, esp. 307-308), on the basis of a careful reconstruction of Cerinthus's views, rejects Irenaeus's claim, implying that it may be an answer to critics like Gaius, who attributed the Fourth Gospel and Revelation to Cerinthus (p. 316). See n. 18, below.

9.   Grant ('Origin', p. 307) dismisses the remark about the Nicolaitans as clearly based on Rev. 2.6 and 15, and because Irenaeus 'equally clearly knew nothing about the Nicolaitans'. This last is presumably based on Irenaeus's extremely brief note on them, following Cerinthus and the Ebionites, in which he quotes Rev. 2.6. Grant fails to note the way Irenaeus links the Nicolaitans with the Gnostics as responsible for the

not only includes tenets attributed to Cerinthus in the catalogue (distinguishing the Creator from the Father of Christ, the Creator's son, Jesus, from the impassible Son, Christ, who descends on Jesus and reascends into the Pleroma), but also adds details which relate to the so-called Barbelognostics and Ophites whose systems are described at the end of the catalogue (1.29, 30: reference to a Beginning, *initium*, i.e. *archē*; Monogenes and Logos the latter's son; and our world being made by the lower ignorant Creator).[10] Of course, Irenaeus's references to Cerinthus and the Nicolaitans as key evidence to support the orthodoxy and antiquity of the Fourth Gospel (and the identity of its author with that of Revelation) may, as Grant suggests, be tendentious, appealing to his own local Asian traditions involving John and supporting the genuineness of Revelation and its millenarianism against anti-Montanist rejection of the Gospel and claims that Cerinthus wrote both.[11] But what is more interesting is his linking of the Nicolaitans with the Gnostics of 1.29, 30 and the relationship he assumes between the Johannine Prologue and the systems of 1.29, 30. These two chapters present two versions of what I would contend is *the* basic Gnostic myth, ch. 29 simply concerned with theogony and cosmogony, ch. 30 relating the whole story.[12] Chapter 29 is remarkably similar to the theogonic section

Fourth Gospel. Did he have information on the Nicolaitans independent of his catalogue, or was he simply trying a two-pronged defence of John's authorship of the Gospel (and Revelation) as (a) countering Cerinthus, who in any case was (b) anticipated by the Gnostics, John's original opponents, whose early date and link with the author of Revelation are guaranteed by the connection with the Nicolaus of Acts 6?

10. Cf. 3.11.1 with 1.26.1 and 1.29.1; 1.30.11-12. As Grant notes ('Origin', p. 311), G. Bardy ('Cerinthe', *RB* 30 [1921], pp. 344-73) had already argued that the Ophite doctrine had been erroneously attributed to Cerinthus, principally because he accepted Gaius's argument. Grant is right to insist that, certainly from Irenaeus's perspective, this need not rule out both groups holding similar views.

11. On the anti-Montanist rejection of the Fourth Gospel, cf. Irenaeus, 3.11.9 (Harvey II, 51); and on the claim that Cerinthus wrote Revelation (and the Fourth Gospel?), cf. Gaius of Rome (c. 200?) and, probably dependent on him, Dionysius of Alexandria, in Eusebius, *H.E.* 3.28.2 (see on this Grant, 'Origin', p. 307, citing also Epiphanius, *Pan.* 51.3.6, the argument of the 'Alogi'); E. Haenchen, *John 1: A Commentary on the Gospel of John Chapters 1–6* (Philadelphia: Fortress Press, 1984), pp. 23-24. Gaius, *pace* Haenchen, was not a bishop.

12. See my unpublished PhD thesis, 'The Development of Gnostic Theology with Special Reference to the *Apocryphon of John*, Irenaeus, *Adversus Haereses* I 29 and 30 and Related Texts' (St Andrews University, 1980). See also B. Layton, *The*

of the *Apocryphon of John* known both from the Berlin Coptic Gnostic Codex version and from no less than three versions from the Nag Hammadi library.[13]

Thus, whether on the basis of independent information or perhaps more likely on the grounds of similarity, Irenaeus interprets the relationship in terms of the Fourth Gospel's having been written to refute the Gnostic myth in its various forms. Certainly he appears to have known two such (1.29, 30) from written sources, perhaps obtained from the Valentinians whose 'commentaries' (*hypomnemata*) he had read;[14] indeed he charges them with having derived their ideas from the Gnostics of 1.29, 30.[15] His argument that the Fourth Gospel was written expressly to answer the spiritual ancestors of the Valentinians would neatly undercut the latter's appeal to it.

Irenaeus's interpretation of the resemblance, implying that the Gnostics even antedated Nicolaus and his followers, might seem to lend some support to the Bultmann thesis of a powerful Gnostic salvation myth underlying the Fourth Gospel, which alone makes sense of it, and which the author, perhaps an ex-Gnostic himself, is criticizing.[16] I hope to show, from the evidence Irenaeus himself supplies, that this further claim is also equally problematical—the Gnostics may be more influenced by John than vice versa. But despite attempts to undermine Bultmann's thesis, on the basis of, for example, the lateness of date or non-Gnostic character of the Mandaean (and Manichaean) parallels he adduces in his 1925 article,[17] that thesis of an underlying myth has, as

Gnostic Scriptures (Garden City, NY: Doubleday, 1987), pp. 5-21.

13. See Berlin Gnostic Codex (BG) 19.1–77.7 in *Die gnostischen Schriften des koptischen Papyrus Berolinensis 8502* (ed. W.C. Till; 2nd edn ed. H.-M. Schenke; Berlin: de Gruyter, 1972); Nag Hammadi Codices (CG) II 1; III 1; IV 1 in *Die drei Versionen des Apokryphon des Johannes im koptischen Museum zu Alt-Kairo* (ed. M. Krause and P. Labib; Wiesbaden: Otto Harrassowitz, 1962); English translation of II.1 supplemented by BG in J.M. Robinson (ed.), *The Nag Hammadi Library in English* (Leiden: Brill, 1977), pp. 98-116.

14. Cf. *Adv. Haer.* praef. (Harvey, I, 4).

15. Cf. 1.30.15 (Harvey, I, 241); 31.3 (I, 243); 2.13.8 and 10 (I, 284 and 286); etc.

16. R. Bultmann, 'Die Bedeutung der neuerschlossenen mandäischen und manichäischen Quellen für das Verständnis des Johannesevangeliums', *ZNW* 24 (1925), pp. 100-46, esp. 102-104; *The Gospel of John: A Commentary* (trans. G. Beasley-Murray; Oxford: Basil Blackwell, 1971), introduction by W. Schmithals, pp. 8-9.

17. See, e.g., E. Percy, *Untersuchungen über den Ursprung der johanneischen*

Wayne Meeks saw in his seminal article of 1972, to be taken seriously, especially as regards the motif of a descending and ascending redeemer figure.[18] He refers to the evidence of the Nag Hammadi library and its support for the view that myths of descending and ascending redeemers flourished in the first century without any Christian influence.[19] He notes the common agreement that 'the Jewish Wisdom myth in some form lies behind both the Johannine christology and the gnostic soul and saviour myths'[20] but insists that the question is whether both the Johannine and the Gnostic myths are independent variants of the Jewish, or whether one has influenced the other.[21] The tentative answer he supplies at the end of his article is that 'it is at least as plausible that the Johannine christology helped to create some gnostic myths as that gnostic myths helped create the Johannine christology'.[22] Only sociological analysis of the function of Gnostic texts, he suggested, might supply the answer.

The Bultmann thesis was regarded by many as not proven, indeed

Theologie (Lund: Gleerup, 1939); C.H. Dodd, *The Interpretation of the Fourth Gospel* (Cambridge: Cambridge University Press, 1953), pp. 121-30; R.E. Brown, *The Gospel according to John I–XII* (AB, 29; Garden City, NY: Doubleday, 1966), pp. lii-lvi, for criticism of the thesis; C. Colpe, *Die religionsgeschichtliche Schule* (Göttingen: Vandenhoeck & Ruprecht, 1961), and 'New Testament and Gnostic Christology', in J. Neusner (ed.), *Studies in the History of Religions*, XIV (Leiden: Brill, 1968), pp. 234-36, for criticism of the Reitzenstein thesis of a pre-Christian redeemer myth accepted by Bultmann; E.M. Yamauchi, *Gnostic Ethics and Mandaean Origins* (HTS, 24; Cambridge, MA: Harvard University Press, 1970), and *Pre-Christian Gnosticism* (London: Tyndale Press, 1973) for rebuttal of the thesis of pre-Christian Gnosticism and the Gnostic character of Mandaeism. However, an expert on Mandaeism, Kurt Rudolph, has argued for the pre-Christian origins of Mandaeism and its attestation of a pre-Christian Gnostic redeemer myth, in 'Stand und Aufgaben in der Erforschung des Gnostizismus', in *Tägung fur allgemeine Religionsgeschichte* (1963), pp. 93-94, 97, cited by J.M. Robinson in J.M. Robinson and H. Koester (eds.), *Trajectories through Early Christianity* (Philadelphia: Fortress Press, 1971), pp. 263-64.

18. W.A. Meeks, 'The Man from Heaven in Johannine Sectarianism', *JBL* 91 (1972), p. 45.

19. Meeks, 'Man from Heaven', p. 45. He refers to G.W. MacRae on the *Apocalypse of Adam* and F. Wisse on the *Paraphrase of Shem*, but see, e.g., Layton, *Scriptures*, pp. 20-21, 52, etc.

20. Meeks, 'Man from Heaven', p. 46.

21. Meeks, 'Man from Heaven', p. 46.

22. Meeks, 'Man from Heaven', p. 72.

weakened by the absence of texts which were both old enough and unified enough to supply a genuine myth of a redeemed redeemer descending and ascending, which could plausibly be argued to be pre-Christian and to have influenced the author of the Fourth Gospel. The Jewish background, it was argued by scholars such as Peder Borgen, offered a more satisfactory solution to the motifs of a heavenly agent or of a descending and ascending redeemer than Gnostic myth.[23] Some German scholars like Bultmann's pupil Ernst Käsemann[24] and Luise Schottroff[25] would go even further than Bultmann. While accepting his analysis of the Gospel and its sources, they would reject his view that its origin, purpose and character are *anti*-Gnostic; rather these are thoroughly docetic and, as Schottroff argues, essentially Gnostic. The discovery of the Nag Hammadi library led many to accept that Gnostic and Mandaean parallels could not be lightly dismissed, nor could the Bultmann thesis of a pre-Christian Gnostic myth underlying the Fourth Gospel.

The most astonishing support for that thesis was to come in 1974 in a claim by Gesine Schenke, a member of the Berlin Arbeitskreis involved in translating the Nag Hammadi library, that the *Trimorphic Protennoia* from Codex XIII, and particularly its third revelatory discourse (see below, p. 134), presented a material parallel to the Prologue which made more sense in itself than the Prologue, and was on the same level as the Gnostic logos hymn assumed by Bultmann to be the source of the Prologue![26] Here was the missing link! But Schenke more cautiously suggested that, laying aside the question of the sources of the Prologue, if one simply examines the similarity of the two texts dispassionately, 'one has the impression that the relevant statements of *Protennoia* stand in their natural context, whereas their parallels in the Johannine

---

23. Cf. P. Borgen, 'God's Agent in the Fourth Gospel', in *Logos was the True Light* (Trondheim: Tapir, 1983), p. 132; also 'The Son of Man Saying in John 3.13-14', in *Logos*, p. 148.

24. *The Testament of Jesus* (London: SCM Press, 1968), pp. 26, 45, 70, which speaks of the 'naive docetism' of the author.

25. *Der Glaubende und die feindliche Welt* (Neukirchen–Vluyn: Neukirchener Verlag, 1970).

26. 'Die dreigestaltige Protennoia: Eine gnostische Offenbarungsrede in koptischer Sprache aus dem Fund von Nag Hammedi', *TLZ* 99 (1974), col. 733, quoted in J.M. Robinson, 'Sethians and Johannine Thought: The *Trimorphic Protennoia* and the Prologue of the Gospel of John', in B. Layton (ed.), *The Rediscovery of Gnosticism*, II (Leiden: Brill, 1981), pp. 650-51.

prologue...seem to have been artificially made serviceable to a purpose really alien to them'.[27] In the same year Carsten Colpe, who had done so much to undermine the foundations of the History of Religions School and hence Bultmann's hypothesis of the pre-Christian myth of the redeemed redeemer, commented on and listed the 'stupendous parallels' between the *Protennoia* and the Prologue.[28] But he refused to draw the Bultmannian conclusion that the evangelist demythologized, Christianized and historicized a Gnostic hymn. He pointed instead to the basic sapiential speculation into which both the Gnostic and Johannine texts seem to fit, which, however, could now be found not scattered among very diffuse streams of the first century AD in the eastern Mediterranean (cf. Dodd's collection of parallels, etc.), but particularly associated with Sethian Gnosticism.

The same year (1974) also saw an edition of the *Protennoia* by the Belgian scholar, Yvonne Janssens, who saw the text rather differently as Barbeloite and hence Christian Gnostic, unaware of the position of the Berlin group and their suggestion that the *Protennoia* had been secondarily Christianized.[29] She has since become acquainted with their position and arguments, but in her edition of the *Protennoia* of 1978 still insisted that it was a matter of Johannine and New Testament echoes in the *Protennoia* and not vice versa.[30] However, in her essay in the Wilson Festschrift of 1983, *The New Testament and Gnosis*, while admitting that she had been one who argued that the *Protennoia* had 'plundered' the New Testament and especially the Fourth Gospel, she is more equivocal, agreeing with R.McL. Wilson that 'there are parallels in thought which may indicate only a common background', leaving the last word on this to specialists in the Fourth Gospel.[31] Wilson himself, in

27. 'Die dreigestaltige Protennoia', in Robinson, 'Sethiams', p. 651.

28. C. Colpe, 'Heidnische, jüdische und christliche Überlieferung in den Schriften aus Nag Hammadi III', *JAC* 17 (1974), pp. 122-24.

29. Y. Janssens, 'Le Codex XIII de Nag Hammadi', *Le Muséon* 7 (1974); revised in a second edition, *La prôtennoia trimorphe (NH, XIII, I)* (Bibliothèque copte de Nag Hammadi, section 'Textes', 4; Quebec: Laval University Press, 1978).

30. Cf. Y. Janssens, 'Une source gnostique du Prologue', in M. de Jonge (ed.), *L'Evangile de Jean: Sources, redaction, théologie* (BETL, 44; Gembloux: Duculot, 1977), pp. 355-58, where she lists the parallels. Cf. *Prôtennoia*, p. 82; Robinson, 'Sethians', pp. 658-59.

31. 'The Trimorphic Protennoia and the Fourth Gospel', in A.H.B. Logan and A.J.M. Wedderburn (eds.), *The New Testament and Gnosis* (Edinburgh: T. & T. Clark, 1983), pp. 229-43, esp. 235, 242-43.

his 1975 paper at the Oxford Patristic Conference, noting Janssens's counter position to the Berlin Arbeitskreis, suggested as an alternative not yet considered that the *Protennoia* may represent an example of secondary de-Christianization.[32]

J.M. Robinson brought the whole matter into the open in his paper on 'Sethians and Johannine Thought' at the International Conference on Gnosticism at Yale in 1978,[33] when in the second section on the *Protennoia* and the Johannine Prologue, he confronted the two—or three—positions and demanded a proper methodology which would help to determine which was the more original. Despite protests of impartiality, he seems more persuaded by the Berlin Arbeitskreis's case and interpretation of the *Protennoia*. He cites in conclusion the Pronoia hymn at the end of the long version of the *Apocryphon of John* (CG II 30.11–31.25; see below, p. 135), whose striking parallels to the *Protennoia* had already been noted by Janssens.[34] As he points out, its parallels to the *Protennoia* are in large part also parallels to the Johannine Prologue, although he insists that the Pronoia hymn is not explicitly Christian. And he asks: 'Is one to classify it as a de-Christianized re-mythologized Gnostic interpretation of the prologue, or is it not more reasonable to see here something like the "natural" context in which this material existed prior to its Christianization?'[35] And he suggests the traces of periodization in the Prologue—the Logos in the primordial period, in the pre-Christian 'spermatic' period and in the incarnate period—as the way the non-Christian tradition was adapted to and unified in Christ, in a way more seemingly 'artificial' when compared to the *Protennoia*.

32. R.McL. Wilson, 'The Trimorphic Protennoia', in M. Krause (ed.), *Gnosis and Gnosticism* (NHS, 8; Leiden: Brill, 1977), pp. 50-54.

33. 'Sethians', pp. 650-64.

34. 'Sethians', p. 661; Janssens, *Prôtennoia*, pp. 11-12.

35. 'Sethians', pp. 661-62. For a recent survey of the relationship of the *Protennoia* and the Prologue, see C.A. Evans, 'On the Prologue of John and *The Trimorphic Protennoia*', *NTS* 27 (1981), pp. 395-401. While sympathetic to Robinson's appeal to a 'Johannine trajectory' in his essay 'The Johannine Trajectory' in *Trajectories through Early Christianity*, pp. 260-66, Evans prefers Colpe's suggestion that the two share a Wisdom trajectory in which a gnosticizing proclivity is evident. The other recent contribution is the paper by Gesine Schenke, published as G. Robinson, 'The Trimorphic Protennoia and The Prologue of the Fourth Gospel', in J.E. Goehring *et al.* (eds.), *Gnosticism and the Early Christian World* (Sonoma, CA: Polebridge Press, 1990), pp. 37-50.

It is Robinson's final point made about the Pronoia hymn in the *Apocryphon* which I wish to focus upon in this article. In all that has been said, the *Apocryphon of John* or the myth underlying it has cropped up as the common factor. Irenaeus suggested—rightly or wrongly, and he was closer to the situation and texts than we are—that the Fourth Gospel was written to refute the Gnostic myth he summarized in a text strikingly similar to the *Apocryphon*; the *Trimorphic Protennoia* as a possible source of the Prologue is also clearly related to the *Apocryphon*, and to its concluding Pronoia hymn in particular (see below, p. 135), and the *Apocryphon* itself has been claimed to represent a Christianization of an earlier non-Christian Gnostic myth. The *Apocryphon*, I would contend, can be seen as a key to the riddle of the relationship of John and the Gnostics.

In this regard it is worth noting that Michel Tardieu, editor of the most recent synoptic version of the *Apocryphon of John* with its four versions and two recensions (a long one including the Pronoia hymn, in Codices II and IV; a shorter one, excluding the hymn, in Codex III and the Berlin Gnostic Codex), rejects the general consensus. He insists that the *Apocryphon* is a *Christian* text composed of the same material as the Fourth Gospel. He claims that it takes up a position at the heart of the Johannine school, and represents the manifesto of those who refused to compromise with Judaism. Further, he argues that its method of exposition is that of the Johannine Prologue, and finally that the Fourth Gospel is the basis of its entire theological argumentation.[36] He would see the Pronoia hymn as going back to a dissident esoteric circle within the Johannine community, around the time of the final redaction of the Fourth Gospel (c. AD 120), and forming the basis of the threefold structure of our present *Apocryphon*.[37]

That may be to go a bit too far. One must be very careful, as Wilson noted in the discussion of Robinson's paper at Yale, in distinguishing different kinds of evidence as regards the Christian character of the text and the matter of literary dependence—we need clear use of quotation to establish the latter: 'Literary allusions can only confirm literary dependence already established by the use of quotation. Given only allusions one must be tentative in drawing conclusions.' As a poor third Wilson notes

---

36. M. Tardieu, *Ecrits gnostiques: Codex de Berlin* (Sources gnostiques et manichéennes, 1; Paris: Cerf, 1984), pp. 10, 33, 35-39.
37. Tardieu, *Ecrits*, pp. 42-43.

parallels in thought which may indicate only a common background.[38]

In what follows, with all these caveats and warnings in mind, I shall attempt first to show, by examining Irenaeus's summary of the Gnostic (or Barbelognostic) myth in *Adv. Haer.* 1.29.1-4 and the Berlin Gnostic Codex version of the *Apocryphon* (the best preserved at this point), that the latter has developed Irenaeus's version of what I contend is an original *Christian* Gnostic myth of Father, Mother/Wisdom and Son/Christ. That myth itself developed, on the basis of materials from the Psalms and Wisdom books (cf. Heb. 1–2) and the birth narrative of Luke in particular, by increasing exposure to Johannine ideas into its present form in the *Apocryphon*. Secondly, I shall try to show how the *Protennoia* reflects that more developed myth and form, and thirdly that the Pronoia hymn, whatever its ultimate provenance, is part of the later development of the text which has become our *Apocryphon*, when it was developed into a treatise on providence by taking over the existing Christian theogonic myth of Irenaeus in *Adv. Haer.* 1.29.1-4. I hope to show that, as Meeks suggests, what is important, and what establishes the Christian character of a text, is not individual elements or more or less clear allusions to the New Testament, but how the text functions in terms of the self-understanding of those using it.

II

Scholarly understanding of the relation between the summary of the main points of the Gnostic myth given by Irenaeus in *Adv. Haer.* 1.29.1-4 as supplying the Valentinian Gnostics, his main target, with their basic mythological substructure, and the *Apocryphon of John* in its two recensions, has varied, from Carl Schmidt's conclusion in 1907, not long after the discovery of the Berlin Gnostic Codex, that Irenaeus had copied the Greek original,[39] to the general consensus of scholars today that the two are related, but that Irenaeus's version is independent, echoing a common source,[40] but casting little light on the *Apocryphon*. Most agree with Wilson, that both Irenaeus's text and the *Apocryphon*

---

38. *Rediscovery*, p. 664.

39. 'Irenaeus und seine Quelle in adv. haer. I 29', in *Philotesia: Festschrift Paul Kleinert* (Berlin: Trowitzch & Sohn, 1907), pp. 315-36.

40. So Tardieu, *Ecrits*, p. 40; cf. M. Krause, 'The Relation of the Apocryphon of John to the Account in Irenaeus', in W. Foerster (ed.), *Gnosis: A Selection of Gnostic Texts*. I. *Patristic Evidence* (Oxford: Clarendon Press, 1972), pp. 100-103, esp. 103.

of John represent a secondary Christianization of an originally non-Christian, perhaps even pre-Christian, document.[41] No one seems to have asked whether, as John Robinson does with regard to the Fourth Gospel in relation to the Synoptics, it might not be a useful hypothesis to reverse the general perspective, which accepts the *Apocryphon*'s version as not only as valid, but even preferable to that of Irenaeus. From long-term wrestling with the complexity of the interrelationships of the four Coptic texts and the Latin version of Irenaeus, I have attempted to argue that Irenaeus's version was nearer the original, and have been led thereby to suggest how the variations in the several Coptic versions might have developed.[42]

But to come to the first point, the development of the myth underlying *Adv. Haer.* 1.29 and the *Apocryphon*. There are certain puzzling features of the heavenly hierarchy in both—especially the confusion between Barbelo and Ennoia: at one point they are identified, at another distinct.[43] So too with Christ, whose position seems anomalous, both a generated being, the Son, and an aspect of the Father, Light (with a female consort; see below, p. 128, *Adv. Haer.* lines 10-15; p. 130, *Adv. Haer.* lines 12ff.). Then again there is in Irenaeus the omission of the appearance of Thelema (see below, p. 130) and the abrupt mention of the Logos (see below, p. 131, *Apoc. Jn* lines 6-7), while the *Apocryphon* clearly obscures the unions of male and female beings (or rather attributes of the supreme Father) which lead to the emission of further beings (see below, pp. 130-31; cf. *Adv. Haer.* lines 3ff. and *Apoc. Jn* lines 6ff.). The unions in the *Apocryphon* have clearly been obscured by the allusion to Jn 1.3 (the Word followed the will, etc.), but traces remain in the linking of Eternal Life and Will, Nous and Foreknowledge. Then again there is the odd pattern of pairing, the first female (Ennoia) with the third male (Logos), the first male (the Light/Christ) with the third female (Aphtharsia/Incorruptibility), whereas the second and fourth pairs are united in a regular way. Finally, there is the confusion over the figure, role and title of the self-originate or Autogenes—clearly distinct in Irenaeus (see below, p. 130, *Adv. Haer.* lines 7-8) but with the odd role of representing the Great Light, and later apparently referred to as

41. But cf. Tardieu, *Ecrits*, p. 10; Layton, *Scriptures*, pp. 5-21.

42. See n. 12, above.

43. Cf., e.g., *Apoc. Jn* BG 27.5-14 (Ennoia = Barbelo); 28.9-13 (Ennoia distinct from Barbelo).

Monogenes,[44] assimilated to Christ in the *Apocryphon* (see below p. 129, *Apoc. Jn* lines 23-33), whose text is evidently confused at this point. Thus he is twice referred to as perfected (see below, p. 129, *Apoc. Jn* line 31; p. 131, *Apoc. Jn* line 11). The status of Truth as his partner in Irenaeus, but as an element in him in the *Apocryphon* (see below, pp. 130-31, *Adv. Haer.* lines 10-11, *Apoc. Jn* lines 14-15), distinct from a prior fifth female heavenly being after Eternal Life in the long version,[45] points to further confusion.

Roel van den Broek has argued that part of the confusion in our texts has been caused by the introduction of the Autogenes figure,[46] but I would go further and argue that it is the growing influence of the Fourth Gospel and its Prologue in particular which has messed up what was a clear and orderly myth of the Father, Mother and Son. That myth, I would argue, originally had no Ennoia, or Logos, or Autogenes, or Truth; it involved the Father, the Invisible Spirit, deciding to reveal himself to Barbelo, that is, the heavenly Wisdom or Sophia of the Wisdom of Solomon, a virginal spirit acting alone (cf. Wis. 7.22-28; etc.). As she is female, his revelatory attributes are three females, Prognosis, Aphtharsia (Incorruptibility) and Eternal Life. As a result, and here the fundamentally *Christian* character of the myth comes into view, she, Barbelo, the *Virgin* Spirit, in a typical Gnostic projection of historical earthly beings and events into the heavenly world, as the archetype of the obedient virgin Mary, delighted with the heavenly revelation and visitation, conceives purely spiritually the only (*monogenes*) Son. The identification of this figure as Light, and the beginning of illumination and generation (see below, p. 128, *Adv. Haer.* lines 11-12), seems a secondary development in line with the introduction of the light motif. Thus it seems odd that the Father should anoint a light rather than his Son with his goodness, so that he becomes perfect and Christ.

What I submit has happened is that under the influence of the Fourth Gospel and its distinctive themes, the Son, Christ, has been assimilated to the male paternal characteristic, Light (the Light, which is Christ), so that the latter and the following characteristic, Thelema, have been omitted in Irenaeus's account. At the same time Logos has been added on to

44. Cf. Irenaeus, *Adv. Haer.* 1.29.4 (Harvey, I, 225).

45. Cf. *Apoc. Jn* CG II 5.32–6.8.

46. R. van den Broek, 'Autogenes and Adamas: The Mythological Structure of the Apocryphon of John', in M. Krause (ed.), *Gnosis and Gnosticism* (NHS, 17; Leiden: Brill, 1981), pp. 16-25.

the end, with an appropriate female counterpart, Ennoia, being inserted before Prognosis and united with Logos. Indeed the Berlin version of the *Apocryphon* reflects the original threesome of male characteristics—will, standing by Nous and *light* (see below, p. 131, *Apoc. Jn* line 5).

As van den Broek saw, Autogenes, the emission of Ennoia and Logos (see below, p. 130, *Adv. Haer.* line 7), is a later addition, but he belongs with Ennoia and Logos as equally arising from the influence of Johannine ideas, particularly the Prologue. I suggest that he is best seen as the heavenly archetype of John the Baptist, later than the Logos and witnessing to the Great Light (the Latin *repraesentatio* of Irenaeus's translator being an attempt to render Jn 1.8b).[47] The presence of Truth as his consort, obscured, as much else in the *Apocryphon*, by its later identification of Christ and Autogenes, is also due to Johannine influence. Having been introduced, Autogenes is given something to do—he it is who emits Adam, the heavenly archetypal man and his consort, rather than, as originally, Prognosis and Nous, an element retained, not in Irenaeus's account, but in the *Apocryphon* (see below, p. 131, *Apoc. Jn* lines 24ff.).

However, as indicated, the *Apocryphon* itself has further confused the—relatively—straightforward version of the original myth in Irenaeus both by adding the Pronoia figure as central to its purpose as a treatise on Providence, *de fato*, as Tardieu has so convincingly shown—hence its use of the concluding Pronoia hymn—and by identifying Christ and Autogenes.

The details are not important. What is important is the attempt to demonstrate how the myth has developed and how Johannine influence is secondary. This must be kept in mind when we come to deal with the *Protennoia* and the Pronoia hymn at the end of the *Apocryphon*.

Finally as regards the original character of the myth, which the consensus of scholars would see as a text secondarily Christianized, the diagram of the structure of the myth as reconstructed by me (see below, pp. 136-37) makes clear, I hope, its basic Christian character. This is evident first in the account of the birth of the Son to the Virgin Spirit, Barbelo, through her exultant response to the Father, the Invisible Spirit, a typical Gnostic back-projection of the birth of Jesus to the virgin Mary

---

47. Van den Broek ('Autogenes', p. 21) suggests it is rendered by the Coptic *eouparastasis* of CG III 11.5, but this is weakened by the fact that the Latin translator later uses *circumstantiam* of the luminaries round Autogenes and *adstare* of the angel standing beside Monogenes.

as referred to in Lk. 1.30-35, 46-49. It is evident secondly in the following episodes of the Son's anointing, perfection and elevation, which do not appear to have a precise parallel in pagan or Jewish theology[48] but can be derived much more plausibly from Christian speculation on the heavenly pre-existent Son in Hebrews 1 and 2. The supreme heavenly figures, as so often in Gnostic myth, are archetypes of the earthly ones, the lower figures negative counterparts of the higher (contrast Barbelo's behaviour with that of Sophia, Adam's [and Christ's] with that of the Protarchon). In a manner strikingly reminiscent of Hebrews 1 and 2, with its similar idiosyncratic combination of Jewish-Christian and Platonic ideas, these Christian Gnostics have constructed a myth of primal Father, Mother and Son as an alternative myth of origins to Genesis 1–5. The latter for the Gnostics properly applied to the later creation of the visible universe and man, reinterpreted as the work of an ignorant and arrogant Demiurge, the Protarchon (or God of the Old Testament). No wonder the whole myth can appear so un-Christian, avoiding reference in its theological and christological speculations to those parts of the Old Testament central to the Jews and favoured by the early Christians, viz. the Law and the prophets.

Nonetheless it does make fundamental use of Wisdom speculation which underlies the myth just as it does the Prologue. However, and this is where the Gnostic approach, while Christian, radically differs from the Johannine scheme, the former uses that speculation not christologically as in the latter but *cosmologically*, to explain the pre-cosmic fall and the presence of the divine spirit or power in this demiurgic creation. Christ and Barbelo/Sophia are *distinct*: in the original, Christ is not the light of Wis. 7.25 and Heb. 1.3 and the Logos is a later addition and entity different from both. But conversely Christ is *not* a later addition, part of a supposed Christianization: the Son is integral and his birth, anointing, perfection and elevation are projections of the Christian Gnostic's own experience and destiny, self-originate like the Son in that he is a spiritual being, but, like the lower Sophia from whom he derives, alienated and lost in matter, seeking a heavenly consort. Then when he is illuminated, he is elevated and freed from this world by the (spiritual?) sacraments of

48. Dr John Muddiman has drawn my attention to the figure of the woman giving birth to the child, his elevation and enthronement and her exile, in Rev. 12.1-6. This image may also have contributed, although it is more eschatological than cosmological, does not imply virgin birth and does not derive the evil principle from the female figure.

anointing, robing, enthroning, etc. (see below, p. 135, *Apoc. Jn* lines 26-27 on the five seals). Conversely the negative experience and response of the lower Sophia and her abortive offspring, the Demiurge or Protarchon, are responsible not only for the lower creation but also for the evil emotions and actions of the one who rejects the Gnostic message—the gracious revelation. Such hypostatization of emotions into the material elements of creation was a major contribution of the Gnostics to the Valentinians.[49]

III

What, secondly, of the evident relationship between the *Apocryphon* and the *Trimorphic Protennoia* noted by Janssens and Robinson, and their mutual relation to John? Tardieu correctly indicates the intention of the author(s) of the *Apocryphon of John* to present it as a revelation to the apostle John, the son of Zebedee, disciple of the Christ, answering his questions about past, present and future, the reasons for Christ's being sent from the Father and the nature of the aeon to which the believers (i.e. Gnostics) will go.[50] I have noted some of the allusions to the Fourth Gospel, and the dialogue in the third part of the *Apocryphon* about the fate of souls who have or have not known the truth or experienced the descent of the saving spirit[51] is close both to the concerns of the Johannine Epistles (a counterfeit spirit like the Antichrist, the need to proclaim Jesus as the Christ, the Son of God, the importance of chrism as imparting knowledge), and to Tatian. He, of course, was the first to set John's Gospel on the same level as the Synoptics, adapting it to his own gnosticizing view of the lower material soul and its need for union with the heavenly Spirit.[52] In its present form the *Apocryphon* is clearly dependent on the Fourth Gospel and the concerns of the Johannine circle and its interpreters.

But what of the relation to the *Protennoia*? The latter is extremely difficult to interpret, as Janssens ruefully admits,[53] and I turn with relief to the outline offered by J.D. Turner, its editor and translator in *The Nag Hammadi Library in English*—'The tractate', he says,

---

49. Cf. Irenaeus, *Adv. Haer.* 2.13.3 (Harvey, II, 282); 8 (*ibid.*, 285); 10 (*ibid.*, 286); etc.

50. *Ecrits*, pp. 33-36.

51. Cf. *Apoc. Jn* BG 64.13–75.10; CG III 32.22–39.10; CG II 25.16–30.11.

52. *Discourse to the Greeks*, 5.7.12–13.15.

53. 'Trimorphic Protennoia', p. 229.

proclaims three descents of the Gnostic heavenly Redeemer Protennoia, who is actually Barbelo, the first thought of the Father...it is divided into three sections, each with individual subtitles and each describing one of the descents of the heavenly redeemer. First she appears as Father, or Voice; second as Mother, or Sound; and third as Son or Word (Logos). Each of these three sections, in turn, is capable of being subdivided into three parts: first an aretalogy (I am); second a doctrinal presentation (on cosmogony, eschatology and soteriology, respectively); and third a concluding revelation.[54]

Again I cannot embark on a detailed examination; as we noted, Robinson and the Berlin Arbeitskreis have the impression that the underlying myth occurs more 'naturally' in the *Protennoia* than in the Prologue, which Robinson seizes on as a criterion to suggest the priority of the former. My simple point is this: the form of the myth presupposed by the *Protennoia*, particularly in the cosmogonic section of the first part (see below, p. 133), is a more developed version of that underlying the *Apocryphon*. Thus, even though only an abbreviated form of the myth is given, Christ identified with the light (and Autogenes?; see below, p. 133, *Trim. Prot.* lines 21-22) is clearly the originator of the four luminaries, who are described as aeons—as in the *Apocryphon* where the original luminaries are being assimilated to aeons (see below, p. 131, *Apoc. Jn* lines 17-33). His consort has dropped from sight and he is explicitly identified with the (Johannine) Word.[55]

Further evidence that the *Protennoia* is developing the form of the myth found in the *Apocryphon* is suggested by the way the former downgrades the primary figures of the Father, Mother and Son into manifestations of Barbelo and attributes Barbelo's titles (threefold male, three powers, names) to apply to the Word (see below, p. 133). This reinterpretation is probably responsible for the fact that it is Barbelo, or Protennoia (a reworking of the *Apocryphon's* Pronoia?), who anoints Christ and not the Father as in the original version in Irenaeus and the *Apocryphon*. Whatever their precise relationship, both the *Apocryphon* and the *Protennoia* can be shown to represent secondary elaborations of the more primary form of the myth found in Irenaeus. And in both of them the figure of the Son or Christ as exemplar/revealer/redeemer is fundamental.[56]

54. P. 461. Cf. Janssens, 'Trimorphic Protennoia', pp. 229-35; Layton, *Scriptures*, pp. 86-87.
55. Cf. *Trim. Prot.* CG XIII 37.3-20.
56. Cf. *Apoc. Jn* BG 32.9-19; 35.13-20; *Trim. Prot.* CG XIII 37.3–39.14. Note

My criterion then for Johannine influence is not the—inevitably—rather subjective one of appeal to individual possible Johannine allusions (as with Colpe and Janssens), where, as Wilson noted, any conclusions can only be tentative, but of appeal to the underlying structure which the myth presupposed. This reflects the stage in the myth underlying Irenaeus's version when I argue it has been subjected to Johannine influence. That myth has a life and logic of its own (Meeks's point), and thus it is not simply a matter of direct literal influence from John's Gospel, but rather of that Gospel as a source among others, working at various levels, offering fresh perspectives in a continuing process of remythologization—the very thing Robinson dismissed as an unreasonable explanation! I have, however, set out (see below, p. 134) the remarkable Johannine parallels, leaving it, like Janssens, to Johannine experts to decide on what they think of the question of the relationship.

IV

I now turn even more briefly to my third point, the Pronoia hymn concluding the long version of the *Apocryphon* (see below, p. 135) which Robinson claims is not explicitly Christian but parallels both *Protennoia* and the Prologue. Tardieu argues, directly reversing Robinson's approach, that the Pronoia hymn is a Gnostic pastiche of the Prologue, itself taken over by the redactor of the *Protennoia* (see below, p. 134). And he gives an impressive list of the allusions he finds in it to Wisdom and Johannine material.[57] Again, whom are we to believe? Surely we must again consider the function of this hymn and the myth the hymn presupposes. It has been used by the author(s) of the *Apocryphon* to express the purpose of the book in its present form as a work on providence, Pronoia, just as the older theogonic myth underlying Irenaeus was adapted and modified: indeed the hymn may have given initial impetus to the production of the *Apocryphon*, as Tardieu suggests. But by itself the hymn already presupposes the kind of myth we find in Irenaeus, which attempts to account for the presence of Gnostics in this evil, material, demiurgic creation, and to explain how revelation and salvation were possible only in terms of periodic visitations at key points by a heavenly revealer/redeemer. The main components of such a scheme

his role in 38.16-33, originating, revealing, glorifying and enthroning the aeons, the archetypes and destinations of the Gnostic elect.

57. *Ecrits*, pp. 340-44.

were not just the Jewish figure of Wisdom with her three sorties into this world (at creation; for all humankind; and finally for Israel), but Christ and his incarnation, the Word made flesh—but in its Gnostic interpretation. Comparison with Tatian and his theory of the soul as darkness, requiring union with the heavenly spirit, related to the Logos in some undefined way, is instructive; both are attempts to solve similar problems: (1) how can one unite primal, continuous and decisive revelation, and (2) how is salvation possible in and from this evil world under the sway of fate, the invention of the archons or demons. Both presuppose an existing mythology into which the Fourth Gospel is fitted as offering illumination, confirmation and support.[58]

By this detailed analysis particularly of Irenaeus 1.29 and the parallel passages in the *Apocryphon of John*, I hope to have given some concrete support to Meeks's suggestion that Johannine christology helped to create or further to develop some Gnostic myths; to have given some reason for thinking that the *Protennoia* is not Bultmann's hypothetical pre-Christian Gnostic *Grundschrift* for the Prologue but in fact presupposes and develops the form of the Christian Gnostic myth found in the *Apocryphon* which is itself dependent on John; and even to have given some support to Wilson's proposal of de-Christianization, in that Gnostic myths, like that underlying Irenaeus's *Adv. Haer.* 1.29, the *Apocryphon of John* and the *Trimorphic Protennoia*, while originating in a Christian milieu, by their own logic moved further and further from the way the theology of Irenaeus and the Catholic Church of the second century developed. As New Testament scholars have rightly insisted, what establishes the character of a text is not individual words but the overall context. Whatever the truth of his contention about the origin of the Fourth Gospel, Irenaeus was surely right to argue that it itself offered the best defence against Gnostic and Valentinian misuse.[59]

---

58. Cf. *Discourse*, 5.7.13.

59. Cf. S.S. Smalley, 'Diversity and Development in John', *NTS* 17 (1971), pp. 276-92; Smith, *Johannine Christianity*, p. 5.

TEXTS

Irenaeus, *Adversus Haereses 1.29.1-3*

> 1) Some of them postulate an Aeon that never grows old in virgin Spirit [i.e. the Spirit] they call Barbelo [cf. Wis. 7.22-28?].
>
> There is, they say, an unnameable Father, and he wished to manifest himself to Barbelo herself [cf. Wis. 9.9?].

5   This Ennoia, however, when she had come forth, stood in his presence and asked for Prognosis.

> When Prognosis had also come forth
>
> Incorruptibility emerged, again at their request,

> and after that Eternal Life.

10   As Barbelo exulted in them and looked at the Greatness, and was delighted at the conception [*conceptus*], she generated for him a light like him. This they say was the beginning both of the illumination and generation of all things [cf. Jn 1.1-4, 9?].

> And when the Father saw this light, he anointed it with his goodness [*benignitas*], that it might become perfect [cf. Ps. 45.7; Heb. 1.9; 1 Jn 2.20,

15   27?]. Now this, they say, is Christ.

Apoc. Jn BG 26.6-19; 27.4-8; 28.4–29.8; 29.18–31.5

[26.6-19] His Aeon [*aiōn*] is incorruptible, at peace, dwelling in silence. He pre-exists the All [cf. Prov. 8.22?]. He is the head of all the aeons [cf. Col. 1.18; 2.10], if there is anything before him [?]. For none of us knew the realm of the Immeasurable One, except him who has dwelt in him. He it is
5   who has told us these things [cf. Jn 1.18?]. He perceives [*noein*] himself in his own [*idios*] light which surrounds him—he is himself the source [*pēgē*] of living water [cf. Jn 4.10, 14; Rev. 22.1?], the light which is full of purity...

[27.4-8] And his thought [*ennoia*] became a work; it appeared and stood
10   before him in the gleam [*lampēdōn*] of the light...

[28.4–29.8] And Barbelo asked [*aitein*] him [the Spirit] to give him [*sic*] a Foreknowledge. He agreed [*kataneuein*]. When he agreed Foreknowledge appeared and stood beside Thought [*ennoia*], which is Pronoia, glorifying the Invisible and the perfect [*teleios*] Power [*dunamis*], Barbelo, because they
15   had come into being through her. Again [*palin*] this power asked that Incorruptibility [*aphtharsia*] be given her, and he agreed. When he agreed Incorruptibility appeared and stood beside Thought and Foreknowledge [*prognōsis*], glorifying the Invisible and Barbelo because she came into being because of her. She asked that Eternal Life be given her. He agreed. When he
20   agreed Eternal Life appeared, and they stood praising him and Barbelo because they had come into being because of her, through the revelation of the Invisible Spirit...

[29.18–31.5] Barbelo gazed intently at him, the purity of the light. She was enveloped [?] by it [cf. Lk. 1.35?] and gave birth to a spark [*spinthēr*] of
25   light, like the blessed light but not equal to it in magnificence. This is the Only Begotten [*monogenēs*], who appeared to the Father [cf. Jn 1.14, 18?], the Self-Originate [*autogenētos*] God, the firstborn Son of the All [cf. Col. 1.15], of the Spirit [*pneuma*] of the pure [*eilikrinēs*] light. The Invisible Spirit rejoiced over the light which had come into being, which was first manifested
30   by the first Power, namely his Pronoia, Barbelo, and he anointed it with his goodness [*chrēstotēs*] so that [*hōste*] it became perfect [*teleios*] and there was no deficiency in it and Christ [*Christos*] because he had anointed him with his goodness for [?] the Invisible Spirit. He revealed himself to him and received the anointing through the Virgin Spirit. He stood in his presence glorifying
35   the Invisible Spirit and the perfect Pronoia through whom he had been manifested.

Irenaeus, *Adversus Haereses 1.29.1-3*

> He again requested, as they say, that Nous be given him as a helper, and
> Nous came forth.

5

> Now in addition to this the Father emits Logos. Unions were now formed
> between Ennoia and Logos and Incorruptibility and Christ, and Eternal
> Life was united with Thelema and Nous with Prognosis. And these glorified
> the Great Light and Barbelo.
> 2) Thereafter, they say, from Ennoia and Logos was emitted Autogenes, to
> represent [*repraesentatio*?] the Great Light [cf. Jn 1.8?], and was greatly
> honoured and all things subjected to him [cf. Ps. 8.6; Heb. 2.7-8;
> Jn. 17.1ff.]. Now Truth [*Aletheia*] was emitted with him and there was a
> union between Autogenes and Truth [cf. Jn 1.14, 17; 5.33; etc.?].

10

> Then from the light, which is Christ, and Incorruptibility four luminaries
> [*phōster*] were emitted to stand around Autogenes, and from Thelema again
> and Eternal Life four emissions were produced to minister to the four
> luminaries, whom they name Charis, Thelesis [MS Thesis], Sunesis,
> Phronesis. Charis was attached to the great first luminary, whom they want
> to be Saviour and call Armoges; Thelesis to the second...

15

> 3) When those had all been established, in addition Autogenes emitted the
> perfect and true Man, whom they also term Adamas...And he was
> removed [?*remotus*] with the First Light by Armoges. Perfect Knowledge
> was put forth by Autogenes and united with him ...also an invincible
> power was given him by the Virgin Spirit. At this they all rejoiced and
> praised the Great Aeon. Hence they say was manifested Mother, Father and
> Son.

20

Apoc. Jn BG 31.5–33.12; 34.19–35.20

[31.5–33.12] And he asked that he be given a helper, Nous. He agreed.
When the Invisible Spirit agreed Nous appeared and stood by Christ,
glorifying him and Barbelo. Now all this came about in silence and a thought
[*ennoia*]. The Invisible Spirit wanted to do a work. His will became
5   embodied and appeared and stood beside Nous and the light glorifying him.
The Word [*logos*] followed the Will because through the Word Christ created
all things [cf. Jn 1.3?]. The self-originate [*autogenēs*] God, and Eternal Life
with Will, but Nous with Foreknowledge [*prognōsis*], stood glorifying
the Invisible Spirit and Barbelo because through her they had come into
10   being. It was through the Spirit that the eternal self-originate God, the Son of
Barbelo, was perfected, for he stood near the eternal virginal Invisible Spirit,
the self-originate from his First Thought [*ennoia*]. It was he who was set as
God over the All by the Invisible Spirit, God of the truth [cf. Jn 17.3?]. He
gave him all authority [*exousia*] and caused the truth that is in him to be
15   subject [*hupotassein*] to him, that he might comprehend [*noein*] the All, him
whose name will be spoken to those worthy of it [cf. Phil. 2.9-11;
1 Cor. 15.27-28; Jn 17.1-6; Heb. 2.7-8]. Now from the light which is Christ,
and Incorruptibility through the light-God, the four great luminaries appeared
from the self-originate God to stand around him, as the triad, Will and
20   Thought [*ennoia*] and Life. Now his four are Grace [*charis*], Insight
[*sunesis*], Perception [*aisthēsis*] and Prudence [*phronēsis*]. Grace is with the
first luminary. Harmozel, the angel of Light is with the first aeon, with which
there are three aeons, grace, truth and form [*morphē*] [cf. Jn 1.16-17]…

[34.19–35.20] But from Foreknowledge and perfect Nous through God and
25   at the resolve [*eudokia*] of the great Invisible Spirit and of the self-originate
[came forth] the perfect [*teleios*] true Man, the first manifestation. He called
him Adam. He set him over the first aeon with the great God, the self-
originate Christ, in the first aeon of Harmozel, and his powers with him.
And the Invisible Spirit gave him an invincible intellectual [*noeron*] power.
30   He said, 'I will glorify and praise the Invisible Spirit for because of you did
all things come into being and all things are in you. Now I praise you and the
self-originate and the aeons, the three, the Father, the Mother, and the Son,
the perfect Power…'

Apoc. Jn BG 27.8–28.4

This is the power which is before the All, which revealed herself, this is the perfect Pronoia of the All, the light the likeness of the light, the image [*eikōn*] of the Invisible [cf. Col. 1.15]. She is the perfect power, Barbelo, the perfect Aeon of glory. She glorified him because she was manifested through
5   him, and she comprehended [*noein*] him. She is the First Thought [*ennoia*], his image [*eikōn*]. She became a First Man, which is the Virgin Spirit [*parthenikon pneuma*], the threefold male, the one with the three powers, the three names, the three begettings, the Aeon that does not grow old, the bisexual, which came forth from his Pronoia.

Trim. Prot. CG XIII 37.20-32; 38.1-28

[37.20-32] Now the Voice which originated from my Thought exists as three permanences [*monē*; cf. Jn 14.2, 23?]: the Father, the Mother, the Son. A Sound existing perceptibly [*aisthēsis*], it has within it a Word [*logos*] possessing every glory, and it has three masculinities, three powers
5 [*dunamis*], and three names. They exist in the form of the triad   which are quadrangles, secretly, in a silence of the Ineffable One. It is he alone who came into being, that is the Christ [*Christos*]. And I anointed him with the glory...

[38.1-28] He who first produced the light of the exalted aeons [*aiōn*], and in
10 a glorious light with a constant strength. And he stood in his own light that surrounds him, who is the Eye of the Light that gloriously illumines me. He gave aeons to the Father of all the Aeons, who is I, the thought of the Father, the Protennoia, that is Barbelo, the perfect glory and the invisible, secret, immeasurable one. I am the image [*eikōn*] of the Invisible Spirit [*pneuma*; cf.
15 Col. 1.15], and it is through me that the All took form [*eikōn*; cf. Jn 1.3?], and the Mother, the light which she established as virgin [*parthenos*], she who is called Meirothea, the intangible Womb, the unrestrained and immeasurable Voice. Then the perfect Son revealed himself to his aeons who had originated through him. He revealed them and glorified them and
20 enthroned [*thronos*] them and stood in the glory with which he glorified himself. They blessed the perfect Son, the Christ, the God who came into being alone [or by himself, i.e., *monogenēs*? cf. Jn 1.14, 18]. And they gave glory, saying 'He is, He is, the Son of God, the Son of God! [cf. Jn. 20.31?]. It is he who is, the Aeon of Aeons! He beholds the aeons which he
25 begot. For you have begotten by your will alone!' [cf. Jn 1.13?]. [Then follows the mention of the four luminaries.]

Trim. Prot. CG XIII 46.5-33; 47.11-32

[46.5-33] 'I am the Word [*logos*] who is [. .] ineffable, being in undefiled [ ], and a thought revealed itself perceptibly [*aisthēsis*] through the [ ] sound of the Mother, although it is a male offspring that supports me [ ]. And it exists from the beginning in the foundation of the All. Now there is a light hidden in Silence [*sigē*]. It was the first to come forth. But whereas she alone
5   exists as Silence, I alone am the Word [*logos*], ineffable, incorruptible, immeasurable, inconceivable, a hidden light, bearing a fruit [*karpos*] of life, pouring forth living water from the invisible, unpolluted, immeasurable spring [*pēgē*; cf. Jn 4.10, 14; Rev. 21.6?], that is the unreproducible Voice
10   of the glory of the Mother, the glory of the offspring of God, a male virgin [*parthenos*] by virtue of a hidden intellect [*nous*], that is the silence hidden from the All, being unreproducible, an immeasurable light, the source [*pēgē*] of the All, the root of the entire Aeon, the foundation [*basis*] which supports every movement [*kinēsis*] of the aeons belonging to the powerful glory. It is
15   the founding of every foundation, the breath of the powers, the eye of the three permanences [*monē*], being a Voice by virtue of Thought. And it is a Word [*logos*] by virtue of the Sound; it was sent to illumine those who dwell in the d[arkness] [cf. Jn 1.5?].

[47.11-32] 'The second time I came in the Sound of my Voice. I gave form
20   [*eikōn*] to those who took form until their consummation [*sunteleia*]. The third time I revealed myself to them in their tents [*skēnē*] as the Word [cf. Jn 1.14] and I revealed myself in the likeness of their image, and I wore [*phorein*] everyone's garment, and I hid myself within them. And they did not know the one who empowered me [cf. Jn 1.10?]. For I am in all the
25   sovereignties [*archē*] and powers [*dunamis*], and in the angels, and in every movement which is in the whole of matter [*hulē*]. And I hid myself in them until I revealed myself to my brethren. And none of them knew me [cf. Jn 1.11?], although it is I who work in them. But they thought that the All had been created by them, since they are ignorant, not knowing their root, the
30   place in which they grew. I am the light which illumines the All [cf. Jn 1.4, 5, 9). I am the light which rejoices in my brethren, for I came down to the world [*kosmos*] of mortals [cf. Jn 1.9?] on account of the Spirit [*pneuma*] that remains…'

Apoc. Jn CG II 30.11–31.25

'I, therefore, the perfect Pronoia of the All changed myself into my seed [*sperma*], for I existed first, going on every road. For I am the richness of the light, I am the thought of the Pleroma. And I went into the realm of the darkness and I endured until I entered the middle of the prison. And the
5 foundations of chaos [*chaos*] shook. And I, I hid myself from them because of their wickedness [*kakia*], and they did not recognize me. Again [*palin*] I returned for the second time, and I went, I went forth from those of the light. I am the thought of the Pronoia—I went into the middle of the darkness and the inside of Hades, since I was seeking my plan [*oikonomia*]. And the
10 foundations of chaos shook, that they might fall down on those who are in chaos and might destroy them. And again I ascended to my root of light lest they be destroyed before the time. Still for a third time I went—I am the light, I am the thought of the Pronoia—that I might enter the middle of darkness and the inside of Hades. I filled my face with the light of the
15 completion [*sunteleia*] of their aeon. And I went into the middle of their prison, which is the prison of the body [*sōma*]. And I said, 'Whoever hears, let him rise up from deep sleep'. And he wept and shed tears. Bitter tears he wiped from himself and said, 'Who is it who calls my name, and from where has this hope come to me, while I am in the fetters of the prison?' And I said
20 'I am the Pronoia of the pure light. I am the thought of the Virgin Spirit [*parthenikon pneuma*] who raised you up to the honoured place [*topos*]. Arise and remember that it is you who heard, and follow your root, which is I, the merciful one and guard [*asphalizein*] yourself against the angels of poverty and the demons of chaos, and all those who ensnare you, and beware
25 of the deep sleep and the enclosure of the inside of Hades.' And I raised him up and sealed [*sphragizein*] him with the five seals that death might not have power over him from that time on.

The Original Form of the Gnostic Myth

The Father [= *Invisible Spirit* = Great Aeon]
reveals himself to
Barbelo [= *Virginal Spirit*, who later becomes the Mother]   [= Higher Wisdom
cf. Wis. 7]

as
Prognosis   ⎫   feminine
Incorruptibility ⎬   aspects
Eternal Life   ⎭   to female

She *delighted, obedient, upward-looking*   [= archetype of
generates by virgin birth   Mary, cf. Lk. 1.30-35]

The Son/Monogenes
he is anointed by the Father with *goodness*   [= archetype of
and made *perfect* as Christ   Christ, cf. Ps. 45.7; Heb. 2.9]
He calls forth from the Father

Nous   ⎫   masculine
Light   ⎬   aspects to
Thelema   ⎭   male

Syzygies are formed:
Incorruptibility and Light
Eternal Life and Thelema
Prognosis and Nous

Incorruptibility and Light emit

4 luminaries to surround Monogenes   [Hebrew names =
archetypes of
archangels? Cf. Ps. 104.4;
Heb. 1.7, 14]

Eternal Life and Thelema emit
4 ministers for the 4 luminaries   [Greek feminines
= archetypes of
ministering angels?
Cf. Heb. 1.14]

Prognosis and Nous emit
Adam/Adamas and consort Perfect Knowledge   [= archetypes of
Adam & Eve?]

For his perfect knowledge of the heavenly world
he is given an invincible power by the Virgin Spirit,
elevated [?] with the Son from the First Luminary
[i.e. angelic realm]   [cf. Ps. 8.5-6;
                                                                                    Heb. 2.5-8]

Adam and Knowledge emit
  The Tree/Knowledge   [= archetype of
                                                                                    tree in Eden?]

Thus is manifested, the | Mother, | the Father, | the Son |

The First Angel standing beside Monogenes (= Harmozel) emits
  Holy Spirit/Sophia/'Prunicus'   [= Lower Wisdom,
                                                                                    Valentinian
                                                                                    Achamoth]

She *disobedient, assertive, downward-looking,*
acts without her consort or the agreement of the Father,
generates by virgin birth, driven by
guilelessness and *goodness,*
an *ignorant* and *bold* work, the Protarchon   [= God of the Old
Demiurge of the visible universe.   Testament]

He steals a great power from his mother, the Holy Spirit,
descends and creates powers, angels and firmaments.

Sophia sadly ascends to become the Ogdoad   [cf. *1 En.* 42]
He, thinking himself the only God, boasts [Exod. 20.5; Isa. 45.5-6; 46.9]

JSNT 48 (1992), pp. 43-65

WITNESSES TO WHAT WAS ἀπ' ἀρχῆς: 1 JOHN'S CONTRIBUTION TO
OUR KNOWLEDGE OF TRADITION IN THE FOURTH GOSPEL

Wendy E. Sproston

The distance from the Synoptics to John's Gospel often seems not so much a step as a quantum leap, for while John also records the life of the historical Jesus he seems to have conceived of its significance independently and on a vastly different scale. As a result the final overall effect is one of transformation and change, and perhaps no more strikingly so than in his presentation of Jesus himself. According to John, Jesus' story begins not in earthly time but with God before all time, and his entry into Palestinian society is the entry of the divine Word into human history. As the Word become flesh Jesus wields the power of God with conscious majesty, seemingly oblivious to human doubt. No intriguing 'messianic secret' keeps the reader guessing about Jesus' identity. On the contrary, his identity, origin and destiny are here openly proclaimed and attention is focused instead on human response to him. For all who encounter Jesus in John a final choice has to be made between stark alternatives—life or death, salvation or condemnation—because by virtue of his very presence in the world the conditions of judgment day have come into force. This is powerful and arresting imagery, but in fact what we see here probably has little to do with the historical Jesus; rather, it is the construct of a remarkable mind which has taken Jesus' story and set it within the framework of God's own confrontation with the world he created, loves and wishes to save.

Even in these few brief remarks the distinctiveness of John's approach becomes apparent and we are easily persuaded that this Fourth Gospel has been executed by a highly original and adventurous exponent of the genre. And yet, eccentric though John's contribution may seem in this context, the mere fact that he has undertaken to produce a Gospel, rather than a dogmatic treatise, has important implications for our attempts to understand his thinking. Specifically, it suggests that John's originality does not consist in inventing *de novo*, but that he has created his Gospel by a process of expanding and expounding on a tradition already known to him as a Christian before he took up his pen.

This view of John as a receiver and interpreter of tradition finds confirmation in certain editorial comments and attitudes in the Gospel itself. As regards his awareness of tradition, it should not be missed that John himself records that the disciples not only witnessed Jesus' words and deeds but also *remembered* them after the event, a remembrance which would subsequently be informed by greater understanding (2.22; 12.16).[1] Furthermore, John's comments in 20.30-31 leave us in little doubt that he knew a number of miracle stories before he began writing, those recorded in the Gospel apparently being the result of the selection of such material as he deemed suitable to his purpose. On the other hand, there are other texts where John's self-perception as an interpreter of tradition is given prominence. The presentation of the so-called Beloved Disciple is a good example of this attitude. This disciple is evidently intended as a key identity figure for Johannine Christianity and is frequently portrayed as the only one of Jesus' followers with the capacity to understand him and grasp his meaning. It is no accident, for example, that in 13.23 this disciple alone lies in Jesus' lap just as in 1.18 Jesus himself is described as in the lap of the Father whom he is uniquely able to interpret.[2] No doubt also the detail on the function of the Spirit-Paraclete in imparting to the faithful a new and hitherto unavailable insight into Jesus' words and deeds would be pointless if John had not thought of himself as a beneficiary of the Spirit's exegetical guidance.[3]

1.   Compare also the injunction to remember Jesus' word in 15.20.

2.   Note also the Beloved Disciple's access to 'inside information' in 13.25-26, his intuitive grasp of the meaning of the discarded graveclothes in 20.8-9 and his quick recognition of the risen Jesus in 21.7. As Mary's adopted son (19.26-27) he is to be seen as Jesus' *Doppelgänger* who faithfully reflects his character and intentions. The overall intention here seems to be to promote the Johannine ideal. See further K. Quast, *Peter and the Beloved Disciple: Figures for a Community in Crisis* (JSNTSup, 32: Sheffield: JSOT Press, 1989), esp. pp. 159-62.

3.   For descriptions of the Spirit's exegetical functions see 14.26; 15.26; 16.12-15. R.E. Brown's comment on this captures the implications well: 'The Fourth Evangelist must have regarded himself as an instrument of the Paraclete when in G John he reported what Jesus said and did but at the same time completely

From our point of view this evidence is valuable because it provides an insight into what has gone into the making of the Fourth Gospel. On this basis we may be confident that two elements will be present in John's text: on the one hand there will be material known from tradition, and, on the other, there will be the fruits of John's own creative interpretation of that tradition. It follows therefore that one very valid point of entry into understanding the workings of John's mind will be provided if we have some means of identifying in his text the tradition on which he has based his exegesis.[4]

However, all is not so simple. The problem is that the distinctive Johannine language and style do not alter significantly throughout the entire Gospel.[5] So consistent is the style, in fact, that translators are occasionally left simply to guess where reported speech has ended and editorial comment has begun. Furthermore, the use and re-use of a limited and theologically-orientated vocabulary strongly suggest a radical re-presentation of source material in the service of theme. None of this augurs well for the 'scissors and paste' approach to detecting John's source material. The stylistic integrity suggests that whatever John has known he has preferred to express in his own idiom. Moreover, the strong thematic interest leaves us with no guarantee that John's exegetical activity has not extended also to the source material itself, with the result that what finally appears in his text has already been recast, and is

reinterpreted it' (*The Epistles of John* [AB, 30; London: Geoffrey Chapman, 1983] p. 287).

4.   This is not to defend the historical-critical method against all comers but merely to affirm its continuing value in John's case in the light of evidence in the text which points to the author's self-perception. However, no attempt to understand the mind of John can afford to ignore his immense literary talent, and I assume that the newer literary-critical approaches to interpreting John can inform already established methods and can in turn be informed by them. See R.A. Culpepper's excellent *Anatomy of the Fourth Gospel: A Study in Literary Design* (FFNT; Philadelphia: Fortress Press, 1983), esp. his remarks on p.5.

5.   So E. Ruckstuhl, *Die literarische Einheit des Johannesevangeliums* (Studia Friburgensia, NS, 3; Freiburg: Paulus, 1951; repr. Novum Testamentum et Orbis Antiquus, 5; Freiburg: Universitätsverlag; Göttingen: Vandenhoeck & Ruprecht, 1987). Ruckstuhl has added two appendices to the reprint. The first (pp. 291-303) is a revision of his list of Johannine style characteristics in *Einheit* itself, and the second (pp. 304-31) is a revision and German translation of his essay 'Johannine Language and Style: The Question of their Unity', in M. de Jonge (ed.), *L'évangile de Jean* (BETL, 44; Leuven: Leuven University Press, 1977), pp. 125-47. For references to these see below.

therefore an interpreted and modified version of what he knew. There is nothing here to encourage us to accept R.T. Fortna's viewpoint that it is possible to reconstruct intact out of John's text some fixed and extensive pre-Johannine *Grundschrift*.[6]

Another approach—and one which injects a proper note of objectivity into the proceedings—is to look beyond the bounds of the Gospel itself to other literature, for example the Synoptic tradition or the Pauline letters, to discover there some correspondence with Johannine statements and so attempt to establish by means of external controls the tradition which John as a fellow Christian is likely to have known and drawn on.[7] This is a well-tried method and the results can be extremely valuable, especially in those areas where John's text appears to correspond closely with the content of these other writings so that the required degree of adjustment to the Johannine idiom is comparatively

6.   Despite heavy criticism along these lines of his earlier book *The Gospel of Signs* (SNTSMS, 11; Cambridge: Cambridge University Press, 1970), Fortna has not substantially modified his position in his recent volume *The Fourth Gospel and its Predecessor* (Edinburgh: T. & T. Clark, 1989), see esp. pp. 6-8. It is particularly unfortunate that he has not devoted more serious consideration to Ruckstuhl's detailed and swingeing criticisms of his handling of style characteristics (see Ruckstuhl, 'Johannine Language', pp. 129-41; and compare Fortna, *Predecessor*, p. 210 n. 509). For criticism of *Predecessor,* see the review by B. Lindars in *SJT* 43 (1990), pp. 526-27; *idem, John* (NTG; Sheffield: JSOT Press, 1990), pp. 32-33; for some searing remarks on Fortna's attitude, see M. Hengel, *The Johannine Question* (London: SCM Press; Philadelphia: Trinity Press International, 1989), p. 201 n. 58.

7.   See W.F. Howard, *The Fourth Gospel in Recent Criticism and Interpretation* (London: Epworth Press, 2nd edn, 1935), pp. 215-29; C.H. Dodd, *Historical Tradition in the Fourth Gospel* (Cambridge: Cambridge University Press, 1963), pp. 335-65. Studies which appeal specifically to the Pauline tradition include M. Wilcox, 'The Composition of John 13.21-30', in E.E. Ellis and M. Wilcox (eds.), *Neotestamentica et Semitica: Studies in Honour of Matthew Black* (Edinburgh: T. & T. Clark, 1969), pp. 143-56; P. Borgen, 'The Use of Tradition in John 12.44-50', *NTS* 26 (1979–80), pp. 18-35; *idem,* 'John and the Synoptics: Can Paul Offer Help?', in G.F. Hawthorne and O. Betz (eds.), *Tradition and Interpretation in the New Testament: Essays in Honor of E. Earle Ellis for his 60th Birthday* (Grand Rapids: Eerdmans, 1988), pp. 80-194. As is well known Barnabas Lindars published extensively in this area. For example, see his 'Traditions behind the Fourth Gospel', in de Jonge (ed.), *L'évangile de Jean,* pp. 107-24; *idem, Behind the Fourth Gospel* (Studies in Creative Criticism, 3; London: SPCK, 1971), esp. pp. 43-60. For further references to Lindars's work, see below.

minor. Much of John's miracles and Passion material has proved amenable to this approach, and even the highly compositional discourse material has to some extent been shown to rest on traditional Jesus sayings.[8]

Finally, however, it has to be questioned whether the actual extent of the tradition as John knew it can always be recovered by this means. Where verbal correspondence between John and the Synoptics is comparatively slight then some degree of speculation beyond these points of contact is inevitable.[9] Moreover, it appears that there is more than Synoptic-type tradition in John.[10] For example, there is no miracle in the Synoptics which compares with the changing of water into wine at Cana in John 2 or with the raising of Lazarus in ch. 11. And how do we come to terms with a passage like Jn 3.16-21? This text is quintessentially Johannine and is usually assumed to represent, at least in part, the so-called Johannine kerygma.[11] The Synoptics cannot help us here, and

8.   See B. Lindars, 'Discourse and Tradition: The Use of the Sayings of Jesus in the Discourses of the Fourth Gospel', *JSNT* 13 (1981), pp. 83-101; *idem, John*, pp. 36-37.

9.   I am indebted to Professor Max Wilcox for the suggestion that Jn 15.13 may be a version of the Son of man logion in Mk 10.45. I note also that Barnabas Lindars published on this, see his 'Mark 10.45: A Ransom for Many', *ExpTim* 93 (1981–82), pp. 292-95; *idem, Jesus Son of Man* (London: SPCK, 1983), p. 79. While I would not disagree with this position (see below n. 43) nevertheless it should be pointed out that actual verbal contact between the Markan and Johannine texts is almost non-existent.

10.   This position is accepted even among those who argue that John composed his Gospel in direct dependence on one or more of the Synoptics. See F. Neirynck, 'John and the Synoptics', in de Jonge (ed.), *L'évangile de Jean*, pp. 73-106 (94); C.K. Barrett, *The Gospel according to St John* (London: SPCK, 2nd edn, 1978), p. 17; see esp. M.D. Goulder's proposals on Gospel interrelationships which allow much more freedom to John in this regard than to Matthew and Luke (*Luke: A New Paradigm* [2 vols.; JSNTSup, 20; Sheffield: JSOT Press, 1989], I, pp. 22-23).

11.   The phrase 'the Johannine kerygma' heads a section in R. Schnackenburg's commentary where he argues that 3.16-21 is part of a discourse composed by the Evangelist which was based on kerygmatic material. See R. Schnackenburg, *The Gospel according to St John* (3 vols.; New York: Herder & Herder; London: Burns & Oates, 1968), I, p. 380. He and others take 3.16 to be the kernel of the Johannine Christian message. See Schnackenburg, *Gospel*, p. 398: G.R. Beasley-Murray, *John* (WBC, 36; Waco, TX: Word Books, 1987), p. 51; B. Lindars, *The Gospel of John* (NCB; London: Marshall, Morgan & Scott, 1972), p. 24; C.K. Barrett, *Gospel*, p. 216; J.H. Bernard, *A Critical and Exegetical Commentary on the Gospel according to St John* (2 vols.; ICC; Edinburgh: T. & T. Clark, 1928), I, p. 117.

while similar statements in the Pauline corpus are enough to persuade us that John's is a version of a common early Christian tradition,[12] precisely what John knew, whether recast or not, continues to remain unclear.

Difficulties such as these serve to highlight the need for a control which is not only external to the Gospel but which is also party to its distinctive style and theological perspective. There is, in fact, one document which fulfils our present requirements. In vocabulary, style and theology its affinity with the Fourth Gospel is undisputed and indeed unsurpassed by any other substantial document known to us. Its origin from within the same matrix which produced the Gospel is thereby declared, and its immediate intelligibility to the Johannine reader thereby guaranteed. It will be obvious by now that the document here referred to is 1 John.

The object of this paper is to propose that the first Johannine epistle can serve as a control which will increase our understanding of the nature of the tradition that has gone into the Fourth Gospel, and hence will also allow us to pry a little further into the thinking of its author. Thus if we wish to learn more about tradition in John we must look first and foremost to 1 John.[13]

When we do turn to 1 John, however, we find that there is much which would seem to confuse our enterprise. We quickly discover that the author of the epistle has not obliged us with a straightforward second edition of the Gospel but that instead he has produced a piece which has an independence of its own.

If we read 1 John with the Gospel freshly in mind we are immediately struck by the absence of reference to what are often substantial areas of the Gospel text. No one, of course, would expect to find narrative here because the epistle is not a narrative piece, but the differences go much deeper than that. Where, we might ask, is the Gospel's identification of Jesus with the divine pre-existent λόγος? The epistle's λόγος τῆς ζωῆς (1.1) is hardly a substitute, especially as other references show that λόγος in the epistle means something like a preached message.[14] And

12. See esp. Rom. 8.31-32; 2 Cor. 5.19; Gal. 1.4; 2.20; 4.4; 1 Tim. 1.15; 2.4; 3.16; Tit. 2.11.

13. In what follows it will be assumed that the Gospel pre-dated the epistle and that the two were not by the same author. However, my eventual conclusions do not rule out alternative views.

14. This meaning is explicit in 2.7 (see also 1.10; 2.5, 14; 3.18). Parallels in the

where do we hear of Jesus as the Lamb of God, the Good Shepherd or the True Vine? Indeed, we search in vain for the whole Gospel presentation of Jesus as sole mediator between God and humanity, who is invested with power over all flesh to give life and to judge, and who declares his authority in the majesty of the 'I am' statements. There is no claim here, for example, that Jesus is the Light of the World but, instead, the epistle's first announcement is that God—and not Jesus—is light (1.5). We do get a description of Jesus as ὁ παράκλητος in 1 Jn 2.1, and this seems to provide some tenuous link with Jn 14.16 where Jesus promises that the Father will send the Spirit as ἄλλος παράκλητος, which implies that Jesus himself is also a paraclete. But then the Gospel goes into some detail in describing the functions of the Spirit as Paraclete (14.16, 26; 15.26; 16.7), and this identification between Spirit and Paraclete is unknown in 1 John.

Reversing the reading process by beginning with 1 John does not seem to improve matters, for the result is much the same. Indeed, considering that the epistle is about one seventh of the length of the Gospel, the incidence of words it contains which are not to be found in the Gospel text is remarkably high (45 in all).[15] Some of these fit in well enough with the Gospel subject matter, but it is not difficult to find others, among them ἀνομία, ἀντίχριστος, βίος, δοκιμάζειν, ἱλασμός and ψευδοπροφήτης, which would seem to indicate real differences.

Given that the epistle does not always reflect the contents of the Gospel, then, it will be in our interest to concentrate on what the two have in common.

What material is common to John and 1 John gives every indication of a strikingly close verbal correspondence. We can trace from one document to the other not only the same words but also often the same

body of the Gospel and elsewhere in the New Testament also support the meaning 'message' for λόγος in 1.1 rather than a reference to the personal Word of the Prologue (so Brown, *Epistles*, pp. 164-65; K. Grayston, *The Johannine Epistles* [NCB; London: Marshall, Morgan & Scott, 1984], pp. 39-40). This is not the only instance where terminology familiar from the Gospel is invested with different meaning in 1 John. See further P. Bonnard's study of these 'mutations sémantiques' in 'La première épître de Jean: Est-elle Johannique?', in de Jonge (ed.), *L'évangile de Jean*, pp. 301-305.

15. See the relevant lists in R. Morgenthaler, *Statistik des neutestamentlichen Wortschatzes* (Zürich: Gotthelf, 3rd edn, 1982).

phrases, and sometimes even whole sentences.[16] Yet in this very feature there lies a further cause for confusion, for neither text will either introduce that common material or continue on from it in the same vein as the other. In each case, therefore, the setting and the surrounding argument are different. The following two examples will demonstrate the point.

If we compare the sentence θεὸν οὐδεὶς ἑώρακεν πώποτε in Jn 1.18 with θεὸν οὐδεὶς πώποτε τεθέαται in 1 Jn 4.12 the correspondence is obvious.[17] But what is equally obvious is that beyond this point all correspondence ceases. For the Evangelist the application of the statement is christological: he uses it as a basis to speak of Jesus as the sole exegete of the Father. This is not the case in 1 Jn 4.12. There the same sentence has been put in the context of the command to love one another and when, in 4.20, the theme of God's invisibility returns, the interest centres on loving one's brother whom one *has* seen.

In 1 Jn 3.14 we note the confident assertion ἡμεῖς οἴδαμεν ὅτι μεταβεβήκαμεν ἐκ τοῦ θανάτου εἰς τὴν ζωήν. Its equivalent is recognizable in the Gospel text at 5.24: μεταβέβηκεν ἐκ τοῦ θανάτου εἰς τὴν ζωήν. In 1 Jn 3.11-18 we find the epistle writer once again concerned with the implications of the love command, and, to that end, this affirmation of the Christian status is directly related to that command in 3.14. In Jn 5.24, however, the love command is not in view. Instead, all hinges on hearing Jesus' word and believing the Father who sent him, by which means judgment is avoided and life guaranteed.

Thus, if we expect the epistle to have a consistent bearing on the Gospel, we will be disappointed. What we have, in fact, are two texts which have evidently issued from the same matrix but which make real contact with one another only intermittently and otherwise can seem to have little or nothing in common. It follows that the degree to which we can allow 1 John to function as a control to isolate tradition in the Gospel will depend on our reaching a much more precise understanding

16. See the comprehensive lists in A.E. Brooke, *A Critical and Exegetical Commentary on the Johannine Epistles* (ICC; Edinburgh: T. & T. Clark, 1957), pp. ii-iv; B.F. Westcott, *The Epistles of St John* (Cambridge: Macmillan, 3rd edn, 1892), pp. xli-xliii.

17. The change in the verb is not significant since no difference in meaning is intended. For the argument that this is true in general of Johannine deployment of these verbs see Brown, *Epistles*, p. 162. 1 John's use of ὁρᾶν as he returns to this theme at 4.20 demonstrates the point well.

of how the contents of the two documents relate to one another.

The clue to the relationship between the two lies, in fact, in the nature and character of the epistle itself, and hence we will now look more closely at 1 John in order to learn a little more about it.

There is evidence in the epistle of a recent schism within the community. It seems that there has been a conflict over christological doctrine (2.22-24; 4.2-3) and several of the group's members have left (2.19). This suggests that what our author is obliged to tackle is the backlash of an exclusively Christian versus Christian controversy. Consequently we find him intent on assuring those who have remained that they alone hold to a proper understanding of the Johannine faith,[18] while also offering advice on how to live out that faith in these new and uncongenial circumstances.

Now this 'in house' controversy does not appear to correspond with the circumstances which precipitated the publication of the Gospel. The Gospel betrays evidence of the community's recent estrangement from contemporary Judaism and of a hostility between Jew and Christian Jew. In the case of the epistle, however, hostility has entered the very ranks of the community and appears to have arisen as a consequence of its own Christian beliefs.[19] At the outset, therefore, we should be aware that the problems which the epistle writer is concerned to resolve will not correspond with those which beset the Evangelist. Nevertheless, the clue to the epistle's relationship to the Gospel does lie in this area. It is not contained in the fact of the schism itself nor in what may have led to it, but it is to be found in the particular method by which the author proceeds with his task of reassuring his own group in the aftermath of the trauma. We will now turn to examine this method in some detail.

18. For the argument that the epistle writer was primarily intent on reassuring his own group rather than on polemizing against its past members, see J.M. Lieu, 'Authority to Become Children of God: A Study of 1 John', *NovT* 33 (1981), pp. 210-28.

19. For a study of John and 1 John as polemical documents directed to entirely different situations, see R.A. Whitacre, *Johannine Polemic: The Role of Tradition and Theology* (SBLDS, 67; Chico, CA: Scholars Press, 1982). Even if Jn 6.66 indicates that the Evangelist himself was no stranger to schism, it can be plausibly argued that the pressure here has resulted from the threat of persecution from outside and not from internal disputes over doctrine; see C.H. Cosgrove, 'The Place where Jesus is: Allusions to Baptism and the Eucharist in the Fourth Gospel', *NTS* 35 (1989), pp. 522-39, esp. pp. 527-30. Thus, it is unlikely that Jn 6.66 and 1 Jn 2.19 are a match in cause as well as in effect (*pace* Hengel, *Question*, p. 52).

The author of 1 John begins by proclaiming himself to his readers as a genuine mediator of the Johannine tradition, for only on this basis can he claim to speak authoritatively to the matter in hand. Once he has assured them of his status, however, any distinction between writer and readers is soon dropped and an exploration of the issues at stake is seen to be undertaken as a joint enterprise.

In his first four verses the epistle writer sets forth his credentials and at the same time announces the benefits which his message will bring for all who heed him. Here the use of the language of original eye-witness together with the authoritative Johannine 'we' (contrast the 'you' who appear to be the addressees) is signally in evidence. Indeed, the words almost tumble over one another in the passage:

ὃ ἀκηκόαμεν, ὃ ἑωράκαμεν...ὃ ἐθεασάμεθα...καὶ ἑωράκαμεν καὶ μαρτυροῦμεν καὶ ἀπαγγέλλομεν ὑμῖν...ὃ ἑωράκαμεν καὶ ἀκηκόαμεν, ἀπαγγέλλομεν καὶ ὑμῖν ἵνα καὶ ὑμεῖς κοινωνίαν ἔχητε μεθ᾽ ἡμῶν...(κοινωνία) ἡμετέρα...γράφομεν ἡμεῖς... (χαρὰ) ἡμῶν...[20]

The author is clearly taking his stand as a true representative of the Johannine tradition. His appropriation to himself of these verbs of perception and proclamation demonstrates that 'what was from the beginning...concerning the word of life' (1.1) has remained unchanged, is therefore reliable, and will be the burden of the witness he himself is about to give.[21] His use of the 'we' here is the prerogative of the tradition bearer,[22] and in that regard is to be compared with the 'we' of apostolic authority which Paul occasionally adopts.[23] In short, the

---

20. There is some textual disagreement over ἡμεῖς and ἡμῶν in v. 4, but the reading given here is probably to be preferred (so Brown, *Epistles*, pp. 172-73).

21. The presence of eye-witness language in a Johannine text need not imply that its author was one of the original disciples. For a discussion on a later generation's capacity to identify with the original witnesses, see Lieu, 'Authority', pp. 213-14; *idem, The Second and Third Epistles of John: History and Background* (Edinburgh: T. & T. Clark, 1986), pp. 143-44; Brown, *Epistles*, pp. 160-61.

22. Brown identifies those who use the 'we' as tradition bearers and interpreters who constitute 'the Johannine school' (*Epistles*, pp. 94-97, esp. n. 221). See also the remarks by J.-W. Taeger on the role and function of the *Traditionsträger* with reference to 1 Jn 1.1-3 in 'Der konservative Rebell: Zum Widerstand des Diotrephes gegen den Presbyter', *ZNW* 78 (1987), pp. 267-87 (284).

23. In 1 Cor. 15.11 the 'we' is used as a guarantee that the tradition conveyed by Paul beginning at v. 3 is genuine apostolic teaching. The same claim to apostolic authority applies in the case of the 'we' in 1 Cor. 11.16; see also 'we preach Christ

author's principal intention in this passage is to establish his undisputed access to the original, and therefore genuine and life-giving, Johannine Christian message. As a result of this the message itself is alluded to only in snatches during the course of this self-advertisement and information on it is kept to a minimum for the moment. In fact, the whole tenor of the beginning of 1 John is one of declaration of the author's authoritative status in relation to his readers, and as such his introduction is perhaps better compared with what Paul has to say about himself at the beginning of Romans rather than treated, as is often the case, as a somewhat lack-lustre version of the Prologue to the Gospel.[24]

Having formally declared his pedigree, the author is now content to put aside the we/you divide between himself and his audience. From 1.5 onwards, with the authoritative proclamation that God is light, this differentiation ceases and where necessary now takes the more personal I/you form.[25] In effect the original 'we' has now been expanded to include the addressees themselves, and so that knowledge of tradition, properly the responsibility of a particular group within the community, is now regarded as the common property of the whole company as receivers of Johannine 'truth'.[26] From now on the author uses the 'we'

crucified' in 1.23. For an examination of Paul's use of 'we' in 2 Corinthians, see M. Carrez, 'Le "Nous" en 2 Corinthiens', *NTS* (1980), pp. 474-86; for doubts on whether the authoritative 'we' of the Johannine authors can be equated with an apostolic claim as such, see Brown, *Epistles*, pp. 94-95, 159.

24. The epistle's introduction inevitably suffers by comparison with the Gospel Prologue; see, e.g., J.L. Houlden, *A Commentary on the Johannine Epistles* (BNTC; London: A. & C. Black, 1973), pp. 45-54; Brown, *Epistles*, pp. 179-80. However, whether its author intended to invite such a comparison is extremely doubtful. He has not used either ἐν ἀρχῇ or πρὸς τὸν θεόν, both of which occur nowhere else in the Gospel *except* in the Prologue (compare 1 Jn 3.21 where πρὸς τὸν θεόν is used but in a different context). Meanwhile, in form and/or meaning his λόγος, ἀπ' ἀρχῆς and πρὸς τὸν πατέρα are all to be found in the Gospel but *not* in the Prologue (for λόγος see n. 14 above, and compare Jn 5.24, 8.51, 52 and 6.63, 68 [with ῥήματα]; for ἀπ' ἀρχῆς and πρὸς τὸν πατέρα see respectively Jn 15.27; 5.45). As for the Prologue's ἐν αὐτῷ ζωὴ ἦν (Jn 1.4), compare rather 1 Jn 5.11c, and even then Jn 5.26 is closer. These examples confirm that the epistle's introduction is a thoroughly Johannine piece; what they do not confirm is that it was intended to direct the mind unerringly to Jn 1.1-18.

25. See, e.g., 2.7, 8, 12-14, 20-21, 26-27; 5.13.

26. This sense of a common cause need not be affected even when the 'we' is used on occasion to declare an adverse position. For the argument that this feature is

to represent both himself and his readers; it will imply the shared experience as well as the shared knowledge of writer and readers alike.

As the epistle writer embarks on his main task, his intention is to teach his group in a manner which not only affords reassurance in a new and unprecedented situation but which also provides a basis for future growth. In practice his campaign is twofold: on the one hand he reminds his readers of what they (and he) already hold to be true, and on the other hand he draws out the implications of those accepted truths in order to speak to contemporary community needs. Two examples of this method should suffice to illustrate the point.

1 John 3.5-8 is part of a wider consideration of the privileged status of the τέκνα θεοῦ. This was begun at 3.1, where it was triggered by the mention of ἐξ αὐτοῦ γεγέννηται in 2.29. In 3.4 the subject of sin has been raised in this connection and sin has been equated with lawlessness. The author is about to assure his readers that those who adhere to the Johannine faith are not susceptible to this kind of sin[27] and at the same time to advise them on how to identify those who are. Accordingly, in v. 5 he appeals to something they know about Jesus as a basis for the argument which will follow: καὶ οἴδατε ὅτι ἐκεῖνος ἐφανερώθη ἵνα τὰς ἁμαρτίας ἄρῃ, καὶ ἁμαρτία ἐν αὐτῷ οὐκ ἔστιν. The ἐκεῖνος here certainly refers to Jesus, and the assumption that Jesus takes away sin is of a piece with the author's previous description of Jesus in 2.2 as the expiation (ἱλασμός) for the sins of the faithful, a statement which he had subsequently expanded at that point to include the sins of the whole world.

As the argument develops throughout vv. 6-8 the positive and negative implications of the Jesus tradition in v. 5 are neatly balanced and the whole is rounded off by a further reference to the original statement. In v. 6 we are told that remaining in Jesus guarantees sinlessness while sinful behaviour demonstrates ignorance of Jesus. After the little warning which begins v. 7 there follows an expanded and modified version of the

part of the author's persuasive style of argumentation, see Lieu, 'Authority', pp. 221-22.

27. This is uncompromisingly stated in 3.9, and is logical in the context of a passage which contrasts the child of God with the child of the devil. This does not prevent the author from insisting in 1.8-10 that the faithful must acknowledge that they do sin. But in this case, as with sin committed by a 'brother' in 5.16-17, matters can be put right. For 1 John the true child of God is always potentially in receipt of God's forgiveness, love and protection (1.9; 4.10; 5.18).

contrast in v. 6, this time placing the emphasis firmly on behaviour. Thus, in v. 7b 'not sinning' has become 'doing righteousness' and is traced to its origin in Jesus (ἐκεῖνος again), while in v. 8a the character of the one who does sin receives a closer definition as originating with the devil, the archetypal sinner. Finally, this allows the ἐκεῖνος ἐφανερώθη ἵνα τὰς ἁμαρτίας ἄρῃ in v. 5 to be re-worked in v. 8b as ἐφανερώθη ὁ υἱὸς τοῦ θεοῦ, ἵνα λύσῃ τὰ ἔργα τοῦ διαβόλου. Taken as a whole this is a typical 1 John 'by their fruits ye shall know them' argument.[28] In this case, however, the argument is based on something the community already believes about Jesus.

In 1 Jn 3.16-18 we find the author in the midst of edifying his readers on how to put into practice the command to love one another. He has reminded them of this command in v. 11 and in vv. 12-15 he has told them how not to do it by citing the example of Cain, after which he has firmly dissociated their own calling from the Cain stereotype. By v. 16 he is ready to provide a positive model. Note again the appeal to something known about Jesus which he now cites as the supreme definition of loving behaviour: ἐν τούτῳ ἐγνώκαμεν τὴν ἀγάπην, ὅτι ἐκεῖνος ὑπὲρ ἡμῶν τὴν ψυχὴν αὐτοῦ ἔθηκεν (v. 16a), after which the reader is exhorted to imitate Jesus with regard to his brother in faith (v. 16b, note the stress in the καὶ ἡμεῖς ὀφείλομεν). In v. 17 he gives an example of how that principle should operate in day-to-day living. He expresses it negatively by way of criticism of those who do not respond in the appropriate manner, but nevertheless the application is clear enough. The principle in v. 16a of expending one's life (τὴν ψυχὴν αὐτοῦ ἔθηκεν) has now become a matter of expending one's *means* of life or livelihood (βίος) so that to do this on behalf of those in need is seen as a practical expression of God's love. At v. 18 the author sums up his argument in a nutshell: the right kind of loving behaviour (i.e. ἐν ἀληθείᾳ) is not lip service but loving 'in action' (ἐν ἔργῳ). Thus, once again, we see the author citing a known tradition and expounding it in terms of ethical behaviour.

We are now in a position to define the character of the epistle a little more closely. In the writer we have an authoritarian figure, a member of the 'we' group who regard themselves as guardians and transmitters of original Johannine tradition. As a member of such a group, the author can legitimately reaffirm those truths shared by himself and his readers

---

28. For other examples of this attitude in 1 John see 1.6; 2.4-6, 9-11, 15-17, 29; 3.12, 14; 4.8, 20.

and accepted by all concerned as the group's basic principles. As he works to meet the demands of new and disturbing circumstances brought about by a recent community crisis, he not only reminds his readers of their tradition but also interprets it afresh to allow it to speak directly to their needs. Thus, as in 1 Jn 2.7-8, the 'old commandment'—the word they have heard from the beginning—can also be expressed as a 'new commandment' inasmuch as it continues to remain true. On this basis we may take it that the epistle writer's work consists essentially of a superstructure of argument built on a foundation of shared principles, and, moreover, that these principles are what the author understands to be basic constituents of the Johannine Christian tradition.[29]

I have suggested that the clue to the real nature of the link between John and 1 John, and hence to the bearing which the epistle can have on the matter of isolating tradition in the Gospel, lies in understanding the epistle writer's methods. For if we think that in thus confining our attention to the epistle we have by now travelled far from the world of the Evangelist, a moment's consideration will tell us that indeed we have not. The fact is that our chief impression of the Gospel is often influenced by the features which strike us most, in particular perhaps the magnificent Prologue and the magisterial 'I am' statements on the lips of the Johannine Jesus. Yet we must not allow our enthusiasm for such artistry to obscure the fact that the real points of correspondence with 1 John are also embedded in the Gospel text. These are the presence of the Johannine 'we' in conjunction with eye-witness language, and certain statements which correspond with the content of what 1 John had appealed to as original tradition.

The Evangelist uses the 'we' to speak on behalf of the faithful community in the Prologue. It appears with an eye-witness verb in 1.14b, 'we have beheld (ἐθεασάμεθα) his glory' (compare ὃ ἐθεασάμεθα in 1 Jn 1.1), and in v. 16 it is used where the faithful (ἡμεῖς πάντες) are described as recipients of grace. Note also that in v. 14a the Evangelist says that the Word dwelt 'among us' (ἐν ἡμῖν), a phrase which finds its parallel in 1 Jn 4.9, 16. It is also worth observing in this context that the 'we' appears again right at the end of the Gospel where the veracity of the Beloved Disciple's witness is guaranteed (21.24). Although this verse is not usually attributed to the Evangelist, in the light of his use of the

29. See further O.A. Piper's excellent defence of the case for treating 1 John as a piece based on known tradition in '1 John and the Didache of the Primitive Church', *JBL* 66 (1947), pp. 437-51.

'we' elsewhere it is surely a possibility that he himself has also penned this final comment.[30]

We can also extend this comparison with the epistle by including the 'you' of direct address to the readers. In 20.31, a passage remarkably similar to Jn 5.13, the Evangelist turns aside from his narrative to tell his readers that he writes 'that you may believe' (ἵνα πιστεύητε)[31] and 'that believing you may have life' (ἵνα πιστεύοντες ζωὴν ἔχητε). We may also choose to add here the little aside to the readers ἵνα καὶ ὑμεῖς πιστεύητε in 19.35, assuming, of course, that that is also original to John.[32]

For the rest of the time the Evangelist does not speak directly to his readers nor represent them in person, and in that regard his work differs from that of the epistle writer. But the difference is only a matter of genre. A Gospel is, ostensibly at least, a narrative of the life of Jesus in times past, and hence its author will tend throughout to assume the low profile of disinterested narrator. It follows that the gospel medium is a form of communication between writer and readers which is primarily indirect. It is not surprising, therefore, to find that the instances where the 'we' and 'you' are used directly in the Gospel occur largely outside the 'time capsule' of the narrative itself. However, this does not mean that the indirect form of communication cannot be effective nor should we take it that the Evangelist has ceased his policy of representing and instructing his community once the narration has begun.

---

30. Among those who identify the 'we' in 21.24 as the Evangelist's trademark as in the Prologue are P.S. Minear ('The Original Functions of John 21', *JBL* 102 [1983], pp. 85-98, esp. p. 95) and P.F. Ellis (*The Genius of John* [Collegeville, MN: Liturgical Press, 1984], p. 308). The reappearance of the 'we' here fits in well with customary devices for framing a narrative (see Culpepper, *Anatomy*, p. 46), and the sentence 'we know that his testimony is true' looks like a typical Johannine endorsement formula which the Evangelist could well have used. J. Chapman points to the parallels in 19.35 and 3 Jn 12 ('We Know that his Testimony is True', *JTS* 31 [1930], pp. 379-87, esp. pp. 380-81) but has overlooked Jn 5.32, which is closer to 21.24 than 19.35, and is indisputably attributed to John himself.

31. The present subjunctive of πιστεύειν, which implies the continuation and strengthening of faith, is to be preferred here to the aorist πιστεύσητε which would be appropriate to conversion to faith (see Barrett, *Gospel*, p. 575).

32. G.R. Beasley-Murray recognizes a 'growing consensus' of opinion among scholars that 19.35 is inauthentic because of its verbal links with 21.24 (*John*, p. 354). This argument relies far too heavily on the unquestioned assumption that 21.24 was not written by the Evangelist (see n. 30 above).

We may be certain that the Evangelist's readers would have identified readily with the faithful in the Gospel story. With this in mind we must surely take careful note of where the 'we' occurs on the lips of the faithful as the narrative proceeds, for this is probably the Johannine 'we' thinly disguised and as such is likely to introduce some known and commonly accepted formula. By the same token, those occasions where the Johannine Jesus addresses his ἴδιοι as 'you' should not be ignored, for these will be the points where the Evangelist offers advice and instruction to his readers.

While the 'we' occurs naturally as part of the inevitable Gospel dialogue, there are occasions where it is used with the language of witness in a way evidently intended to resound beyond the confines of the historical setting. For example, in 4.42 we read that the Samaritan villagers have heard (ἀκηκόαμεν) for themselves and now know (οἴδαμεν) that 'this is truly the Saviour of the world'. There is also the confession of Peter in 6.69 who, as spokesman for the disciples, affirms that they have believed and have come to know (ἡμεῖς πεπιστεύκαμεν καὶ ἐγνώκαμεν) that Jesus is the Holy One of God. Furthermore, in view of the presence of eye-witness language, it may be feasible also to include in this category one of the instances where Jesus himself speaks in terms of 'we'. Jn 3.11 begins with an address specifically to Nicodemus (ἀμὴν ἀμὴν λέγω σοι) but in what follows the personal pronouns change abruptly to the plural, and this has the effect of raising what is said to the level of general comment.[33] Note how close the ὃ ἑωράκαμεν μαρτυροῦμεν here comes to the καὶ ἑωράκαμεν καὶ μαρτυροῦμεν in 1 Jn 1.2.[34] Thus, the 'we' here is probably to be regarded as introducing an attitude of the Johannine faithful. The conviction that their witness is not received is certainly not untypical of the author's own stance in the Prologue and elsewhere.[35]

While Jesus does address his disciples as 'you' earlier in the Gospel,[36] this feature is signally in evidence in the last discourse material where Jesus instructs them privately and at length (chs. 13–16). The tone of

33. See also v. 12 where the second person plural persists.

34. Compare also ἡμεῖς τεθεάμεθα καὶ μαρτυροῦμεν in 1 Jn 4.14.

35. See Jn 1.11 and compare both 1.11 and 1.12 with 3.11 and 3.32-33. See also 12.37-40 where this attitude is underpinned by two texts from Isaiah. Presumably this thinking is also behind the epistle writer's assumption that the world will listen only to false prophets (1 Jn 4.5).

36. Note, for example, the sudden shift in address from singular to plural at 1.51.

assurance in these passages is quite marked, and the object seems to be not only to ensure community' survival beyond the recent trauma of rejection by Judaism but also to provide a basis for the community's continuing growth and development into the future.[37] Indeed, not only in tone but also in actual content, this relatively narrative-free area of the Gospel approximates most closely to 1 John.[38]

On this evidence we may assume that the first point of correspondence between Gospel and epistle is confirmed. It seems that the Evangelist has also felt free to adopt the language of guarantee with which 1 John had defended his position as guardian and transmitter of original tradition. He has used the Johannine 'we' to represent his readers, he has also addressed them as 'you' and, as with 1 John, he has taken pains to encourage and instruct them. Moreover, he has pursued this policy not only directly but also indirectly by working through the Gospel medium. Both authors, it would seem, are tradition bearers who can address the community and put its case in the interests of providing a blueprint for the future against a background of recent crisis.

We now turn to examine the second point, namely, that the two texts coincide specifically in the terms of the tradition which the epistle writer has appealed to as the basis for his argument. With that in mind we must return to the two examples from the epistle given earlier in order to remind ourselves of the content of the traditional material cited by 1 John and to draw comparisons with relevant texts from the Gospel.

In 1 Jn 3.5 the author referred to his readers' knowledge (καὶ οἴδατε) that Jesus was manifested 'in order to take away sins' (ἵνα τὰς ἁμαρτίας ἄρῃ). I suggested that this bore on a previous statement in 2.2 where Jesus was described as the expiation not only for the sins of the faithful but also for the sins of the whole world (περὶ ὅλου τοῦ κόσμου). If we take the ἵνα τὰς ἁμαρτίας ἄρῃ of 3.5 together with the reference to ὁ κόσμος in 2.2, we come up with something

---

37. For the general tone of comfort and assurance, see, for example, 14.1, 3, 18, 27; 16.33. Note also how the subject of persecution is tackled here in a way designed to encourage fortitude and to ward off dismay at its onset (15.18–16.4).

38. As in 1 John note the use of the affectionate τεκνία (13.33), the emphasis on the love command (13.34; 15.12), the theme of possession of the Spirit (14.16, 17, 26; 15.26; 16.7-15), the expectation of joy fulfilled (15.11; 16.20, 22, 24) and the assurance that prayer will be answered (14.13-14; 15.7, 16; 16.23, 24). For a chart of themes common to 1 John and the final discourses, see S.S. Smalley, *1, 2, 3 John* (WBC, 51; Waco, TX: Word Books, 1984), p. xxx.

remarkably similar to the declaration of John the Baptist in Jn 1.29 that Jesus, the Lamb of God, 'takes away the sin of the world' (ὁ αἴρων τὴν ἁμαρτίαν τοῦ κόσμου). Thus, we have good reason to assume that this part of Jn 1.29 was not newly minted by the Evangelist when he wrote but that at this point he was repeating the essential elements of a statement of a confessional nature about Jesus which was already part of the Johannine Christian tradition. Moreover, judging by the way it has been reflected with only minor variation in both writings, it would seem that the verbal form of this statement has been fairly fixed. There are other indications in both texts which would support such a conclusion. For example, it is worth noting that, while both authors faithfully retail this information, neither consistently makes full use of the entire content of what he reports. Thus, in the Gospel the atoning quality of Jesus' death is not denied but at the same time it is not a major theme, while in the epistle the sense of outreach to the world is almost wholly absent and hence the writer's reference to ὁ κόσμος in 2.2 is untypically benevolent for him.[39] It is also significant that neither author puts αἴρειν together with ἁμαρτία in any other context—indeed in 1 John αἴρειν never occurs outside 3.5 where this tradition is cited. Finally, it is also relevant to observe that outside these two references αἴρειν and ἁμαρτία are never found together anywhere else in the New Testament.

In 1 Jn 3.16 the model behaviour of Jesus (ὅτι ἐκεῖνος ὑπὲρ ἡμῶν τὴν ψυχὴν αὐτοῦ ἔθηκεν) is cited as the starting point of a brief treatment of the nature of loving in action. The most prominent Gospel reference to this is as a laudable principle placed on Jesus' lips at 15.13 where, as in 1 John, it not only connects with the love command but serves as a definition of loving in action. Indeed, *mutatis mutandis* the two texts are very similar:

ἐν τούτῳ ἐγνώκαμεν τὴν ἀγάπην,
ὅτι ἐκεῖνος ὑπὲρ ἡμῶν τὴν ψυχὴν αὐτοῦ ἔθηκεν (1 Jn 3.16)

---

39. See especially J.M. Lieu's remark that 1 John's references to the world in 2.2 and 4.14 'sound like statements which have survived in tradition and they have no effect on the theology of the immediate context or of the Epistle as a whole' (*Second and Third Epistles*, p. 183). We have already seen good reason to identify the title σωτὴρ τοῦ κόσμου in 4.14 as tradition because of the 'we' and the eye-witness language which herald it in Jn 4.42 (see p. 57).

μείζονα ταύτης ἀγάπην οὐδεὶς ἔχει,
ἵνα τις τὴν ψυχὴν αὐτοῦ θῇ ὑπὲρ τῶν φίλων αὐτοῦ
(cf. v. 14a, ὑμεῖς φίλοι μού ἐστε) (Jn 15.13).

The Gospel makes other references to this principle of laying down life. For example, it is present in ch. 10 where it is applied to Jesus as the Good Shepherd who lays down his life for the sheep:

10.11 ὁ ποιμὴν ὁ καλὸς τὴν ψυχὴν αὐτοῦ τίθησιν ὑπὲρ τῶν
       προβάτων
10.17 ἐγὼ τίθημι τὴν ψυχήν μου
10.18 ἐγὼ τίθημι αὐτήν...θεῖναι αὐτήν.

It also appears in 13.37, again in the context of the love command (vv. 34, 35), where it supplies the verbal form of Peter's foolhardy declaration of loyalty to Jesus, and in v. 38 Jesus echoes these words in querying Peter's competence to perform the act:

13.37 τὴν ψυχήν μου ὑπὲρ σοῦ θήσω
13.38 τὴν ψυχήν σου ὑπὲρ ἐμοῦ θήσεις;[40]

Here again we are almost certainly in touch with an element of Johannine Christian tradition which has been picked up by both authors and differently applied. Again we have language peculiar to the group (τίθημι ψυχήν is uniquely Johannine)[41] in which they expressed their belief that Jesus had loved them by sacrificing his life on their behalf.

On this evidence it seems that our second point of correspondence can also be confirmed. In the two examples from 1 John where it was possible to detect that the epistle writer was appealing to tradition, the close verbal correspondence with the Gospel has emerged precisely in the content of the tradition cited and *not* in the surrounding argument. We may also pause to reflect that, since in these two cases the tradition in question has been expressed in an idiom distinctive to the Johannine writings, then it could not immediately have been discerned by adducing Synoptic or Pauline parallels.

We have attempted to achieve a more precise understanding of the relation between John and 1 John by concentrating first on the epistle writer

40. Note also the formal similarity between these examples and the dictum of Caiaphas ἵνα εἷς ἄνθρωπος ἀποθάνῃ ὑπὲρ τοῦ λαοῦ in 11.50. The application of this 'prophecy' to the τέκνα τοῦ θεοῦ in 11.52 certainly implies that it is intended to bear the same meaning.

41. So Ruckstuhl, *Einheit*, p. 298.

and his methods, and it seems that this approach has served us well. In 1 John we have seen a tradition bearer at work seeking to reassure his community in the wake of a crisis by citing known tradition and interpreting it to meet their needs. In the Gospel we have seen another tradition bearer at work similarly bent on reassurance, and on his own showing already known to us as a receiver and highly creative interpreter of tradition. Further comparisons have shown that material which the author of 1 John had appealed to as the basis of his argument may be recognized in the Evangelist's text also. In other words, what the epistle writer identifies as original tradition the Gospel also contains.

In view of these and our earlier findings it seems feasible to describe John and 1 John in the following terms. We are dealing with two documents which belong to different literary types and which have been addressed to the Johannine church at different stages in its fortunes. Thus, in terms of genre and orientation to particular circumstances, they are not alike. Nevertheless, they can be compared in certain fundamental respects as follows: in both cases the author responsible has had access to community tradition, and in both cases the procedure of citing tradition and interpreting it to meet present needs has been adopted. These common features have given rise to a third point of comparison and, in this case, a phenomenon which has, in effect, forged the link between John and 1 John as they are now known to us in their final form. This is the fact that there have been occasions when Gospel and epistle have coincided in reflecting tradition with the same content.

Thus, a picture emerges of John and 1 John as independent productions, which relate to one another by virtue of their mutual reliance on a body of tradition which was known to both authors and to their readers before either document was written. Moreover, it is a picture which makes sense of the results of my earlier attempts to compare them directly. It plausibly explains the pattern of striking but intermittent contact between them that we observed at that point, for it allows us to understand how material traceable directly from one text to another can be found in contexts where no such correspondence exists.

It hardly needs to be stressed that this perspective on John and 1 John does not accord with the majority view that the epistle is directly related to the Gospel and was intended as some kind of explanatory adjunct to it.[42] But there again we have seen no evidence to suggest that

---

42. There are, however, dissenting voices. See, e.g., G. Strecker, 'Die Anfänge der johanneischen Schule', *NTS* 32 (1986), pp. 31-47, esp. pp. 40-41, and J.M. Lieu, *The*

this was so. Neither 1 John's declaration of his status as tradition bearer nor the terms in which he has couched his message have conveyed any impression that he has needed to defer to the work of a predecessor to make his case. More specifically, it seems that the verbal parallels which exist between Gospel and epistle cannot be claimed as evidence that the epistolary author was referring directly to the Gospel itself. On the contrary, these are best described as instances of tradition overlap: they are points where the author of 1 John has repeated certain elements in the tradition ἀπ᾽ ἀρχῆς which the Evangelist, writing in another context, had also known and reproduced. In sum, our findings indicate that what links the epistle materially to the Gospel is the Johannine Christian tradition, or at least certain important aspects of it.

Having thus specified the nature of what is common to John and 1 John I have at the same time supplied the evidence in favour of my initial proposal that the epistle could be made to function as a control to isolate tradition in the text of the Gospel. On this basis we may assume that where the epistle writer reminds his readers of what they 'know', or speaks of what they have 'heard from the beginning', or simply takes for granted a particular attitude, and where the equivalent (or near equivalent) occurs in the Gospel, then at such points the Evangelist has included known community tradition as part of his text. We will then be in a position to judge how the Evangelist himself has chosen to build on this material in the process of composing the Gospel. To this extent, then, 1 John is surely qualified to take its place alongside other means of identifying the tradition known to the Fourth Evangelist, and therefore it remains only to add some brief remarks on the potential value of the epistle's contribution in this regard by way of conclusion.

As with our other resources, the epistle offers only a limited insight into what the Evangelist knew. It cannot help us in terms of narrative, nor will it teach us anything radically new about the essentials of Johannine faith compared with what we could reasonably have guessed from passages elsewhere in the New Testament which express the same

---

Theology of the Johannine Epistles (NT Theology; Cambridge: Cambridge University Press, 1991), esp. p. 101. Both scholars have also found reason to regard the epistle as an independent piece which reflects community tradition. Even Raymond Brown, undoubtedly the most influential exponent of the direct dependence theory, does not exclude this position as a possible alternative to his own thesis (see *Epistles*, p. 86 n. 190).

Christian sentiments.[43] Nevertheless, in one important respect the epistle's contribution is of outstanding value, because at the level of *diction* 1 John as a control is unsurpassed. In other words, given that the epistle is another Johannine piece, then in this instance we have a control in which the tradition is articulated using the distinctive style and vocabulary with which the Evangelist himself was familiar. This means that in those areas where 1 John does come into play we can be clearer than otherwise would be possible about the precise wording of the tradition the Evangelist knew, and hence can more easily discern its presence in his text. With this in mind, it is worth remembering that 1 Jn 4.9-10 offers the closest available parallel to Jn 3.16-17 in which the 'Johannine kerygma' is thought to be represented.[44] As I hinted in my opening paragraph, this seems to have helped to provide the conceptual framework for John's distinctive presentation of Jesus. Among other examples we may note that the Johannine version of the 'ask and it will be given' logion is common to both,[45] as is also a jaundiced outlook on the world as the sphere of inevitable opposition and hatred towards the faithful.[46] In short, this is the stuff of which the Fourth

---

43. For example, Jn 1.29/1 Jn 2.2; 3.5 can be compared with 2 Cor. 5.19 and 1 Tim. 1.15, both of which are also assumed to reflect traditional formulae; for Jn 15.13 etc./1 Jn 3.16 compare esp. Gal. 2.20; Eph. 5.2 and the Son of man logion in Mk 10.45 (cf. 1 Tim. 2.5-6). This agreement over fundamentals is hardly surprising; it simply confirms that the Johannine group was a branch of the early Christian tree and not an alien life form.

44. As is often remarked, the benefits of the mission of the Son in the 1 John passage are confined to the believing community and do not extend to the world. However, this particularization looks like a deliberate modification. 1 Jn 4.14 shows that the author is fully aware of the universal scope of the divine intention (compare Jn 3.17; 4.42). Note, significantly, that this is precisely the point where the language of original eye-witness makes its appearance in his argument.

45. For the full range of references to this well-attested logion together with a proposal that it is an item of early tradition which was probably original to Jesus, see D. Goldsmith, '"Ask, and it will be Given...", Toward Writing the History of a Logion', *NTS* 35 (1989), pp. 254-65.

46. The world's hatred is introduced in Jn 15.18-19 and 1 Jn 3.13 as an accepted fact of life whose abiding relevance is merely confirmed by present difficulties (see also Jn 7.7; 17.14). Barnabas Lindars describes this attitude as a Johannine 'maxim' which in this case has its roots in traditional Jesus logia; see Lindars, 'The

Gospel was made, and which was no less influential in the Evangelist's thinking than other aspects of the early Christian tradition on which he drew.

Persecution of Christians in Jn 15.18–16.4a', in W. Horbury and B. McNeil (eds.), *Suffering and Martyrdom in the New Testament* (Cambridge: Cambridge University Press, 1981), pp. 48-69 (58).

THE REVELATION OF JOHN

JSNT 11 (1981), pp. 3-20

THE ELDER JOHN, AUTHOR OF REVELATION

John J. Gunther

A. Harnack, W. Bousset, G. Baldensperger, J. Weiss, W. Bauer, E. Lohmeyer, and E. Lohse[1] have considered the Elder the best candidate to identify with John of Patmos. The issue is complicated by the Ephesian-Johannine school hypothesis;[2] but there is no reason to equate the Elder John and the anonymous Elder of 2 and 3 John if all Johannine writings except for Revelation are dissociated from Ephesus.[3]

In seven biographical points internal data from Revelation matches ecclesiastical tradition, although admittedly the latter became confused concerning his relationship to John of Zebedee (see below).

(1) John was a 'brother' (1.9) to the seven churches in Asia who shared in their tribulation. He felt well-informed of the churches' history and current situation, and he expected them to recognize his name and authority. Eusebius credibly reported the tradition[4] that when Nerva

---

1. C. Brütsch, *La clarté de l'Apocalypse* (Geneva: Labor et Fides, 1966), p. 400; U.B. Müller, *Zur frühchristlichen Theologiegeschichte* (Gütersloh: Gerd Mohn, 1976), p. 48.

2. R.A. Culpepper, *The Johannine School* (SBLDS 26; Missoula, MT: Scholars Press, 1975), pp. 1-34.

3. J.J. Gunther, 'The Alexandrian Gospel and Letters of John', *CBQ* 41 (1979), pp. 581-603; 'Early Identifications of Authorship of the Johannine Writings', *JEH* 31 (1980), pp. 1-21.

4. Eusebius's sources included Irenaeus (*Adv. Haer.* 5.30.3), Clement (*Quis Dives* 42), Hippolytus (*ap.* Dionysius Bar-Salibi; cf. *Antichr.* 36: by or from Rome, as in Tertullian, *Praescor.* 36.3; cf. *Apol.* 5.5: Domitian restored those whom he had banished) and probably Melito (R.H. Charles, *A Critical and Exegetical Commentary on the Revelation of St John* [ICC; New York: Charles Scribner's Sons, 1920], I, p. xcii) and Hegesippus (H.J. Lawlor, *Eusebiana* [Oxford: Clarendon Press, 1912], pp. 53-54, 96). John Malalas (*Chron.* 11), appealing to Irenaeus and Julius Africanus,

succeeded Domitian, the apostle John, who had been sentenced to 'banishment on the island, took up his residence at Ephesus' (*H.E.* 3.18.1; 3.20.7-9; 3.23.1). In the prologue to his *Expositions* (*ap.* Eusebius 3.39.4), Papias used the aorist εἶπεν to distinguish (1) what the Twelve disciples did say, from (2) what John and Aristion (who represent 'a living and surviving voice') were saying (λέγουσιν) when Papias made his inquiries. 'At the time of Papias' inquiries they were the only two surviving disciples of the Lord' to whose teaching he had access.[5] Travellers through Papias's area of Phrygia who had been followers of the elders were habitually questioned by him. Eusebius (*H.E.* 3.39.7; cf. 1) reports that Papias 'says that he himself was an actual hearer' of Aristion and the elder John. Papias, in referring to 'the elder', meant John (*H.E.* 3.39.15). Irenaeus also read the work of Papias and called him 'a hearer of John' (*Adv. Haer.* 5.33.4).

In his *Dialogue with Trypho* (81.4), which occurred at Ephesus, Justin claimed 'a certain man among us named John...prophesied in a revelation' about the millennium in Jerusalem. According to tradition, he had been with the local community. His 'is the only book of the New Testament to which Justin specifically refers', as E. Osborn observes.[6] Justin, who had been converted at Ephesus, witnesses to the fact that this community did not consider the Apocalypse to be pseudonymous. According to Irenaeus (3.3.4) John remained with the church in Ephesus 'until the times of Trajan'. 'Those men who saw John face to face bear their testimony' to ancient texts of Rev. 13.18 (5.30.1). The Montanist Proclus held that John had been in Asia and was buried there (Eusebius, *H.E.* 3.31.4; cf. 2.25.7; 7.25.16). Apollonius quoted from the Apocalypse of John and told how 'a dead man was raised by John himself at Ephesus' (Eusebius, *H.E.* 5.18.13-14). Bishop Polycrates of Ephesus (Eusebius, *H.E.* 5.24.2-3) confirms that John 'has fallen asleep at Ephesus'. As he begins his list saying 'in Asia great luminaries have fallen asleep', and refers to only one John, little credence can be given to speculation about two local luminaries and tombs (Dionysius Alex.; Eusebius, *H.E.* 3.39.5-6; 7.25.16; Jerome, *De Vir. Ill.* 9, *Ap. Const.*

specifies Trajan's second year. On the dating, see B. Reicke, 'Die jüdische Apokalyptik und die johanneische Tiervision', *RSR* 60 (1972), pp. 174-79. Did John see Rome (16.19; 17.9; 18.9-24)?

5.   J.F. Bligh, 'The Prologue of Papias', *TS* 13 (1952), p. 239.

6.   *Justin Martyr* (Tübingen: Mohr–Siebeck, 1973), p. 137; he notes three apparent 'main points of contact', all in eschatology.

7.46). F.M. Braun[7] notes that the existence of two Peters cannot be inferred from the fact that his trophies were honoured at the Vatican and on the Ostian Way (Gaius of Rome *ap.* Eusebius, *H.E.* 2.25.7). No Asian writer supports the guess about two Johns, though two would be more of a credit than one. The theory arose from the need to distinguish between 'Johannine' authors.

(2) John claimed to be an inspired prophet (Rev. 1.1-3, 10; 2.7, 11, 17, 29; 3.6; 4.2; 10.7, 11; 14.13; 17.3; 19.10; 21.10; 22.6-7, 9-10, 18-19).[8] His 'words are trustworthy and true' (21.5; 22.6) and cannot safely be added to or taken away (22.18-19). Blessed are those who read, hear and obey the words of this prophecy (1.3).

Eusebius (*H.E.* 3.39.5-6) believed it likely that the Revelation was seen by the elder John. He believed Papias got his ideas of a material millennium 'through a misinterpretation' of tradition (*H.E.* 3.39.11-12). Papias states that he wrote down what he learned and recalled well from the elders, including interpretations (ἑρμηνεία). He inquired about the discourses of the elder John, 'a living and abiding voice' (*H.E.* 3.39.3-4). He relied on travellers' interpretations of the elder John's oral eschatological teachings. It is unlikely that the author of Revelation, the travellers *and* Papias all distinguished between the prophetic words of the earthly and the heavenly Christ.

According to Andrew of Caesarea,[9] 'Regarding the divine inspiration of the book [the Apocalypse of John], Papias...bears witness to its trustworthiness (ἀξιόπιστον)'. The traditions of the elder John were often apocalyptic.[10] Papias's chiliasm sensationalizes that of Rev. 3.12;

---

7. *Jean le Théologien et son évangile dans l'église ancienne* (Paris: Lecoffre, 1959), I, p. 363. See also R. Eisler, *The Enigma of the Fourth Gospel* (London: Methuen, 1937), pp. 120-27; F.F. Bruce, 'St John at Ephesus', *BJRL* 60 (1978), p. 352.

8. J.E. Carpenter, *The Johannine Writings* (London: Constable, 1927), pp. 35-40; A. Satake, *Die Gemeindeordnung in die Johannesapokalypse* (Neukirchen–Vluyn: Neukirchener, 1966), pp. 67-72; L.J. Thompson, 'Cult and Eschatology in the Apocalypse of John', *JR* 49 (1969), pp. 345-49; D. Hill, 'Prophecy and Prophets in the Revelation of John', *NTS* 18 (1972), pp. 403, 411, 415-16; Müller, *Theologiegeschichte*, pp. 31-35, 49-50.

9. *Praef. in Apoc.*, in Migne, *PG* 106. 217B. Andrew (*In Apoc.* 34.12) quoted from Papias a passage clarifying 12.9 (on the overthrow of angels who misruled the earth).

10. B. Bacon, 'The Elder of Ephesus and the Elder John', *HibJ* 26 (1927), pp. 128-29.

5.10; 19.7, 9; 20.1-9; 21.1-2, 14, 17. 'The elders who had seen John'
received from him a supposed saying of Jesus promising a fantastic
growth of vines and grapes, each giving 200 gallons of wine' (Irenaeus
5.33.3-4).[11] Some who are worthy 'will enjoy the delights of Paradise'
(5.36.1). 'There will be enjoyment of material foods' in the Kingdom,
according to Papias[12] (cf. Rev. 3.20; 19.9; 22.2, 14). Although he
accepted Revelation as inspired, Papias was more impressed by the
independent oral traditions from John; they were more concrete and clear.

The Asiatic chiliastic 'school' traceable to the prophet John included
the elders, Papias, Justin, Montanists, Irenaeus and Melito. Justin (*Dial.*
81.4–82.1; cf. 80.5) related that John 'prophesied in a revelation made to
him that they who have believed in our Christ will spend a thousand
years in Jerusalem and afterwards the...resurrection...and the judgment
also will occur... For the prophetic gifts remain with us even to the
present time.' The local John was clearly a prophet.[13] The punishment of
the devil is taught 'in our writings' (*Apol.* 28.1; cf. Rev. 12.9; 20.3).

(3) The author of Revelation probably functioned as an apostolic or
patriarchal elder *par excellence* (cf. 1 Pet. 1.1; 5.1) in leading worship
and in interpreting and enforcing Christ's teaching among a group of
churches (Rev. 1.4). The court of white-robed, enthroned 24 elders surrounds God (4.4) and worships him (4.10; 11.16-18; 19.4) and the Lamb
(5.8-10, 13-14) in song, as do angels (5.11-12; 7.11-12) and martyrs (7.9-
10; 14.2-3; 19.6). Probably this picture was suggested by the 24 Levites
who prophesied and led the Temple worship of praise and thanks to the
Lord in music (1 Chron. 25; cf. Rev. 5.8).[14] One of the elders makes
revelations to the prophet John (5.5; 7.13-14), who in turn acts as
mediator to the church. The heavenly pattern of worship and instruction
is analogous to the earthly. Church elders held seats of honour
(*Herm. Vis.* 3.9.7), presumably in leading the liturgy (cf. *Ign. Eph.* 4.1;
Magn. 6.1; *Smyrn.* 8.1). Their teaching role appears in 1 Tim. 5.17;

11. Similar prophecies appear in rabbinic literature, *1 En.* 10.18-19; The Syriac
Apocalypse of Baruch (*2 Bar.* 29.5-8) (J. Klausner, *Jesus of Nazareth* [London:
George, Allen & Unwin, 1947], p. 401) and an Apocalypse of James (M.R. James,
The Apocryphal New Testament [Oxford: Clarendon Press, 1960], p. 37).

12. Maximus, *Schol. in Dion. Areop.* 7; Preuschen, *Analecta*, p. 61; Stephen
Gobarus, cited by Photius, *Biblioth.* cod. 232 (Migne, *PG* 103.1104A).

13. Osborn, *Justin*, p. 93.

14. G. Bornkamm, 'πρέσβυς', *TDNT*, VI, p. 669; Satake, *Gemeindeordnung*,
p. 150. Bornkamm (pp. 669-70) finds church structure in Revelation was based on
Palestinian tradition.

Tit. 1.5-9; *2 Clem.* 17.3. *Did.* 10.7; 15.1-2 reflect the stage in which prophets (when available: 13.4) offer thanks at the Eucharist (10.7); the institutional leaders perform tasks of the more honoured apostle-prophets and teachers (15.1-2; cf. ch. 11). John, who claimed to be *the* prophet (Rev. 22.6),[15] necessarily exercised a dominant liturgical and didactic role which he was apt to interpret in terms of the presbyteriate (Rev. 5.5; 7.13-14). As a prophet and as an elder John interpreted the words of Jesus and applied them to the churches' needs: Rev. 1.3b; 22.10 and Mt. 26.18; Lk. 21.8; Rev. 1.7 and Mt. 24.30; Rev. 1.16 and Mt. 17.2; Rev. 1.18; 3.7 and Mt. 16.19; Mk 10.33-34; Lk. 24.25-26; 39; Rev. 2.5 and Mt. 21.41; Lk. 13.3, 5; Rev. 2.9 and Lk. 12.21; Rev. 2.10 and Lk. 12.4-5; 21.12, 16; Rev. 2.23 and Mt. 16.27; Rev. 2.26 and Mt. 19.28; Rev. 3.3; 16.15 and Mt. 24.42-43, 50; 25.13; Lk. 12.39-40; Rev. 3.5 and Mt. 10.32; Lk. 12.8; Rev. 3.18 and Mt. 13.44; 25.9; Rev. 3.20 and Lk. 11.7, 9; 12.36-37; 22.29-30; Jn 10.1-9; 14.23; Rev. 3.21 and Mt. 19.28; Lk. 22.28-30. That is, Jesus in these passages spoke anew through John his traditional message of: persecution; hearing the voice of him who opens and shuts the door to salvation; his face shining like the sun; spiritual treasure; the mourning of all tribes of the earth when he comes with the clouds; because the time is near, watching for him who soon will come as a thief and who will repay and grant thrones; his acknowledging the names of the faithful before the Father and his angels. God will soon vindicate the persecuted who cry unto him (Rev. 6.10; Lk. 18.3-8). No one in Asia had greater authority than John to state, interpret and apply Christ's teachings on his behalf. 'He who has an ear let him hear!' (Rev. 2.7, 11, 17, etc. and Mt. 11.15; 13.9, 43; Lk. 8.8; 14.35).

The elders, according to Papias (*ap.* Eusebius, *H.E.* 3.39.3), 'repeat the commandments given to the faith by the Lord himself and derived from the truth itself'. Aristion and John, like other elders, transmitted various traditions from the Twelve: narratives, Dominical λογία, authoritative interpretations, etc. According to Eusebius (3.39.14), 'Papias gives us in his work accounts (διήγησις) of the aforesaid Aristion of the sayings of the Lord, and traditions of John the elder'.

For Irenaeus the elders were custodians of apostolic tradition (4.26.2 and 4-5; 4.32.1); he called them 'the elders the disciples of the apostles' (4.27.1; 4.31.1; 4.32.1; 5.5.1; 5.33.3; 5.36.1-2; *Dem. Apost. Pr.* 3). 'The elders who saw John the disciple of the Lord' (2.22.5; 5.30.1) 'related

---

15. Satake, *Gemeindeordnung*, pp. 62-64, 73.

what they heard from him' (5.33.3); Irenaeus then sets forth a story generally recognized as coming from Papias. Irenaeus and Papias looked to the same John as a major source of the elders' traditions. But as the designation, 'elder', did nothing to enhance his status and antiquity of witness, Irenaeus dropped the term and reduced 'the elders' to an intermediate position between John (now glorified as the Beloved Disciple) and Papias. Polycarp becomes an 'apostolic elder' who heard from 'John and the others who had seen the Lord' about 'His mighty works and teaching' (Epistle to Florinus *ap.* Eusebius, *H.E.* 5.20, 5.6-7). G. Bornkamm[16] believes that, for Papias and Irenaeus, 'presbyter' 'is not a title for office-bearers in the local congregation but for members of the older generation who are regarded as mediators of the authentic tradition and reliable teachers'. This second century conception of 'elder' partially corresponds with that of Acts 15 and 16.4, where they function, together with the apostles, as authoritative teachers.[17] In the Letters of John 'the elder' is the foremost witness and defender of tradition in his area. As late as Polycrates (*ap.* Eusebius, *H.E.* 5.24.3) John was viewed as διδάσκαλος. This tradition preserved the primary, didactic content of John's understanding of his role as 'the elder'. But he considered his teachings true, not simply because he was an old man with good sources and memory, but primarily by virtue of Christ's applying through him, his prophet, his teachings to current critical problems. This was a more critical function than recitation of unwritten Logia. Thus the roles of elder and prophet overlapped. 'The elder John' was known as 'Bishop John'; Timothy, Titus and Aristo were also regarded as bishops (*Apost. Const.* 7.46). Clement (*Quis Div. Salv.* 42, *ap.* Eusebius, *H.E.* 3.23.6-8) has John appointing bishops, one of whom is called 'the elder'.[18]

Though the name was common in Palestine, B. Bacon was probably correct in identifying Papias's Elder John with one of the 'bishops' of the Jerusalem church who succeeded James (see below). John's name was on a lengthy list (Eusebius, *H.E.* 4.5.3; Epiphanius, *Haer.* 66.20) of those who led the faithful at Jerusalem, Pella, Capernaum and/or

16. Bornkamm, *TDNT*, VI, p. 676; cf. H. von Campenhausen (*Ecclesiastical Authority and Spiritual Power* [Stanford: Stanford University Press, 1968], p. 122): 'a man of the Spirit, a prophet or teacher of the earlier type…spiritual father.'

17. Bornkamm, *TDNT*, VI, p. 663.

18. The originally Jewish term, 'elder', 'designates the office' of one functioning as 'bishop' (R.E. Osborne, 'Is the Bishop "Mod"?', *CJT* 14 [1968], pp. 131-34).

Kokaba.[19] Such official status would entitle him to honour in the Asian churches when he was banished to the penal colony of Patmos (Pliny, *Nat. Hist.* 4.12.23; Tacitus, *Ann.* 3.68; 4.30; 15.71) from Pella because of his preaching (Rev. 1.9). Generally, prominent churchmen would be the most likely to be so treated legally. See n. 4.

(4) Although John did not claim to be among the twelve apostles (Rev. 21.14), he probably included himself among the persecuted 'apostles and prophets' (18.20; cf. Lk. 11.49) and the class of teachers 'calling themselves apostles' (Rev. 2.2). The liars who were not apostles are implicitly contrasted with true apostles. Among the traditional signs qualifying John to be an 'apostle' are: a special authority from Christ,[20] ecstasy (2 Cor. 12), prophecy (Acts 15.22, 27, 32; 1 Cor. 12.28-29; 14.18-19; *Did.* 11),[21] preaching (Mk 3.14; Lk. 9.2), miracles (Lk. 10.17; Acts 8.13; 2 Cor. 12.12; cf. Rev. 13.14; 16.14; 19.20), tribulation and poverty (2 Cor. 12.10; cf. Rev. 1.9; 2.9; 3.17-18; 6.15; 18.3-11, 19) and seeing the Lord (1 Cor. 9.1; on Revelation see next page).

Justin (*Dial.* 81.4) called John, who prophesied in a revelation, 'one of the apostles of Christ'. The context suggests that his apostleship was closely allied to his receiving revelations from Christ and transmitting them authoritatively. For Justin the Synoptic Gospels and Revelation were scriptural (see above). At worship services 'the memoirs of the apostles or the writings of the prophets were read' (*Apol.* 1.67; cf. Muratorian Canon on the Apocalypses of John and of Peter). The apostles are 'those who have written memoirs of all things concerning the Savior' (*Apol.* 1.33; cf. 66). The author of Revelation was 'the apostle', John of Zebedee was the 'disciple' in 16 references in Justin.[22]

19. J.J. Gunther, 'The Fate of the Jerusalem Church', *TZ* 29 (1973), p. 92 n. 27. In a future publication the present writer hopes to show the first four after James and Symeon (Judas of Justus, Zacharias, Tobiah, Benjamin) led the Galilean church and were likewise relatives of Jesus. John, Matthias, Philip and Seneca led the progressively Hellenized Pellan church after AD 93 (when Symeon was crucified), while Justus, Levi, Ephraim, Joseph and Judas led those who returned to Jerusalem ca. 120. See n. 59 below.

20. G. Bornkamm, 'ἀπόστολος', *TDNT*, I, pp. 427, 432, 436, 437, 445-46.

21. W.G. Manley, *A Dissertation on the Presbyterate* (Cambridge, 1886), pp. 39-42. In Syria and Palestine prophet and apostle were apparently more overlapping, if not synonymous, than elsewhere.

22. Of Justin's 47 mentions of 'John', only on one other occasion is 'the apostle John' found (D. Guthrie, *New Testament Introduction: Hebrews to Revelation* [Chicago: Inter-Varsity Press, 1962], p. 254 n. 3).

Apollonius (*ap.* Eusebius, *H.E.* 5.18.3-4), too, viewed John as a charismatic. The author of the Apocalypse raised a dead man by divine power (cf. Acts of John 19–24, 40, 46–47, 48–54, 62–80, 81–83; Latin XVI, XVII).

According to Irenaeus John was among the apostles who instructed Polycarp and the elders (see above; 3.3-4; *ap.* Eusebius, *H.E.* 5.24.16). His emphasis was on apostolic tradition.

(5) John claimed to have been a μάρτυς (Rev. 1.2) who had seen Christ (1.12-18; 19.11-16; 21.16, 20) and received 'a revelation of Jesus Christ' (1.1). Thus he could write the words of Jesus (1.5, 8, 19; 2.8, 12, 18; 3.1, 7, 20; 16.15). The μάρτυς in persecution proclaims the truth (11.7; 12.11). M. Dibelius perceived that readers of the Apocalypse 'may have confused these [heavenly] revelations with his experiences of long ago, and have held his part in the life of Jesus as greater than it was'.[23]

Eusebius (*H.E.* 3.39.5) was certain that the elder John was distinguished by Papias (3.39.4) from the John who was listed among seven members of the twelve. The elder John and Aristion were not disciples of Jesus in the same sense as were members of the Twelve. They were disciples in a broader sense than the Twelve, but in a narrower sense than the Asian elders; they were closer to Jesus than the elders were; hence they were singled out as authoritative. They belonged to the large group of disciples who followed Jesus during his ministry (e.g. Lk. 6.17; 7.11; 14.27; 19.37; Jn 6.66-67; 7.3; 8.30-31; 19.38-39) or at least in the very early Jerusalem church (Acts 6.1-2, 7; 9.1; cf. 1.15).[24] Papias (*ap.* Eusebius, *H.E.* 3.39.15) relates that Mark, the interpreter of Peter, 'neither heard the Lord, nor was he a follower of his'. Papias implied that the elder John was closer to the Lord than Mark was. The elder, representing 'a living and surviving voice', was among 'not those who recalled the commands of others, but those who delivered the commands given by the Lord'. Aristion was portrayed as one of the 72 disciples of Christ[25] and as the first bishop of Smyrna (*Apost. Const.*

23. *A Fresh Approach to the New Testament and Early Christian Literature* (New York: Charles Scribner's Sons, 1936), p. 108. P. Vielhauer ('Jesus und der Menschensohn', *ZTK* 60 [1963], pp. 171-72) believes Synoptic tradition confused words of Jesus and of prophets (cf. Mk 13.11).

24. J. Munck, 'Presbyters and Disciples of the Lord', *HTR* 52 (1959), pp. 239ff.; K.H. Rengstorf, 'μαθητής', *TDNT*, IV, pp. 57-60.

25. The Roman Martyrology attributes this tradition to Papias (J. Drummond, *An Inquiry into the Character and Authorship of The Fourth Gospel* [London: Williams & Norgate, 1903], p. 198 n.).

7.46: Aristo).[26] To him were attributed the longer ending of Mark[27] (wherein all Resurrection appearances occur in Jerusalem) and the story of the miraculous drinking of poison by Justus Barsabbas.[28]

The allegedly superior discipleship and historical witness of Aristion and the elder John are not proven by Papias's record. Bacon observed:[29] 'This Elder John never comes forward with a single instance of personal attestation...to a fact of Jesus' career...' Even the most credible tradition attributable to the elder, on the origin of the Gospels of Mark and Matthew, need not have come from a first generation 'disciple'. Yet the credibility of the elder John and the scope of his traditions have been undermined by the appetite for the bizarre and the 'exceedingly small intelligence' of Papias (Eusebius, *H.E.* 3.39.13) and/or his travelling informants.

Irenaeus's description, *Ioannes Domini discipulus in Apocalypsi* (4.20.11; 4.30.4; 5.26.1; 5.35.2), reflects a later merger of Papias's elder-disciple and the Beloved Disciple. Similarly Polycrates (*ap.* Eusebius, *H.E.* 5.24.1) boasts of the John who 'leant back' on the Lord's 'breast', who was a μάρτυς and teacher, and 'has fallen asleep at Ephesus'. John's suffering on Patmos as a witness (Rev. 1.2, 9) made him a μάρτυς. He was aggrandized as the Beloved Disciple in order to be a source of local tradition and in response to the anti-Johannine Alogi.[30] Nevertheless, the persecuted 'apostle' who saw Christ in visions was rightly remembered as an early believer.

(6) The author of Revelation was from Palestine. Bacon[31] pointed out that 'the whole geographical standpoint of "the prophet" is exclusively Palestinian'. Jerusalem is 'the city' (11.13; 14.20), 'the holy city' (11.2), 'the beloved city' (20.9) and 'the great city...where their Lord was crucified' (11.8). On its walls the names of the Twelve would be engraved (22.14). It is to be the center of the Kingdom (21.22-26),

26. F.X. Funk, *Patres Apostolici*, I (Tübingen: Mohr-Siebeck, 1901), p. 353 n.; B.H. Streeter, *The Four Gospels* (London: Macmillan, 1930), p. 446; E. Peterson, 'Aristione', *EC* i (1948), p. 1908.

27. J. Moffatt, *Introduction to the Literature of the New Testament* (New York: Charles Scribner's Sons, 1911), pp. 240-42; Streeter, *Four Gospels*, pp. 345-47.

28. Related by Papias (Eusebius, *H.E.* 3.39.9) and attributed to Aristion by a manuscript of Rufinus's *Historia eccles.*

29. 'The Elder', p. 131.

30. Gunther, 'Early Identifications', pp. 5-10, 13, 20-21.

31. *The Fourth Gospel in Research and Debate* (New Haven: Yale University Press, 1918), p. 180.

where the son of David (3.7; 5.5; 12.5; 19.15; 22.16) would be enthroned in a world theocracy. The Lamb will stand on Mt Zion with the elect (14.1-5) and lead a marriage feast (19.7, 9; cf. 3.20; 22.2, 14). 'The wilderness' into which the church fled (12.6, 14) was the wilderness of Judea.[32]

In opposing teachers who permitted the practices of immorality and eating of food sacrificed to idols (2.14-15, 20), John applied the decision of the Jerusalem Council (Acts 15.28-29) and laid no other burden on his readers (2.24).[33] He emphasized 'perfect works before God' (3.2; cf. 2.2, 5, 9, 19, 23, 26; 3.1, 8, 15).

The vocabulary and style of Revelation abound in Semitisms.[34] C. Torrey cogently noted:[35] 'According to well-established Jewish doctrine, composition in Hebrew or Aramaic was an absolutely essential feature of any work claiming inspiration'. E. Lohmeyer,[36] C.G. Ozanne[37] and G.J.M. Bartelink[38] have argued that John imitated the sacred Hebrew style. Torrey concluded that there were deliberate 'offences against Greek grammar'; he held the work to be a translation from an Aramaic text.[39] G.R. Driver[40] disagreed, but concurred on the relevance of both Aramaic and Hebrew 'in considering the background of the author's language'. G. Mussies[41] judges it 'highly probable that our phrase "Hebrew or Aramaic" suggests a problem which does not exist: both languages most likely influenced an author who was so well versed in Ezekiel *and* Daniel, and who lived in a period when both languages

32. J.J. Gunther, 'The Fate', *TZ* 29 (1973), pp. 87-88.

33. As noted by W. Ramsay, A. Harnack, M. Goguel, C.K. Barrett and F.F. Bruce.

34. E.B. Allo, *Saint Jean, l'Apocalypse* (Paris: Gabalda, 3rd edn, 1933), pp. clxiv-clxvii; M. Zerwick, *Biblical Greek* (Rome: Pontifical Biblical Institute, 1963), pp. 15, 40, 52, 65, 95, 149, 154.

35. *The Apocalypse of John* (New Haven: Yale University Press, 1958), p. 58.

36. *Die Offenbarung des Johannes* (HNT; Tübingen: Mohr–Siebeck, 2nd edn, 1953), pp. 198-99.

37. 'The Language of the Apocalypse', *TynBul* 16 (1965), p. 4.

38. *VC* 21 (1967), pp. 247-49.

39. *The Apocalypse*, pp. 13, 16, 27-58.

40. In his review of Torrey's book, *JTS* 11 (1960), pp. 387-89. 'The author was equally at home' in both languages.

41. *The Morphology of Koine Greek as Used in the Apocalypse of St John* (NovTSup, 27; Leiden: Brill, 1971), pp. 352-53; cf. p. 312.

were used by each other's side'. A. Lancelotti[42] supports Charles's hypothesis[43] that John was intimately acquainted with the Hebrew Old Testament text and, 'though no doubt he used the Aramaic of his day...he thought in Hebrew and translated its idioms literally into Greek'. L.P. Trudinger,[44] finding that John's Old Testament quotations and allusions are akin to midrashim, Aramaic Targum texts and a non-Masoretic textual tradition which is often close to the Qumran texts, concluded that the author of Revelation knew thoroughly the Palestinian synagogue tradition.

Papias's traditions are often of Palestinian derivation;[45] e.g. on the millennial wondrous growth of vines and grapes.[46] Papias's belief in John's special relation to the Twelve presupposes his contact with them outside of Asia; his discipleship or apostleship placed him closer than the other elders to the Holy Land. His Judean origin is implicit in his final trait:

(7) The author of Revelation had priestly interests, as evidenced by his many references to the temple, altars, priests and sacrificial Lamb.[47] Their spiritual heavenly nature makes it more likely that John's background was in sectarian (Zadokite?) than in official Judaism. Numerous parallels have been found in Revelation to the Scrolls of Qumran,[48] a seat of sectarian apocalypticism.[49] In Revelation John uses some of the

42. *Sintassi ebraica nel greco dell' Apocalisse. I. Uso delle forme verbali* (Assisi: Studia Theologica 'Porziuncula', 1964); 'L'Antico Testamento nell' Apocalisse', *RivB* 14 (1966), pp. 369-84.

43. *Revelation*, I, p. xliv.

44. 'Some Observations concerning the Text of the Old Testament in the Book of Revelation', *JTS* 17 (1966), pp. 82-88. John used the Hebrew Old Testament and Aramaic Targums ('*Ho Amēn* [Rev. III: 14], and the Case for a Semitic Original of the Apocalypse', *NovT* 14 [1972], pp. 277-79). On contacts with the Targums see M. McNamara, *Targum and Testament* (Shannon: Irish University Press, 1972), pp. 142, 144, 148, 155-56.

45. A. Schlatter, *Die Kirche Jerusalems vom Jahre 70–130* (Gütersloh: Bertelsmann, 1898), pp. 48-49, 53-57; B. Bacon, 'Date and Habitat of the Elders of Papias', *ZNW* 12 (1911), pp. 180-83, 186-87; *idem*, 'The Elder', pp. 129-30.

46. See n. 11 above.

47. A. Feuillet, *L'Apocalypse: État de la question* (Paris: Desclée de Brouwer, 1963), p. 72; J.J. Gunther, *St Paul's Opponents and their Background* (Leiden: Brill, 1973), p. 157; J. Ford, *Revelation* (AB, 38; Garden City, NY: Doubleday, 1975), p. 34 ('...intimate knowledge of the liturgy and the temple; its author was probably a priest').

48. H. Braun, 'Qumran und das neue Testament...', *TRu* 30 (1964), pp. 118-36.

49. Gunther, *St Paul's Opponents*, pp. 49-51.

language of Paul's Christianized Essene opponents.[50] In such circles favouring apocalyptic priestly purity, abstinence was expected from a prophet.[51] Our John was a virgin (Rev. 14.3-5; 19.14; Acts of John 63, 107, 113).[52] He presented his prophetic teaching in priestly terms. As Christ made the church a kingdom of priests to God (Rev. 1.6; 5.10; 20.6; cf. Exod. 19.6) who are led by prophets (11.18; 16.6; 18.20, 24), John as *the* prophet (–elder) could readily view himself as a sort of high priest. John included himself among the priests (1.4-6; 5.10-11) and he mediated the revelations to his addressees. The prayers of the saints were offered by elders in gold bowls (5.8) and by angels (standing before God) on the gold altar (8.3-4). Elders (4.4) and an angel (14.14-15) wore gold crowns. The Spirit wrote to the angelic mediator-guardian (the leading elder or bishop)[53] in each church about the need to turn from their sins (2.4-5, 14-16, 20-22; 3.1-3; 15.19). Thus John potentially filled an angelic and high-priestly role of approaching God as mediator of prayer on behalf of his penitent people.

Bishop Polycrates (*ap.* Eusebius, *H.E.* 5.24.3) boasted that John 'was a priest, wearing the sacerdotal plate'. That is, his descent and/or function was priestly. The ceremonially pure high priest made atonement and sprinkled sin offerings on the mercy seat for the people so that through their mediating representative they might be holy to the Lord (Exod. 29.36). The high priest wore the gold πέταλον so that the people's offerings would be acceptable to the Lord (29.38). Wearing the

---

50. Gunther, *St Paul's Opponents*, pp. 116-17, 157, 184-85, 229-30, 263, 280. But John's teaching was less Judaizing and more Christocentric.

51. Gunther, *St Paul's Opponents*, pp. 118-19, 122-25, 127, 272, 274, 276, 281, 297.

52. Gunther, *St Paul's Opponents*, pp. 116-17; Müller, *Theologiegeschichte*, pp. 21, 36.

53. J. Colson, *L'évêque dans les communautés primitives* (Paris: Cerf, 1951), pp. 81-86; A. Erhardt, *The Apostolic Succession* (London: Lutterworth, 1953), pp. 79, 107 ('because the Jewish High Priest was regarded as the angel of God'); W.H. Brownlee, 'The Priestly Character of the Church in the Apocalypse', *NTS* 5 (1958–59), pp. 224-25 ('priestly role of bishops'); A. Kragerud, *Der Lieblingsjünger im Johannesevangelium* (Oslo: Universitatverlag, 1959), p. 100 n. 4 (bibliogr.). As representative of the church for which he is responsible, each is held fast by the Son (1.16) and receives a letter. Elders (19.4-5), like angels or stars (1.16, 20), praise God (Ps. 148.2-3). John established the Asian monarchial episcopate (Tertullian, *Adv. Marc.* 4.5; Clement, *Quis Div Salv.* 42; Manley, *Dissertation*, pp. 26-34), which was of Palestinian origin.

πέταλον was a sign of high priesthood which John shared with James the Lord's brother (Hegesippus *ap.* Epiphanius, *Haer.* 29.4; 78.13-14),[54] who was also a virgin (78.13). James 'asked forgiveness for the people' in the Holy of Holies (Hegesippus *ap.* Eusebius, *H.E.* 2.23.4-6). He was surrounded by elders (Acts 21.18). The high priest, acting as president of the sanhedrin, had his seat of honour (*Kethidra*, Hebr.); cf. Mt. 23.2. Bishop James of Jerusalem had his also (Eusebius, *H.E.* 7.19), as do the elders in Rev. 4.4; 11.16. James taught *ex cathedra* 'on Moses' seat', so to speak, at the Jerusalem Council (Acts 15.19). Did John play a similar, though more prophetic, role as mediator in the leadership of the exiled Jerusalem believers and/or in Asia? He acted as a proto-archbishop toward its seven churches (Rev. 2–3). Patterning Ephesus after Jerusalem (i.e. James and the Jewish high priest), did he make the πέταλον and throne part of his regalia as *the* Ephesian elder? Hippolytus, who called John 'Ephesian High Priest',[55] wrote that the succession of the apostles participates in the high priesthood and offices of teaching and guarding church doctrine (*Philos.* I, proem. 6).[56] According to the *Didache*, some members may be holy and their sacrifices (prayers) pure, their transgressions were repented of and confessed in the church (4.14; 10.6; 14.1-3; cf. 15.4) before the Eucharist, at which prophets, 'who are your *high priests*' (13.3), gave thanks (10.7), speaking in the Spirit (11.7) (see above). Prophets became rivals to local church leaders when they settled down (13.1-4; 15.1-2). From these analogies we may imagine that at the Eucharist the prophet John, who resided in his later years in Ephesus as the (first) elder-bishop and who received divine admonitions, would wear the golden πέταλον and offer intercessory prayer like the high priest for the sins of his people, who were to become a holy priesthood (1.6; 5.8-10; 8.3-4; 11.18; 16.6; 18.24; 20.6).

John of Patmos was probably a successor to John the Galilean fisherman in personality and millenarian, apocalyptic outlook. Their Palestinian school of prophecy may be called 'Johannine'. 'The author of Revelation is a volatile, imaginative man of great virility, quick to anger and terrible in condemnation.'[57] His eagerness for divine wrath to

54. Lawlor, *Eusebiana*, pp. 10-14, 99.

55. Fragmentary *Odes on all the Scriptures*; cited by Eisler, *The Enigma*, p. 55.

56. Tertullian (*De Bapt.* 17) called the bishop a high priest; cf. *Adv. Marc.* 4.23-24.

57. G. Schofield, *It Began on the Cross* (New York: Hawthorne, 1960), p. 138.

fall upon persecutors reveals the same mentality as that of the Sons of
wrath (or thunder) who in Samaria wished fire to come down from
heaven and consume those who would not receive the Lord (Lk. 9.54).
Their request to sit at the right and left of Jesus in glory (Mk 10.35-40)
is reminiscent of Revelation's kingly Word (19.11-16) and thirty-eight
mentions of thrones. The content of the preaching of John and James
must have been so offensive to Jewish religious sensitivities and to
Herod Agrippa that it led to martyrdom. The teaching most objection-
able to Romans and Jews alike concerned Jesus as returning military
Messiah, judge of the earthly Jerusalem and ruler over the descending
heavenly Jerusalem. Both Johns, then, may have been apprehended for
the same teaching.[58] Moreover, in light of the earthliness of some
Galilean political Messianic views (Jn 6.15), it is fair to presume that the
eschatological kingdom over which the sons of Zebedee wished to rule
was in some way earthly and millenarian.[59] Jesus' reference to rule over
the Gentiles (Mt. 20.25; Mk 10.42) presupposes that this was the expectation of James and John.

The Boanerges probably had the gift of prophecy. Some charismatic
power is apparent from the fact that the Holy Spirit was received by the
Samaritans through John's laying on of hands (Acts 8.14-18; cf. 19.6;
1 Cor. 12.1ff.): a curious counterpart to *his* power of calling down the
fire of judgment (Lk. 9.53; Rev. 11.5). Moreover, would the sons of
Zebedee have requested to sit next to Jesus in his kingdom if they
lacked spiritual gifts (Mt. 20.21; cf. 10.1; Mk 6.7; 10.37; Acts 3.1-11)?

The hypothesis[60] that Revelation 11 is based on the martyrdom of the

58. Christ is the military King of Kings (Rev. 1.5; 15.3; 17.14; 19.11-19).
Domitian banished John for preaching Christ's return to rule (22.3) over a new
earthly Jerusalem after the destruction of Rome (16.12–19.21). Were James and John
(Mk 13.3-4) primarily responsible for the formulation of the 'Little Apocalypse'
(13.6-8, 14-20, 24-27) ca. October 40 (vv. 14, 18), which prophesied unparalleled
tribulation, especially to childbearing Judeans, manifestations of heavenly power (cf.
Rev. 6.12-14) and the universal gathering of the elect at the Parousia?

59. Jewish teachings on eschatological abundance (see n. 11 above), prophecies
about Jerusalem and Zion (Ps. 2.6; Isa. 37.31-32; Mic. 4; Zech. 1.14; ch. 2; 8.2-3;
Joel 2.28-32; cf. Acts 2.16-21) and Ebionite belief in the physical Jerusalem millennium (Jerome, in Migne *PL* 24, pp. 150-56, 390, 609, 689, 917) suggest its acceptance among Palestinian Christians, especially those who later returned to Jerusalem
and built a church on Mt Zion (Epiphanius, *Mens. et Pond.* 14; *Haer.* 29.7).

60. Eisler, *The Enigma*, pp. 86-89; Bacon, *The Fourth Gospel*, pp. 177, 181;
idem, 'The Elder John in Jerusalem', *ZNW* 26 (1927), p. 189; A. Greve, '"Mine to

Christian prophets James and John (vv. 3, 10) is well-founded. Jerusalem is the holy city (11.2; cf. 21.2, 10; 22.19; Neh. 11.1, 11; Dan. 9.24; Mt. 4.5; 27.53), the great city (Rev. 11.8; cf. *Sib. Or.* 5.154, 226, 413)[61] of 70,000 inhabitants (11.13)[62] where the Lord was crucified (Rev. 11.8). It resembles Sodom (11.8; Isa. 1.9-10; Ezek. 16.46, 48) in being doomed from sin. Herod Agrippa's three and one-half year defiling, profaning reign (πατέω; cf. Dan. 8.13-14; 1 Macc. 3.51) over Jerusalem (11.2) and its church lasted from his appointment at the accession of Claudius in January 41 to ca. June 44.[63] During this period, dressed in sackcloth like Elijah (2 Kgs 1.8), the witnesses mourned the pending destruction of the city and called for repentance (cf. Jon. 3; Mt. 3.4-10; Lk. 19.41-44; 21.20-24). James and John, who had seen Elijah at the Transfiguration (Mk 9.2-4), had his power to prophesy woes. John and Peter were beaten and almost killed (Acts 5.33) after being forbidden to preach Christ (3.1ff.; 5.17-42) and to blame the Jews (especially Sadducees and high priests) for his death (3.15; 4.10; 5.28, 30), while calling for their repentance (3.19; 5.31), lest they be destroyed (3.23). The fire pouring out of the prophets' mouth and consuming their foes (Rev. 11.5) is reminiscent of the words of the sons of thunder: 'Lord, do you want *us* to bid fire come down from heaven and consume' the Samaritans? (Lk. 9.54). They were as zealously and exclusively loyal to Jesus (9.53-54; Mk 9.38) as Elijah[64] was to Yahweh. Hence they could be seen in the form of Elijah, who called down a consuming fire from heaven (2 Kgs 1.12). Their 'power to shut up the sky, that no rain may fall during the days of their prophesying', may be explained by the prophecy of drought which prompted the sending of relief to the Jerusalem church (Acts 11.27-29; cf. Mk 13.8; see n. 58), which in turn occasioned the persecution in AD 44.[65] Herod (the beast opposing God and vested with imperial authority) killed James and was killed (11.5). A

vidner": Et forsog pa at identificere de to jerusalemitiske vidner (Apok. 11, 3-13)', *DTT.* 40 (1977), pp. 128-38. First suggested by E. Hirsch.

61. Ford, *Revelation*, p. 180.

62. J. Wilkinson, 'Ancient Jerusalem: Its Water Supply and Population', *PEQ* 106 (1974), pp. 33-51.

63. J.J. Gunther, *Paul: Messenger and Exile—A Study in the Chronology of his Life and Letters* (Valley Forge, PA: Judson, 1972), p. 36.

64. Elijah and Enoch do not appear elsewhere in Revelation. Their martyrdom is not known in pre-Christian Jewish tradition (R. Bauckham, 'The Martyrdom of Enoch and Elijah: Jewish or Christian?', *JBL* 95 [1976], pp. 447-58).

65. Gunther, *Paul*, pp. 40-43.

case has been made[66] for the inclusion of Ἰωάννην καί from the original text of Acts 12.2. 'James and John the brother of James' appears in Mk 5.37 (cf. 3.17). Why would Agrippa, in ill-treating some Jerusalem believers, leave John unharmed while seizing his brother and Peter? John had gained pre-eminence over James (Acts 3.1-11; 4.13ff.; 8.14; Gal. 2.9). The 'men from the peoples and tribes and tongues and nations (who) gaze at their dead bodies and refuse to let them be placed in a tomb...and rejoice over them and make merry' (Rev. 11.9) are the Jews who were pleased (ἀρεστός) at James's death during the days of unleavened bread (Acts 12.3), when the Dispersion gathered in the holy city (Rev. 11.9-10, 13; cf. Acts 21.7). Earlier an enraged mob had stoned the visionary Stephen when he denounced the murderers of the Son of Man, who was seen as standing ready to return (7.52, 55-56). Agrippa was smitten by an angel for not giving glory to God (Acts 12.23), but those remaining alive in the city 'gave glory to the Lord of heaven' (Rev. 11.13). The resurrection and ascent of the two martyrs (11.11-12), like Elijah (2 Kgs 2.9-12), may have found corrupt expression in the ending of the Acts of John ('we went forth and found not his body, for it was translated by the power of our Lord Jesus Christ').

The visionary John deemed these two martyrs who prophesy (Rev. 11.3, 10) and witness to Christ (11.7) as his personal ideal or model. As exemplary Christian witnesses who 'stood up' they were vindicated in terms of Ezekiel's (37.5, 10) vision of the resurrection of the righteous Israel of God, whom they represent;[67] that is, 'the prophets and the saints' who will be rewarded in the Kingdom (Rev. 11.15-18; cf. Dan. 7.27). John had been deeply moved when he beheld in Jerusalem the scene of rejoicing over 'their dead bodies', and he expected his readers to know their identity from their importance and from his traditions about John's death, which Papias (*ap.* Philip of

---

66. Eisler, *The Enigma*, pp. 73-77; cf. H.L. Jackson, *The Problem of the Fourth Gospel* (Cambridge: Cambridge University Press, 1918), p. 143 n. 2; J. Colson, *L'énigme du disciple que Jésus aimait* (Paris: Beauchesne, 1969), p. 66. Our text probably is abbreviated since Codex D explains that ἡ ἐπιχείρησις αὐτοῦ ἐπὶ τοὺς πιστούς pleased the Jews; ἐπιχειρέω is a peculiarly Lukan word (Lk. 1.1; Acts 9.9; 19.13).

67. M. Black, 'The "Two Witnesses" of Rev. 11.3f. in Jewish and Christian Apocalyptic Tradition', in *Donum Gentilicum: New Testament Studies in Honour of David Daube* (ed. E. Bammel, C.K. Barrett and W.D. Davies; Oxford: Clarendon Press, 1978), p. 236.

Side and George Hamartolus) preserved.[68]

The Evangelists (Mk 10.39; cf. Mt. 20.23) recorded Jesus' prophecy of their baptism in blood partly because it had already been fulfilled. H.L. Jackson[69] commented: 'The figure of "the cup" has but one meaning on his lips (cf. Mk 14.36), and the recorded pregnant saying, Lk. 12.50 ("I have a baptism to be baptized with, etc.") points to their anticipated death'.

68. Jackson, *The Problem*, pp. 142-48; Charles, *Revelation*, I, pp. xlv-xlix; Eisler, *The Enigma*, pp. 60-72; N.P.V. Nunn, *The Authorship of the Fourth Gospel* (Eton: Alden & Blackwell, 1952), pp. 87-95.

69. *The Problem*, p. 142 n. 4. See E. Lipinski, 'L'apocalypse et le martyre de Jean à Jerusalem', *NovT* 11 (1969), p. 227. Supported by A. Réville, E. Schwartz, J. Wellhausen, J. Moffatt, B. Bacon, F.C. Burkitt, C.F. Burney, B.H. Streeter, R. Bultmann, M. Enslin *et al.*

JSNT 37 (1989), pp. 103-16

THE PROPHETIC CIRCLE OF JOHN OF PATMOS
AND THE EXEGESIS OF REVELATION 22.16

David E. Aune

David Hill has cautiously argued that the nine references to 'prophets' in Revelation (10.7; 11.10, 18; 16.6; 18.20, 24; 22.6, 9) refer primarily to Christian prophets who constituted a special group within the churches of the Roman province of Asia, though they did not hold formal offices or exercise institutional authority over other Christians.[1] Hill also suggested that John addressed his apocalypse directly to these community prophets (1.1; 22.16), whose task it was to mediate John's revelatory message to the seven churches.[2] He maintains, however, that John himself was not a typical Christian prophet, but rather a prophet who consciously stood in the Israelite-Jewish prophetic tradition. Since Christian prophets were subject to community authority and restricted themselves to oral prophesying, John did not compose his book in his capacity as a Christian prophet, but rather (on analogy with the ancient Israelite prophets) in direct response to the command of the risen Lord 'with authentic prophetic consciousness'.[3] My purpose in the present article is

1. David Hill, 'Prophecy and Prophets in the Revelation of St John', *NTS* 18 (1971–72), pp. 406-11.
2. Hill, 'Prophecy', p. 413.
3. Hill, 'Prophecy', pp. 415-16; *idem, New Testament Prophecy* (Atlanta: John Knox, 1979), p. 87. This is undoubtedly the weakest of Hill's three proposals. The view was first proposed in 1959 by Gerhard Friedrich (*TDNT*, VI, pp. 849-50), generally approved by Elizabeth Schüssler Fiorenza ('The Quest for the Johannine School: The Apocalypse and the Fourth Gospel', *NTS* 23 [1977], p. 425), and defended more recently in a particularly imaginative and vulnerable form by Wayne A. Grudem (*The Gift of Prophecy in 1 Corinthians* [Washington, DC: University Press of America, 1982], pp. 106-109). For a critique of this view, see M. Eugene Boring, 'The Apocalypse as Christian Prophecy', in *SBLSP* 13 (ed. George MacRae;

to focus on a close reading and exegesis of Rev. 22.16 in defence of what I take to be Hill's essentially correct understanding of that passage, an interpretation which has been disputed by a number of other scholars.[4]

I

Rev. 22.16 reads as follows: ἐγὼ Ἰησοῦς ἔπεμψα τὸν ἄγγελόν μου μαρτυρῆσαι ὑμῖν ἐπὶ ταῖς ἐκκλησίαις, 'I, Jesus, sent my angel to attest this message to you for the churches'. This statement, attributed to the exalted Jesus, is metatextual since the pronoun ταῦτα probably refers to the entire message of Revelation which has just been presented (1.4–22.5).[5] Along with 22.6 this verse has several similarities to 1.1 which (in the context of 1.1-3) is also a metatextual statement which explicitly introduces the book which follows, presented as a statement of the author to his audience.[6]

The central problem in interpreting Rev. 22.16 is that of determining the referents of the plural pronoun ὑμῖν (a dative of indirect object) and the plural noun ταῖς ἐκκλησίαις. The options are limited. Commentators usually understand ὑμεῖς to refer either to a group of Christian prophets (who mediate John's message to the seven churches),[7] or to the Christian members of the seven churches to whom

Cambridge, MA: Society of Biblical Literature, 1974), II, p. 56; David E. Aune, *Prophecy in Early Christianity and the Ancient Mediterranean World* (Grand Rapids: Eerdmans, 1983), pp. 205-208; Adela Yarbro Collins, *Crisis and Catharsis: The Power of the Apocalypse* (Philadelphia: Westminster Press, 1984), pp. 39-40.

4.   Most recently by Yarbro Collins, *Crisis*, pp. 34-46.

5.   While most commentators interpret ταῦτα in this way, some argue that it refers only to the immediate context, i.e., the promises and threats in 22.12-15; see Bernhard Weiss, *Die Johannes-Apokalypse: Textkritische Untersuchungen und Textherstellung* (TU, 7.1; Leipzig: J.C. Hinrichs, 1891), p. 112, and Martin Karrer, *Die Johannesoffenbarung als Brief* (Göttingen: Vandenhoeck & Ruprecht, 1986), p. 224 n. 14.

6.   A helpful analysis of the literary framework of Revelation is that proposed by Lars Hartman, 'Form and Message: A Preliminary Discussion of "Partial Texts" in Rev. 1–3 and 22.6ff.', in J. Lambrecht (ed.), *L'Apocalypse johannique et l'Apocalyptique dans le Nouveau Testament* (BETL, 53; Leuven: Leuven University Press; Gembloux: J. Duculot, 1980), pp. 129-49; cf. David Hellholm, 'The Problem of Apocalyptic Genre and the Apocalypse of John', in *SBLSP* 21 (ed. K.H. Richards; Chico, CA: Scholars Press, 1982), pp. 157-98.

7.   Wilhelm Bousset, *Die Offenbarung Johannis* (Göttingen: Vandenhoeck &

John addressed his book (1.4).[8] With a few exceptions, most scholars simply choose one of these two views without providing supportive arguments.[9] These are not the only possible views, however, and we will introduce other possibilities below.

The exegesis of the phrase μαρτυρῆσαι ὑμῖν ταῦτα ἐπὶ ταῖς ἐκκλησίαις must begin with the recognition that in Greek it is only a remote linguistic possibility that the plural dative pronoun ὑμῖν and noun ταῖς ἐκκλησίαις can refer to the same entity. While the author of Revelation was not a native speaker of Greek and consequently his composition exhibits numerous syntactical irregularities,[10] the

Ruprecht, 6th edn, 1906), p. 459; Isbon T. Beckwith, *The Apocalypse of John* (New York: Macmillan, 1919), p. 777; R.H. Charles, *A Critical and Exegetical Commentary on the Revelation of St John* (ICC; Edinburgh: T. & T. Clark, 1920), II, p. 219 (a secondary possibility); Martin Kiddle, *The Revelation of St John* (London: Hodder & Stoughton), p. 454; Ernst Lohmeyer, *Die Offenbarung des Johannes* (Tübingen: J.C.B. Mohr [Paul Siebeck], 3rd edn, 1970), p. 180; Schüssler Fiorenza, 'The Quest for the Johannine School', p. 425; Ugo Vanni, *La Struttura Letteraria dell'- Apocalisse* (Brescia: Morcelliana, 2nd edn, 1980), p. 80; Elisabeth Schüssler Fiorenza, 'Apocalypsis and Propheteia: The Book of Revelation in the Context of Early Christian Prophecy', in Lambrecht (ed.), *L'Apocalypse johannique*, pp. 120-21; Müller, *Offenbarung*, p. 370; David E. Aune, 'The Social Matrix of the Apocalypse of John', *BR* 26 (1981), p. 19; Ulrich B. Müller, 'Literarische und formgeschichtliche Bestimmung der Apokalypse des Johannes als einem Zeugnis frühchristlicher Apokalyptik', in *Apocalypticism in the Mediterranean World and the Near East* (ed. David Hellholm; Tübingen: J.C.B. Mohr [Paul Siebeck], 1983), p. 616.

8.   Henry Barclay Swete, *The Apocalypse of St John* (repr. Grand Rapids: Eerdmans, n.d.), p. 309; Charles, *Revelation*, II, p. 219: Akira Satake, *Die Gemeindeordnung in der Johannesapokalypse* (Neukirchen–Vluyn: Neukirchener Verlag, 1966), p. 25; Eduard Lohse, *Die Offenbarung des Johannes* (Göttingen: Vandenhoeck & Ruprecht, 1976), p. 113; Robert H. Mounce, *The Book of Revelation* (NICNT; Grand Rapids: Eerdmans, 1977), p. 394; J.P.M. Sweet, *Revelation* (Philadelphia: Westminster Press, 1979), pp. 315, 317; G.R. Beasley-Murray, *The Book of Revelation* (Grand Rapids: Eerdmans, 1981), p. 342; Jürgen Roloff, *Die Offenbarung des Johannes* (Zürich: Theologischer Verlag, 1984), p. 212. Pierre Prigent (*L'Apocalypse de Saint Jean* [Lausanne and Paris: Delachaux & Niestlé, 1981], p. 357) argues that the ὑμεῖς in 22.16 is modelled after 22.6 and represents a secondary addition which accompanied the inclusion of the proclamations to the seven churches, and therefore it refers to the churches.

9.   Three exceptions are Beasley-Murray, *Revelation*, p. 342, Vanni, *La Struttura*, p. 180, and Yarbro Collins, *Crisis*, p. 39.

10.   On this problem, see T. Cowden Laughlin, *The Solecisms of the Apocalypse* (Princeton: C.S. Robinson, 1902), and G. Mussies, *The Morphology of Koine Greek*

phraseology of Rev. 22.16 is unusual but clearly within the boundaries of conventional Greek usage. The presence of the preposition ἐπί indicates that the substantive ταῖς ἐκκλησίαις is more remote from the action described by the infinitive μαρτυρῆσαι than is the pronoun ὑμεῖς. This means that the view that ὑμεῖς and αἱ ἐκκλησίαι *both* refer to Christians in general is *a priori* untenable.[11] Since αἱ ἐκκλησίαι very probably refers to the seven Christian communities in the Roman province of Asia, ὑμεῖς must refer to a *different* group.

The problematic character of the phrase ἐπι ταῖς ἐκκλησίαις centers on the relatively uncommon use of the preposition ἐπί. There are several ways in which ἐπί with the dative can be construed. (1) ἐπί with the dative can function as a marker of persons *benefited* by an event, that is, the *dativus commodi*. μαρτυρῆσαι ὑμῖν ταῦτα ἐπὶ ταῖς ἐκκλησίαις can therefore be translated 'to testify *for* [the benefit of] the churches',[12] or even 'on account of', or 'for the sake of the churches'.[13] This is the preferable way of understanding ἐπί, one which assumes that the referent of ὑμεῖς mediates revelation to the referent of αἱ ἐκκλησίαι. (2) ἐπί can also function as 'a marker of the experiences, often with the implication of an action by a superior force or agency'.[14] Though this way of construing the significance of ἐπί is less probable, the problematic phrase could then be translated 'to testify *to* the churches'. (3) Several scholars have argued that ἐπί with the genitive can mean 'about, concerning', citing Jn 12.16 in addition to Rev. 10.11 and 22.16.[15] According to Yarbro Collins, 'The testimony is

as Used in the Apocalypse of John: A Study in Bilingualism* (NovTSup, 27; Leiden: Brill, 1971).

11. Most of the commentators cited above in note 7 (with the exception of Swete) hold that both ὑμῖν and ταῖς ἐκκλησίαις refer to Christians in the seven churches.

12. Johannes P. Louw and Eugene A. Nida (eds.), *Greek–English Lexicon of the New Testament Based on Semantic Domains* (2 vols.; New York: United Bible Societies, 1988), I, §90.40.

13. Moses Stuart, *Commentary on the Apocalypse* (2 vols.; Andover: Allen, Morrill & Wardwell, 1845), II, p. 393; Paul S. Minear, *I Saw a New Earth: An Introduction to the Visions of the Apocalypse* (Washington and Cleveland: Corpus Books, 1968), p. 364, provides this translation of Rev. 22.16a: 'It is I, Jesus, who sent my angel to confirm these things to you, for the sake of the congregation'.

14. Louw-Nida, *Greek–English Lexicon*, I, §90.57.

15. Charles, *Revelation*, I, p. cxxxiii; ἐπί in Rev. 22.16 is translated as 'au sujet de' by Allo (*L'Apocalypse*, pp. 359-60) and Prigent (*L'Apocalypse*, p. 357), both of whom refer to the parallel use of ἐπί in 10.11. Walter Bauer, *Wörterbuch zum Neuen*

thus not given to others "for" the congregations, but to them, and is "about" them'.[16] The chief difficulty with this view is that the message of Revelation (with the exception of Rev. 2–3) is not primarily *about* the churches, though it is clearly *for* them.[17] Though ἐπί in Rev. 10.11 is often referred to as a parallel usage,[18] that assumption is problematic. Rev. 10.11 reads: 'It is necessary that you prophesy again to many peoples [ἐπὶ λαοῖς...πολλοῖς] and nations and tongues and kings'. Since the content of Revelation from that point on fits that injunction, in this context ἐπί can reasonably be construed to mean 'about, concerning, on the subject of'.[19] This is an unusual meaning of ἐπί with the dative, however, which would normally be expressed with ἐπί and the genitive.[20] Since John's message to the nations is primarily one of *judgment*, however, the use of ἐπί with the dative in 10.11 is best construed in the sense of 'to prophesy *against* the people' (i.e., ἐπί with the *dativus incommodi*).[21]

The difficulty of understanding how to construe ἐπί with the dative in Rev. 22.16 is reflected in the variant readings for ἐπί. The original reading was certainly ἐπί,[22] which is the *lectio difficilior* because of the

Testament (ed. K. and B. Aland; Berlin and New York: de Gruyter, 6th edn, 1988), col. 582 (II.1.b.δ); this meaning of ἐπί, however, is both rare and problematic. Of the six texts cited by Bauer–Aland as examples of this usage, both Rev. 22.16 and Heb. 11.4 do not fit the gloss. On the latter passage, see Harold W. Attridge, *The Epistle to the Hebrews* (Hermeneia; Philadelphia: Fortress Press, 1989), pp. 316-17; ἐπί τοῖς δώροις probably means 'upon the gifts', or 'over the gifts', perhaps referring to a legendary fire sent to consume the offering.

16. Yarbro Collins, *Crisis*, p. 39; cf. Satake, *Gemeindeordnung*, p. 24, who then translated 22.16a: 'Ich, Johannes [sic!], sandte euch meinen Engel, um dieses zu bezeugen, nämlich über die Gemeinden (über das Schicksal der Gemeinden)'.

17. Satake (*Gemeindeordnung*, p. 24) anticipates this objection and argues that the author is less interested in the entire Cosmos than he is in the fate of Christians, and therefore he directs his book to them.

18. Bousset, *Offenbarung*, p. 166; Allo, *L'Apocalypse*, p. 360; Prigent, *L'Apocalypse*, p. 357 n. 19; Kraft, *Offenbarung*, p. 281; Bauer–Aland, *Wörterbuch*, col. 582 (II.1.b.δ).

19. Bauer–Aland, *Wörterbuch*, col. 582 (II.1.b.δ).

20. Bauer–Aland, *Wörterbuch*, col. 580 (I.1.b.γ).

21. Louw–Nida, *Greek–English Lexicon*, I, §90.34: ἐπί + dative or accusative can function as 'a marker of opposition in a judicial or quasi-judicial context' meaning 'against', i.e., with the *dativus incommodi*.

22. Josef Schmid, *Studien zur Geschichte des griechischen Apokalypse-Textes* (Munich: Karl Zink, 1955), II, p. 134.

relatively unusual meaning of the preposition in this context.[23] The easiest scribal correction was the simple omission of the problematic ἐπί, a textual alteration found in the influential *Commentary on the Apocalypse* by Andreas of Caesarea (written ca. AD 600).[24] This omission was probably motivated by a desire to read ταῖς ἐκκλησίαις in apposition to ὑμῖν, 'to you, that is, to the churches'. This scribal alteration suggests the difficulty which native speakers had in understanding ὑμῖν and ἐπὶ ταῖς ἐκκλησίαις as referring to the same group.

Another widespread correction, which has found some modern scholarly support, was the substitution of ἐν for ἐπί.[25] This substitution was a correction which could mean 'I, Jesus, have sent my angel to you in the churches', that is, it stresses the fact that individual Christians are members of the seven Christian communities.[26] The view that it could mean '*before* the churches', that is, 'in the community gatherings',[27] involving the oral reading of Revelation before the assembled Christian communities by lectors, is problematic since the term ἐκκλησία does not have that meaning elsewhere in Revelation.[28]

While the occurrence of ὑμεῖς in 22.16 is unexpected, second-person

23. ℵ 1611 1854 2050 2053-2062 (a small but very important group of witnesses); *Andreas family f*2023; *Byzantine*; the reading is accepted by most modern editions.

24. 051 209 598 *Andreas*; cf. Josef Schmid, *Der Apokalypse-Kommentar des Andreas von Kaisareia*, Part I.1 of *Studien zur Geschichte des griechischen Apokalypse-Textes* (Munich: Karl Zink, 1955), p. 260; *Arethas*; *Primasius* (*vobis septem ecclesiis*); Heinrich J. Vogels, *Untersuchungen zur Geschichte der Lateinischen Apokalypse-Übersetzung* (Düsseldorf: L. Schwann, 1920), p. 164.

25. ἐν is supported by A (lacuna in C) 1006-1841 (these, with 911 which has a lacuna here, constitute an important family); 2329 *Andreas family f*2073 i l 94 (for a list of MSS comprising these families, see Schmid, *Studien*, I, 2, pp. 1-78; *gig* (*testari haec in ecclesiis*; Vogels, *Untersuchungen*, p. 175); *Tyconius*[2] (*testari vobis haec in ecclesiis*; Vogels, *Untersuchungen*, p. 190); *Beatus* (*testari vobis haec in ecclesiis*; Vogels, *Untersuchungen*, p. 208); *vulg* (*testificari vobis haec in ecclesiis*). This reading is accepted as original by B. Weiss, *Johannes-Apokalypse*, p. 244; Charles, *Revelation*, II, p. 382; Hadorn, *Offenbarung*, pp. 217-18 (it is also included as a marginal reading in Westcott and Hort).

26. Satake, *Gemeindeordnung*, p. 24.

27. Weiss, *Johannes-Apokalypse*, pp. 112, 224; Hadorn, *Offenbarung*, p. 218.

28. While ἐκκλησία can mean 'assembly' in the sense of a group of citizens gathered for social or political activities (cf. Acts 19.39; Louw–Nida, *Greek–English Lexicon*, I, §11.78), there are no instances in Revelation in which ἐκκλησία means 'Christian assembly'; cf. Karrer, *Johannesoffenbarung*, p. 244 n. 13.

plural pronouns (and verb forms) are used in direct address in two different contexts in Revelation, in the epistolary prescript (1.4) and in some of the proclamations to the seven churches (2.12-29). The closest apparent parallel to 22.16 is found in 1.4 in the epistolary prescript: 'John to the seven churches [ταῖς ἑπτὰ ἐκκλησίαις] which are in Asia, grace to you [ὑμῖν] and peace'.[29] Here, in contrast to 22.16, the plural dative noun ταῖς ἐκκλησίαις and pronoun ὑμῖν clearly refer to the same entity; ταῖς ἐκκλησίαις is a dative of indirect object, while ὑμῖν is a *dativus commodi*. Furthermore, this is the only place in Revelation where all seven Christian communities are collectively addressed with a plural pronoun. However, ὑμεῖς occurs here within a nominal clause which constitutes a stereotypical epistolary salutation of the kind typical of early Christian letters, particularly those attributed to Paul. The second context within which second-person plural pronouns are used in Revelation is in the proclamations to the seven churches in 2.12-29. Though the author uses the literary device of addressing each proclamation to an angel who functions as the *alter ego* of each community, he does not consistently maintain that fiction. He can refer to the *entire* community with second-person plural verbs (2.10) and pronouns (παρ' ὑμῖν; 2.13), or he can address a particular group within a community in a similar way (2.10, 14-15, 20-22, 24). None of these uses of ὑμεῖς can be regarded as a satisfactory parallel to the ὑμεῖς of Rev. 22.16.

II

Since it is virtually certain that ὑμεῖς and αἱ ἐκκλησίαι in Rev. 22.16 must be understood as referring to two *different* (though possibly overlapping) entities, we must evaluate the various proposals which have been made in the attempt to identify the two groups. H.B. Swete, aware that two groups are necessarily in view, distinguishes the ὑμεῖς, which he thinks refers to Christians in the seven communities addressed by John, from the αἱ ἐκκλησίαι immediately following, which refers to Christians everywhere, the church universal.[30] The term αἱ ἐκκλησίαι occurs thirteen times in Revelation (only in 1–3 and 22.16), seven times in the formula 'what the Spirit says to the churches' (2.7, 11, 17, 29; 3.6, 13, 22). In four of the remaining occurrences, the *seven* churches to

29. Vanni, *La Struttura Letteraria*, p. 180.
30. Swete, *Apocalypse*, p. 309.

whom the Revelation is addressed are specifically in view (1.4, 11, 20 [2x]); the two remaining occurrences are 2.23 and 22.16). In all these references with the possible exception of 22.16, it is either clear or probable that the seven churches are specifically in view. There is no evidence to suggest that αἱ ἐκκλησίαι as a collective term refers to any group other than the seven specific Christian communities to whom the book as a whole is addressed.

Since the phrase αἱ ἐκκλησίαι in Rev. 22.16 undoubtedly refers to the seven Christian communities of Roman Asia addressed by John, ὑμεῖς must refer to a *different* group. There are four possible options which have been suggested: (1) *potential martyrs*, that is, particularly faithful Christians who faced the possibility of dying for their faith, (2) *lectors* whose task it was to read Revelation to the congregations, (3) *envoys* whose task it was to deliver copies of Revelation to each of the seven churches, or (4) a group of John's *prophetic colleagues*.

1. G.B. Caird is alone, so far as I can determine, in proposing that the testimony is given only to those who are ready and willing to lay down their lives for their faith.[31] Though he does not support this opinion with evidence, it is true that particular rewards are promised to 'the one who conquers' (2.7, 11, 17, 26-27; 3.5, 12, 21; cf. 16.15), and martyrs are certainly accorded special status in the author's eschatological scenario (20.4-6). However, there is nothing to suggest that the ὑμεῖς of 22.16 should be identified with this elite group.

2. Theodor Zahn is one of the few who have suggested that ὑμεῖς refers to the *lectors* whose task it would be to read the book of Revelation to Christians at their assemblies.[32] This proposal has the advantage that 'the one who reads' and 'those who hear', referred to in Rev. 1.3, are two distinct entities. Since the author intended that Revelation be read in assemblies of all the seven churches by different lectors, they could conceivably be referred to as a group, that is, οἱ ἀναγινώσκοντες. Further, since several verbal and thematic links exist

31. G.B. Caird, *A Commentary on the Revelation of St John the Divine* (HNTC; New York: Harper & Row, 1966), p. 286.

32. Theodor Zahn, *Die Offenbarung des Johannes* (Leipzig and Erlangen: A. Deichert, 1st, 2nd, 3rd edn, 1924–26), II, pp. 626 n. 89, 628. This view was briefly articulated earlier by Weiss (*Johannes-Apokalypse*, pp. 112, 224) and also appears to be the view of Johannes Panagopoulos, 'Die urchristlich Prophetie: Ihre Charakter und ihre Funktion', in *Prophetic Vocation in the New Testament and Today* (ed. J. Panagopoulos; NovTSup, 45; Leiden: Brill, 1977), p. 22.

between 22.16 and 1.1-3, this view would tie them even closer together.

3. While no commentator to my knowledge has suggested that the ὑμεῖς of Rev. 22.16 could refer to the *envoys* responsible for carrying copies of Revelation to their destinations, that possibility deserves consideration. While there is no way of knowing whether or not John was still an exile when Revelation was completed, it is nevertheless likely that others were entrusted by him to deliver copies of the book to some if not all of the seven churches. Who these individuals were cannot be determined, and how they performed their task cannot be known, except by analogy. In the ancient world private letter carriers often played an active role in the delivery of a written message by accompanying it with an oral message.[33] Paul's letters reflect a network of Christian communities interconnected by frequent visits by Christians of various stations, travelling for secular as well as for religious reasons, among whom were messengers carrying letters from those unable to be physically present.[34] Tychicus is an example of a Christian who is presented as an envoy of Paul whose task it was to carry a letter to the Colossians and provide an oral report of Paul's personal situation (Col. 4.7).[35] Further, Tychicus is not presented as a subordinate, but as a 'beloved brother, faithful minister and fellow servant [σύνδουλος]' of Paul. Perhaps the closest analogy to the envoys of John who must have delivered copies of Revelation to their destinations is found in *Herm. Vis.* 2.4.3, where the Ancient Lady tells Hermas what to do with the revelation she has given him:

> You shall therefore write two little books and send one to Clement and one to Grapte. Clement shall then send it to the cities abroad for that is his duty; and Grapte shall exhort the widows and orphans; but in this city you shall read it yourself with the elders who are in charge of the church.

---

33. John L. White, *Light from Ancient Letters* (Philadelphia: Fortress Press, 1986), p. 216. White translates the closing lines of a letter written in 257 BC: 'The rest (i.e., anything else that remains) learn from the one who carries the letter to you. For he is no stranger to us.'

34. Wayne A. Meeks, *The First Urban Christians: The Social World of the Apostle Paul* (New Haven: Yale University Press, 1983), pp. 109-10.

35. E.A. Judge, 'The Early Christians as a Scholastic Community', *JRH* 1 (1960–61), pp. 134-35. Though Colossians is probably pseudonymous (cf. Mark Kiley, *Colossians as Pseudepigraphy* [Biblical Seminar, 4; Sheffield: JSOT Press, 1986]), that would have had little or no effect on the presentation of typical social customs and roles.

Those whom Hermas is instructed to send out with copies of his book are envoys and lectors, though not prophets. Another close parallel from Graeco-Roman paganism, from second-century AD Anatolia, involves envoys who are prophets. Lucian reports that the oracular prophets Alexander of Abonuteichos sent χρησμολόγοι (roughly 'collectors and interpreters of oracles') to cities throughout the Roman empire with predictions of plagues, fires and earthquakes (*Alex.* 36). Understanding the ὑμεῖς of Rev. 22.16a as envoys coheres well with the way in which that passage should be translated: 'I, Jesus, sent my angel to attest this message to you for the churches'.

4. The widespread view that the ὑμεῖς of Rev. 22.16a refers to a group of prophets associated with John,[36] is usually based on two inferences: (a) Rev. 22.9 indicates that John is one of several Christian prophets, and (b) the term 'servants' in Rev. 22.6, like the phrase 'servants of God' elsewhere in Revelation, refers to Christian prophets.

a. In Rev. 22.9, the angelic revealer claims that 'I am [εἰμι] a fellow servant [σύνδουλος] of you and your brothers the prophets and those who obey the contents of this book'. By including this statement, John clearly implies that he is a prophet, a self-conception corroborated by his characterization of the book he is writing as a 'prophecy' (1.3) and a 'prophetic book' (22.7, 10, 18, 19). While it is clear that a plurality of prophets is in view in Rev. 22.9, the problem is whether this refers to (a) John and ancient Israelite prophets, (b) John, other contemporary Christian prophets and ancient Israelite prophets, or (c) John and other contemporary Christian prophets. While some scholars think that all nine references to prophets in Revelation refer to Christian prophets,[37] others argue that these references (with the exception of 11.10) can be understood as referring exclusively to ancient Israelite prophets.[38] It is important to note that the phrase 'your brothers the prophets' is coordinated with 'those who obey [τῶν τηρούντων, a present substantival participle] the words of this book'. Since the latter group is one contemporaneous with John, the likelihood that the former phrase also describes contemporaries is increased. This interpretation is confirmed by Rev. 19.10, which not only contains verbal parallels to 22.9, but which also is one of two structurally similar conclusions of a pair of

36. See note 7 above.
37. A.T. Nikolainen, 'Über die theologische Eigenart der Offenbarung des Johannes', *TLZ* 93 (1968), pp. 161-70.
38. Yarbro Collins, *Crisis*, p. 44.

angelic disclosures (17.1–19.19; 21.9–22.9).[39] Rev. 22.9 therefore has an important parallel in 19.10;

> Then I fell down at his feet to worship him, but he said to me, You must not do that! I am a fellow servant [σύνδουλος] with you and your brothers who hold the testimony [τὴν μαρτυρίαν] of Jesus. Worship God. For the testimony [ἡ μαρτυρία] of Jesus is the spirit of prophecy.

Here a single group contemporaneous with John is mentioned, 'your brothers who hold the testimony of Jesus'. Their prophetic function is suggested by the gloss with which the verse concludes, which identifies ἡ μαρτυρία Ἰησοῦ (a subjective genitive) with τὸ πνεῦμα τῆς προφητείας. The conclusion is inescapable that the glossator is trying to make it abundantly clear that the 'brothers who hold the testimony of Jesus' are *prophets*. This strengthens the case that the prophets mentioned in 22.9 are Christian prophets contemporaneous with John, and further that they are the most likely group referred to by the ambiguous ὑμεῖς of 22.16.

b. If 'servants' (δοῦλοι) in 22.6 is intended to refer to 'prophets', that would provide further evidence for a prophetic community associated with John in Asia:

> And the Lord, the God of the spirits of the prophets [τῶν πνευμάτων τῶν προφητῶν], has sent his angel to show [δεῖξαι] his servants [τοῖς δούλοις] what must soon take place.

This statement has close verbal parallels with both 22.16 and 1.1, and in all likelihood belongs to the final redaction of Revelation. The term 'servants' is used in several ways in Revelation: (1) literally of 'slaves' (6.15 [sing.]; 13.16; 19.18), (2) figuratively of Christians generally (2.20; 7.3; 19.5; 22.3); (3) figuratively in the phrase '[God's] servants the prophets' of prophets (10.7; 11.18);[40] (4) figuratively of John himself (1.1), (5) figuratively of Moses (15.3). The ambiguous passages (1.1; 22.6) could thus refer to Christians generally (2), or to prophets (3) and (4). The use of the verb δεικνύναι narrows the choice somewhat, for it is used six times of visionary revelations to John (4.1; 17.1; 21.9, 10;

---

39. Charles H. Giblin, 'Structural and Thematic Correlations in the Theology of Revelation 16–22', *Bib* 55 (1974), pp. 487-504; cf. Vanni, *La Struttura Letteraria*, pp. 283-86.

40. In Rev. 11.18, the phrase τοῖς δούλοις σου τοῖς προφήταις refers to *one* group rather than two, since lists of groups of people found in Revelation are polysyndetic, with καί consistently used to link each individual group.

22.1, 8), and twice with the ambiguous term δούλοις used as an indirect object (1.1; 22.6). If the term 'servants' in 22.6 and 1.1 refers to prophetic associates of John, then it is clear that Revelation has been entrusted by John to prophetic colleagues and envoys for distribution and presentation to the seven churches. This understanding has the advantage of providing a reason why John prefaced an apocalypse framed as a letter with a prologue in 1.1-3. The prologue functions to legitimate the fact that the revelation which John has received and written is in possession of prophetic envoys charged with its dissemination.

III

References to prophets and prophecy in Revelation are both maddeningly general and intriguingly ambiguous. Only one prophet, 'Jezebel', is specifically mentioned, though with a pejorative codename (2.20). She has followers (2.22-23), but they are not styled prophets, though the original Jezebel did maintain a stable of 450 prophets of Baal and 400 prophets of Asherah (1 Kgs 18.19). The Two Witnesses of Revelation 11 are presented as Christian prophets (11.3, 10), and regardless of their symbolic significance, suggest that John's conception of the prophetic role was modelled after Old Testament prototypes. Prophetic guilds led by master prophets are religious phenomena found in ancient Israel and early Christianity. There is considerable evidence in the Old Testament for the existence of prophetic schools (called 'sons of the prophets'), which sometimes practised group prophecy and were led by master prophets given the title 'father'.[41] Elisha led one such school (1 Kgs 20.35; 2 Kgs 2.3, 5, 7, 15; 4.1-38). Even classical prophets such as Isaiah had disciples (Isa. 8.16-18), who were probably responsible for writing down, collecting and editing of their oracles into the complex and layered books which bear their names.

Groups of prophets also functioned in early Christianity, though the evidence is scanty and problematic. Migaku Sato has recently argued that the sayings source Q arose in just such a prophetic community.[42] 1 Cor. 14.29-33 suggests that a group of prophets functioned in a special way in the Corinthian church. The odist responsible for the *Odes of Solomon* seems to represent a group of inspired singers, perhaps as their

41. Aune, *Prophecy in Early Christianity*, p. 83.
42. Migaku Sato, *Q und Prophetie: Studien zur Gattungs- und Traditionsgeschichte der Quelle Q* (WUNT, 29; Tübingen: J.C.B. Mohr [Paul Siebeck], 1988).

leader, who constituted a distinct group within the community (cf. *Odes* 7.16b-20).[43] A similar prophetic school may lie behind the pseudony-mous *Ascension of Isaiah* (cf. ch. 6), a Jewish work with an extensive Christian addition completed in the second century AD. While little is known of any of these Christian prophetic groups, they do provide a model for understanding the prophetic circle of John of Patmos.

IV

In this article I have argued for the following positions: (1) From a syn-tactical standpoint it is highly unlikely that both ὑμῖν and ταῖς ἐκκλησίαις in Rev. 22.16 refer to the same group or entity. (2) Since αἱ ἐκκλησίαι in all probability refers to the seven Christian congrega-tions addressed by John, the ὑμεῖς necessarily refers to a *different*, though perhaps overlapping, group or entity. (3) Of the groups which have some claim to be identified with the ὑμεῖς of Rev. 22.16 (envoys, lectors and prophets), the prophets referred to in 22.9 have the strongest claim, though it is likely that they also served both as envoys and lectors in the distribution and presentation of Revelation to the seven churches. (4) The existence of such a prophetic circle is made more probable by hints of analogous prophetic groups in Judaism and early Christianity.

43. David E. Aune, 'The Odes of Solomon and Early Christian Prophecy', *NTS* 28 (1982), pp. 448-49.

JSNT 25 (1985), pp. 105-24

REVELATION 4–5 IN THE LIGHT
OF JEWISH APOCALYPTIC ANALOGIES

L.W. Hurtado

In an essay on 'The Visions of God in Apocalyptic Literature', Christopher Rowland makes two assertions that provide us with handy theses to test in this paper:[1] (a) the vision in Revelation 4 'shows no evidence whatsoever of Christian influence';[2] and (b) Revelation 4 is 'incidental to the overriding purpose of the work as a whole'.[3] Nearly all scholars recognize that the most transparent evidence of Christian theology in the vision of God in Revelation 4–5 is in ch. 5, with the appearance of the Lamb and the worship directed 'to him who sits on the throne and to the Lamb' (5.13); and implicit in Rowland's understanding of Revelation 4 is the notion that *only* in Revelation 5 do the writer's Christian experience and theology come to expression. The concern in this paper will be to determine whether this notion is correct, or whether, on the contrary, the writer's Christian point of view influences the whole of Revelation 4–5. Rowland's conviction that there is nothing of any theological distinction in Revelation 4 seems to be the basis for his view that this passage is incidental to the rest of the book. Therefore, if it can be shown with some plausibility that Revelation 4, like Revelation 5, is shaped by the author's Christian convictions, this will provide a basis for re-evaluating the importance of the heavenly vision in these chapters for the remainder of Revelation. The procedure

1.   *JSJ* 10 (1979), pp. 137-54. Rowland takes the same positions in his book, *The Open Heaven: A Study of Apocalyptic in Judaism and Early Christianity* (London: SPCK, 1982), pp. 222-25, 420-21, 425-26.
2.   'The Visions of God', p. 145. Rowland does not deal with Revelation 5 in this essay.
3.   'The Visions of God', p. 150.

to be followed here will be to try to isolate and interpret those features of Revelation 4–5 that seem to be unique to this passage (within the limits of the available evidence), the working assumption being that any major distinctives in the passage may be indicators of the author's theology and purposes in writing. Before we address these chapters in detail, however, it may be helpful to describe briefly the evidence concerning visions of God in Jewish apocalyptic and mystical literature that provides a background for the scene in Revelation 4–5.

Heavenly Visions in Ancient Jewish Apocalyptic Writings

The idea of heavenly journeys is not limited to Jewish and Christian writings in ancient times, being reflected in various traditions in the Graeco-Roman world, though with many variations.[4] The form of heavenly ascent tradition most significant for Revelation 4–5, however, seems to be found in the ancient Jewish writings that describe a vision of the throne of God.

The Old Testament provides us with evidence that visions of God and his throne were a venerable aspect of ancient Jewish religious tradition (e.g. Exod. 24.9-18; 1 Kgs 22.19-22; Jer. 23.16-22; and, most important, are Isa. 6.1-13; Ezek. 1.1-28; 10.1-22; Dan. 7.9-10). The study of the subsequent development of the fascination with visions of God and his throne in Jewish tradition of the Hellenistic and later periods is not entirely new to our time, but in recent decades has taken on a lively pace, largely due to the impetus given by Gerschom G. Scholem.[5] Scholem was interested in showing that the fascination with the heavenly world and the throne of God evident in the Jewish literature known as the Hekalot, of the fourth century CE and later, was reflected also in Talmudic tradition he traced to the second century CE, and may have been shared by Jewish circles of still earlier centuries.[6] Although his

---

4.   See A.F. Segal, 'Heavenly Ascent in Hellenistic Judaism, Early Christianity and their Environment', in *ANRW* II.23.2, pp. 1333-94, and literature cited there.

5.   Scholem's most frequently cited works are *Major Trends in Jewish Mysticism* (New York: Jewish Theological Seminary, 1941, 1954), and *Jewish Gnosticism, Merkabah Mysticism, and Talmudic Tradition* (New York: Jewish Theological Seminary, 1960, 1965).

6.   Scholem, *Jewish Gnosticism*, pp. 1-8. On the Hekalot, see M. Smith, 'Observations on Hekalot Rabbati', in *Biblical and Other Essays* (ed. A. Altmann; Cambridge, MA: Harvard University Press, 1963), pp. 142-60; and now especially I. Gruenwald, *Apocalyptic and Merkavah Mysticism* (AGJU, 14; Leiden: Brill, 1980),

handling of the Talmudic material has been subjected to criticism,[7] he is to be credited at least with generating a great deal of interest in the early roots of what is known as Merkabah mysticism.

The study of the roots of this Merkabah mysticism takes us into the world of Jewish apocalyptic literature. Here we are indebted to the work of Ithamar Gruenwald, who, following the lead of Scholem, has traced the indications of an interest in visions of God and his throne in this material, producing a book that must now be regarded as required reading for students of apocalyptic,[8] and the work of C.C. Rowland, whose Cambridge dissertation gives a meticulous examination of ancient texts that exhibit the influence of the vision of God's throne in Ezekiel 1.[9] Although there are still other very early indications of Jewish interest in heavenly visions of God's throne, it is accurate to say that the primary evidence is in apocalyptic material.[10] In the following paragraphs we shall look at this Jewish apocalyptic evidence as background for our examination of Revelation 4–5, which we shall take up in the

and P. Schäfer, *Synopse zur Hekhalot-Literatur* (TSAJ, 2; Tübingen: Mohr, 1981). Translated selections of Hekalot texts appear in D.R. Bluementhal, *Understanding Jewish Mysticism: A Source Reader* (New York: Ktav, 1978). On *3 Enoch* and its place in the Hekalot texts, see P.S. Alexander, 'The Historical Setting of the Hebrew Book of Enoch', *JJS* 28 (1977), pp. 156-80. A brief introduction to Merkabah tradition is in J.W. Bowker, '"Merkabah" Visions and the Visions of Paul', *JSS* 16 (1971), pp. 157-73. One must also mention here J. Maier, *Vom Kultus zur Gnosis: Studien zur Vor- und Frühgeschichte der 'jüdischen Gnosis'* (Kairos, 1; Salsburg: Müller, 1964).

7.   J. Neusner, 'The Development of the *Merkavah* Tradition', *JSJ* 2 (1971), pp. 149-60; E.E. Urbach, 'Traditions about Merkabah Mysticism in the Tannaitic Period', in *Studies in Mysticism and Religion Presented to G.G. Scholem* (Jerusalem, 1967), pp. 1-28 (Hebrew); D.J. Halperin, *The Merkabah in Rabbinic Literature* (AOS, 62; New Haven: American Oriental Society, 1982); I. Chernus, *Mysticism in Rabbinic Judaism* (SJ, 11; Berlin: de Gruyter, 1982).

8.   I. Gruenwald, *Apocalyptic and Merkavah Mysticism*; see n. 7 above.

9.   C.C. Rowland, 'The Influence of the First Chapter of Ezekiel on Jewish and Early Christian Literature' (PhD dissertation, Cambridge University, 1971). Rowland's a massive introduction to apocalyptic, *The Open Heaven: A Study of Apocalyptic in Judaism and Early Christianity*, embodies much of his dissertation, and advances the study of apocalyptic significantly, although the present essay shows that I find his views on Rev. 4 less than satisfying.

10.   See, e.g., Gruenwald, *Apocalyptic and Merkavah Mysticism*, pp. 127-33, for hints in Philo and in Ezekiel the Tragedian. See also D.J. Halperin, 'Merkabah Midrash in the Septuagint', *JBL* 101 (1982), pp. 351-63.

next section of this essay. This brief discussion draws upon an examination of *1 Enoch* 14 and 71; *2 Enoch* 1–20; *Testament of Levi*; *3 Baruch*; *Apocalypse of Abraham*; *Testament of Abraham*; and *Ascension of Isaiah* (with due allowance for the Christian influence in these last two writings). We have also taken into account more fragmentary evidence, such as the Angel Liturgy from Qumran, and later tradition in the Talmud and in *3 Enoch* (*Sepher Hekalot*). Rather than attempt to give here a detailed discussion of these texts *ad seriatim*, we shall simply list and describe briefly some major characteristics of the heavenly visions in them to assist in our major task, the examination of Revelation 4–5.[11]

The first and most obvious characteristic of the primary texts mentioned above is that they all describe a heavenly ascent. In describing the ascent, the writers characteristically take an interest in detailing the manifold structure of the heavens and the various inhabitants in each layer of the heavenly world. *1 Enoch*, with its description of a lesser and greater house in heaven (14.8-25), appears to give the simplest picture, the other writings usually mentioning a multiple of heavens (e.g. *T. Levi* 2.7–7.10, three heavens [or more?]; *2 En.* 1–22, ten heavens). Although a great deal of effort has been spent on explaining the sources of this metaphysical stratification, the more important but often neglected question, so it seems to me, is the religious meaning of description of the heavenly world for the writers and ancient readers of these texts. In view of our major purpose in this essay, this question cannot detain us long here, but I suggest that the answer may have something to do with a desire to emphasize God as utterly exalted above all other metaphysical powers and religious systems familiar to the readers. There are no hard data to

11. For this study, I have used the following widely available translations and editions of the works listed above: for *1 Enoch*, *2 Enoch*, *3 Enoch*, *Testament of Levi*, *3 Baruch*, *Testament of Abraham* and *Apocalypse of Abraham*, the translations in J.H. Charlesworth (ed.), *The Old Testament Pseudepigrapha*. I. *Apocalyptic Literature and Testaments* (Garden City, NY: Doubleday, 1983); also R.H. Charles (ed.), *Apocrypha and Pseudepigrapha of the Old Testament* (2 vols.; Oxford: Clarendon Press, 1913); G.H. Box, *The Apocalypse of Abraham* (London: SPCK, 1919); 'The Testament of Abraham', from A. Roberts, J. Donaldson (eds.), *The Ante-Nicene Fathers* (New York: Christian Literature, 1896), IX, pp. 183-201; R.H. Charles, *The Ascension of Isaiah* (London: SPCK, 1919); H. Odeberg, *III Enoch or the Hebrew Book of Enoch* (New York: Ktav, 1973 [1928]); J. Strugnell, 'The Angelic Liturgy at Qumran', *VTSup* 7 (1960), pp. 318-45. The most extensive Talmudic passage is *b. Hag.* 11b-16a.

justify the view that this exalted picture of God involved a sense of alienation from him, or that these attempts to picture his transcendence *necessarily* meant that the readers had a lessened sense of God's nearness to their concerns.[12] The complex structure of the heavens in these writings may be the projection of the writers' and readers' experience of their world, a world of complex and conflicting religions and values, made more complex in the Hellenistic period by closer contact of various cultures. Thus, the picture of the heavens as multi-layered may reflect, not a notion of God as distant, but rather an attempt to display sophistication and complexity in the portrayal of heavenly realities.[13]

Along with the interest in the structure of the heavens seems to go a fascination with the number and kinds of heavenly inhabitants. In addition to references to thousands of angels (*1 En.* 14.21-23; 71.8), there is evident interest in the various higher ranks of heavenly beings (e.g. archangels, 'angels of the presence', 'thrones', 'dominions', cherubim, seraphim, ophannim).[14] The influence of Ezekiel 1 is quite evident in many of these visions, with the mention of the 'living creatures' (Ezek. 1.5-14), which are always described as standing in close proximity to the very throne of God, and whose main task is the singing of praises to God (e.g. *1 En.* 71.1; *2 En.* 19.3–22.3; *Apoc. Abr.* 18; *T. Abr.* 20). Here again, we are constrained to inquire briefly after the religious meaning of these descriptions of the hosts of heaven who stand at God's bidding. Once more, the purpose seems to be to emphasize how awesome and formidable God himself is who has such a vast and powerful retinue as his servants and courtiers. Of course, the interest in other heavenly beings could always have been in danger of becoming such a preoccupation as to obscure the uniqueness of God, but the mere presence of a multitude of ranked angelic beings in visions of heaven is not automatically to be taken as evidence that the seer's view of God's uniqueness

12. Note the still valuable study by H.J. Wicks, *The Doctrine of God in the Jewish Apocryphal and Apocalyptic Literature* (New York: Ktav, 1971 [1915]).

13. The fullest discussion of the cosmology reflected in these and other ancient Jewish texts is H. Bietenhard, *Die himmlische Welt im Urchristentum und Spätjudentum* (WUNT, 2; Tübingen: Mohr, 1951).

14. D.S. Russell, *The Method and Message of Jewish Apocalyptic* (Philadelphia: Westminster Press, 1964), pp. 235-62. Cf. Bietenhard, *Himmlische Welt*, pp. 101-42; H.B. Kuhn, 'The Angelology of the Non-Canonical Jewish Apocalypses', *JBL* 67 (1948), pp. 217-32; P. Schäfer, *Rivalität zwischen Engeln und Menschen: Untersuchungen zur rabbinischen Engelvorstellung* (SJ, 8; Berlin: de Gruyter, 1975).

was clouded by these other heavenly figures.

A third feature of all these visions is the sense of heaven as utterly 'other' and as 'off-limits' for mere mortals. Thus, for example, in *1 En.* 14.9-25, the writer describes heaven as 'hot like fire and cold like ice', a place where 'there was no pleasure of life in it', the 'second house [the place where God himself dwells] which is greater than the former...was built with tongues of fire'. Into God's presence even angels could not go (14.21-22), and 'no one of the flesh can see him'. This emphasis makes the ascent of the visionary to heaven and to the throne of God all the more remarkable. In his heavenly visions, the hero usually sees no other human, only the awesome and sometimes terrifying heavenly hosts, although we occasionally are shown glimpses of Old Testament heroes who are given exalted status in the heavenly realms (e.g. *T. Abr.* 11–13, referring to Adam and Abel; *3 En.* 4; 10–15, referring to Enoch's trans-formation into Metatron; cf. *2 En.* 22.8-12). The point of this emphasis seems to be to make the ascent and vision of the hero all the more impressive and meaningful; and once more we must ask after the meaning. Likely, the answer has to do with the representative signifi-cance of the hero making the ascent. The fact that the ascending figure in Jewish apocalyptic texts is always an Old Testament worthy, a great figure from Israel's past, suggests that the readers were intended to identify themselves with the hero, seeing in his ascent the assurance of God's interest in Israel, the reality of heavenly things, and therefore the trustworthiness of the promise that God will someday act to establish his glory upon the earth and to exalt Israel in divine favor.[15]

At the same time, we must note that these visions seem very little concerned with the Messiah or any equivalent figure. Although there is sometimes a reference to a chief angel, such as Jaoel in the *Apocalypse of Abraham* (10), or Gabriel and Michael in *2 Enoch* (21–24) and *3 Baruch* (11–15), and although in *3 Enoch* there is a notable interest in Enoch/Metatron, none of these figures is described in a way that finally threatens God's uniqueness or makes the being anything more than God's chief steward. That is, the visions are thoroughly theocentric and, though they may have held eschatological implications for ancient readers, their primary purpose was to hold forth a vision of God's

15. Of course, in the later mystical literature it is likely that the tradition of the heavenly ascent of ancient figures served as inspiration for similar mystical feats among the practitioners of *Ma'aseh Merkavah*, and the earlier eschatological significance was eclipsed somewhat by this mystical interest.

exalted place above all other symbols of power and veneration.[16]

With the preceding general observations in mind, we shall now examine the vision in Revelation 4–5, highlighting in more detail where it seems to offer significantly distinctive features in comparison with the other examples of heavenly vision, and attempting to describe the religious meaning of these features in the context of the author's theological emphases as they are evident in this vision and elsewhere in Revelation.

The Heavenly Vision in Revelation 4–5

Nearly all scholars recognize in Revelation 5 clear indications of the writer's Christian views, especially in the description of the Lamb (5.6-12), the content of the hymns (5.9-10, 12-13), and the fact that they are sung *to the Lamb* as to God, and even in the sealed book which can be opened only by the Lamb (5.1-5, 7-10). As mentioned earlier, Rowland has asserted that the Christian features of the vision of the heavenly throne are confined to ch. 5, and that Revelation 4 is totally unaffected by Christian beliefs. Because there is such wide support for the notion that Revelation 5 is heavily conditioned by the writer's Christian beliefs, we shall reserve our discussion of this chapter until later and concentrate first on Revelation 4, in the interest of determining whether Rowland's view is correct.

Before we look at the details of the passage, we should note the place of the chapter in the structure of Revelation. In chs. 1–3, the writer describes a vision of the exalted Christ and relays a series of messages to seven churches of the province of Asia. Chapter 4 begins a new major section of Revelation that extends to 22.5, although there are several obvious sub-sections in this material. This means that Revelation 4 is not simply one scene among others, but it is the initial scene in a new major section and constitutes, therefore, a major turning point in the text. Our expectations of a writer must not determine our interpretation of what he has written, but it would seem to be a legitimate expectation for the initial scene in a major new section of his writing to reflect something of the important convictions that determine the content of that section. Thus, the vision of the risen Christ in Revelation 1 certainly determines the content and imagery employed in the following messages to the seven churches, as the commentaries demonstrate.

Further, ch. 4 seems integrally related to ch. 5, these two chapters

16. Note the sensitive discussion in Bietenhard, *Himmlische Welt*, pp. 255-72.

constituting two closely related scenes in one unified vision of God's throne. Precisely because the author's Christian convictions have so radically determined the scene in Revelation 5, it seems proper to inquire more closely whether ch. 4 likewise is influenced by those same convictions, forming as it does an integral unit of the same vision. To approach Revelation properly, we must make allowance not only for the rich background in Judaism (and indeed perhaps in other traditions) from which the author draws, but also for the Christian convictions of the author which shape fundamentally what he does with the material inherited from his background. The clear indebtedness of Revelation 4 to the Jewish apocalyptic background of heavenly visions should not stop us from inquiring whether and, if so, how the distinctive features of the passage arise from the Christian faith of the author. Similarly, the more transparently Christian features of Revelation 5 should not blind us to what may be (for us) less easily recognized but important distinctives of Revelation 4.[17]

The first thing to notice about Revelation 4 is the simplicity of the description of heavenly ascent. The writer is called up into heaven in 4.1, and immediately thereafter gives his vision of the throne of God and its attendants. This is quite striking in comparison to the more detailed ascent descriptions in the Jewish apocalyptic material, where we learn about various heavenly layers and the inhabitants of each layer. It has been suggested that the author may not have been aware of the latest developments in Jewish apocalyptic, and so incorporated a somewhat earlier and outmoded description of a single heaven, instead of three or more.[18] But this suggestion is highly implausible, for nearly all commentators emphasize how very much the author seems thoroughly familiar with the rich apocalyptic tradition of his time and of earlier decades. It would see, therefore, much more likely that the author has consciously chosen to describe his ascent in simple terms, and that the description of multiple heavenly layers simply forms no part of his purpose (or perhaps no part of his religious experience).[19] The author amply demonstrates

---

17. Cf. the discussion of Rev. 4 in Bietenhard, *Himmlische Welt*, pp. 56-63, where he concludes that, although the writer clearly draws upon the Old Testament tradition, he also exercised full freedom in the creative ways he used the traditional elements in conveying his message, which was grounded in his Christian religious experiences.

18. See, e.g., Gruenwald, *Apocalyptic and Merkavah Mysticism*, p. 48.

19. In this paper, we treat Revelation as literature resulting from the authorial

that he is capable of substantially modifying the imagery and tradition he inherited.[20] The stark simplicity of the author's heavenly ascent is therefore probably to be understood as another example of his distinctive literary purpose and/or religious experiences. The conclusion that the author's simple description of heavenly ascent is purposeful does not yet tell us what his purpose was; but we may be better able to say something about his purpose after looking closely at other features of his vision.

Most students of Revelation recognize that, though the writer's description of God's throne is very similar to descriptions of it in Jewish apocalyptic literature (except that the author is very reserved about any anthropomorphic imagery such as we sometimes find),[21] the twenty-four elders represent a distinctive feature of the scene, not being found in any example of Jewish apocalyptic visions of heaven.[22] But not only are the twenty-four elders a distinctive element in the author's vision, there are indications that they are a most important element. We should

purposes of the writer. This does not foreclose the question of what kinds of religious/visionary experiences lie behind the text before us.

20. To select only one proximate example, the four creatures of Rev. 4.6-8, though clearly 'borrowed' from Ezek. 1.4-14, are modified, having six wings instead of four (an indication that they are to be linked also with the seraphim of Isa. 6.1-5), and each creature has one face instead of four. Further, they are 'full of eyes all round and within', a detail taken from the description of the wheels of the divine throne in Ezek. 1.18. Finally, the living creatures of Rev. 4 occupy themselves purely with praising God, in words adapted from Isa. 6.3 (and modified substantially!), though in Ezek. 1, they are primarily the accompaniment of the movable throne, which in Rev. 4 appears to be a stationary throne!

21. Bietenhard (*Himmlische Welt*, p. 62) also draws attention to the fact that the divine throne in Revelation is not described as a movable one, something very different from what we often find in Merkabah texts.

22. In light of the view taken in this essay that the elders represent the elect in some way, it is interesting to note *1 En.* 60.2, where the writer describes a scene with God 'surrounded by the angels and the righteous ones', the latter term likely referring to human elect (cf. the use of the term in *1 En.* 60.24; 61.3; 70.3-4; 71.17). This section of *1 Enoch* (37–71) is notoriously difficult to date, but if the Similitudes of Enoch date from the same approximate period as Revelation, the scene would show that the general idea of the elect being represented in some way before God's throne was not entirely unfamiliar among Jewish apocalyptic circles of that time. It is still true that the particular way of representing the elect in Rev. 4, and the emphasis placed upon the twenty-four elders there, are distinctive among all other examples of apocalyptic heavenly visions.

note that the elders are given a very prominent place in the vision, being mentioned right after the reference to God's throne, and being referred to several times in the vision (4.10-11) and elsewhere in Revelation (7.11-13; 11.16; 14.3; 19.4). Charles noticed their early appearance in the vision, immediately after the description of God's throne, but wrong-headedly attributed their placement in the vision to the writer's suppos-edly poor literary skill, and suggested that the author had stitched the description of the elders into an earlier draft of the vision, thereby incor-rectly mentioning them before the four living creatures, who are in fact closer to the throne.[23] But the author's failure to describe the figures in the scene in concentric circles outward from the throne, as Charles wished him to have done, does not necessarily mean that the author was simply illogical or careless. Again, his demonstrated skill elsewhere in modifying apocalyptic imagery suggests that the irruption of the elders into the description of the heavenly scene right after the reference to the throne of God was deliberate, and conveys something of the author's own message and purpose in delivering his vision.

The early and prominent mention of the elders in the scene, together with the fact that they appear to be a unique feature of the writer's vision, suggest that the elders are important, indeed, that they may be the point of emphasis in the scene, second only to the throne of God. Surely, ancient readers familiar with Jewish apocalyptic visions like this one would have recognized that this author had no interest in specula-tions about heavenly stratifications and their inhabitants, and that, like-wise, though he attributed to God a marvellously large heavenly retinue (e.g. 5.11-12), complete with the then standard accompaniment of the divine throne, the four living creatures (4.6-8), he did not offer another attempt to rank and describe in detail the angelic host. Further, they would have noticed that the elders were a new and unparalleled group before the throne, whose prominence is all the greater precisely because the author otherwise mentions specifically so few categories of heavenly beings in his vision. Nearly every example of heavenly vision in the apocalyptic texts has its own distinctive features, usually minor variations in language or in the description of the throne, and most of these may be rather insignificant. But in the case of the twenty-four elders here in Revelation 4, we are dealing with what constitutes a major feature of the vision, and it is therefore likely that this is a very significant

---

23. R.H. Charles, *A Critical and Exegetical Commentary on the Revelation of St John* (ICC; Edinburgh: T. & T. Clark, 1920), I, pp. 104-105.

variation in the pattern of apocalyptic visions.

If it is correct that the twenty-four elders are the major, significantly distinctive feature in Revelation 4, it is important to know what they represent; but the commentaries exhibit the present lack of consensus on how to identify them.[24] Some have attempted to determine the meaning of these figures by the process of first trying to project the background of the image of a group of twenty-four heavenly beings, for example, in ancient astrological thought (so Gunkel and Bousset). But it may be more profitable to take another course of action and establish a tentative meaning of these figures on the basis of internal clues in the book of Revelation itself, afterwards considering the question of whether proffered backgrounds for the figures illumine them further.[25]

To anticipate the conclusions of the following investigation, in spite of the similarities between the angels and these figures (heavenly status, proximity to God's throne, participation in the heavenly liturgy), I suggest that the twenty-four elders are to be viewed as heavenly representatives of the elect. They are always distinguished from the angels (5.11; 7.11), and the facts that elders (not angels!) announce the appearance of the sacrificed Lamb (5.5), identify the elect (7.13-17), and strike up a praise chant to God at the announcement of his coming triumph on behalf of his saints (11.15-19) suggest strongly that the elders are to be thought of as connected somehow with the elect and their salvation.

The association of the elders with the elect is reinforced by the items mentioned in the description of these heavenly figures: the thrones, the garments, and the crowns (4.4). In the letters to the seven churches, the elect are promised white garments (3.5), crowns (3.11), and a throne

---

24. Thus, for example, Charles, *Revelation*, I, pp. 129-33, regards the elders as 'heavenly representatives of the whole body of the faithful'. In H.B. Swete, *The Apocalypse of St John* (London: Macmillan, 1908), they are 'the church in its Totality', 'idealized', reflecting a 'potentially realized' state (pp. 68-69). For J. Sweet, *Revelation* (Pelican Commentaries; London: SCM Press, 1979), they are 'OT worthies' (p. 118). R. Mounce, *The Book of Revelation* (NICNT; Grand Rapids: Eerdmans, 1977), sees them as 'an exalted and angelic order', 'the heavenly counterpart to the twenty-four priestly and twenty-four Levitical orders (1 Chron. 24.4; 25.9-13)' (pp. 135-36). For I.T. Beckwith they were 'angelic kings', and he regarded the passage as 'conceived throughout on the traditional lines of Hebrew angelology' (*The Apocalypse of John* [London: Macmillan, 1919], pp. 498-99; and likewise M. Kiddle, *The Revelation of St John* [New York: Harper & Row, 1940], pp. 76-84).

25. Bietenhard subjects the theories of Gunkel and Bousset to telling criticism (*Himmlische Welt*, pp. 57-59).

seat (3.21), and, coming as it does right after these promises, the vision of the twenty-four elders seems to be assurance of the heavenly reality of the promises.[26] The reference to the thrones of the elders is especially important, and, as Gruenwald recognizes,[27] seems out of keeping with the more frequently attested Jewish apocalyptic picture of heaven, in which God is seated and all other creatures there spend their whole time standing.[28] These figures are thus given a status and honor denied to the highest angels, even to the living creatures; but their status and honor correspond perfectly to the promises made just a bit earlier in Revelation to the elect.

Further, the association of the elders with the elect may help explain the fact that the figures are called 'elders'. The description of angels as 'elders' is without parallel in Jewish apocalyptic visions of the time,[29] as is reference to a group of twenty-four heavenly beings of any kind. The Old Testament does, however, have a tradition of the elders of ancient Israel participating with Moses in a vision of God (Exod. 24.10), and this tradition seems to be what is referred to in Isa. 24.23 (LXX), which mentions God in eschatological victory, ruling in Zion and 'glorified before the elders', these passages likely supplying at least part of the

26. In what is very possibly an allusion to Rev. 4, *Ascension of Isaiah* refers to heavenly garments, crowns, and thrones for the elect of the Old Testament, to be received after the exaltation of Christ (8.26; 9.7-18), indicating that the author of the latter writing may have seen the elders of Rev. 4 as proof of Christ's exaltation, since they are pictured as possessing these honors now. For Jewish references to the elect receiving crowns in the age to come, see 1QS 4.7; 1QH 9.25; *b. Ber.* 17a; *T. Benj.* 4.1 (also Gruenwald, *Apocalyptic and Merkavah Mysticism*, p. 128 n. 2).

27. Gruenwald, *Apocalyptic and Merkavah Mysticism*, pp. 66-67.

28. The reference to a throne in each of seven heavens in *Asc. Isa.* 7.13-22 seems intended to show that God rules at all heavenly layers. The references to Adam and Abel as seated on thrones (chs. 11–13) are both later than Revelation and do not picture these thrones as in the same scene with God's throne. The references to the throne of Metatron/Enoch in *3 Enoch* are far too late to be of relevance, and likewise do not place Metatron's throne in the same proximity to God's throne as we see done in Rev. 4, where the elders are given thrones in the very presence of God.

29. The reference to elders in *2 En.* 4.1 provides the only other example known to me of figures bearing this label in apocalyptic visions of the heavens, but it is not clear what class of beings these figures are. Further, it should be noted that, whatever kind of beings they are, they do not seem very important, being placed in the lowest of several heavens, and being charged merely with managing stellar orders. For these reasons, this reference is no true parallel to the elders of Rev. 4.

inspiration for the presence of a group of elders in the heavenly scene in Revelation 4.[30]

Additionally, the well-established usage of the term 'elder' to describe the leaders in the synagogues and churches of the late first century (if not earlier) seems to give us the most immediate association of the term for the first readers.[31] That is, it does not seem difficult to think that the readers would have found the reference to heavenly 'elders' immediately meaningful on the basis of their familiarity with Jewish and Christian traditions, and would easily have taken these elders as playing a role in heaven similar to that of the earthly elders of Jewish and Christian groups.

That there are *twenty-four* elders in the vision is not so easily explained; but the facts that the figures are clad as priests (in white) and are described here as participating in a heavenly liturgy (4.11) make the suggestion entirely reasonable that their number is an allusion to the number of the courses of priests and Levites in the Old Testament (1 Chron. 24.4-6).[32] The writer was certainly familiar with the Old Testament,[33] and loved to use bits of Old Testament imagery in new ways, rather like the way a stained-glass craftsman constructs new images out of the colored glass with which he works. It is not, therefore,

---

30. So also Bietenhard, *Himmlische Welt*, pp. 58-59.

31. Especially interesting are the uses of 'elders' and 'presbytery' in Ignatius (*Eph.* 2.2; 4.1; 20.2; *Magn.* 13.1; 2.1; *Trall.* 2.2; 7.2; 13.2; *Phld.* 3.1; 5.1; 7.1; *Smyrn.* 8.1), who pictures the presbyters of the church as the 'council of the bishop' (*Phld.* 8.1), and the 'council of God' (*Trall.* 3.1), the latter image strikingly similar to the scene in Rev. 4. The fact that the author of Revelation does not elsewhere refer to church elders cannot be taken to mean that the writer and readers were unfamiliar with the use of the term 'elder' to refer to leaders of synagogues and churches, because the author simply had no occasion to refer to the church organization familiar to him. In any case, it is clear that the readers were familiar with synagogues (e.g. 2.9), and thus would likely have known of 'elder' as a term for synagogue leaders. The further fact that the readers were encouraged to see themselves as the true 'Jews' (2.9; 3.9) suggests that they would not have found it strange to read of heavenly elders representing the elect.

32. So also Rowland, *The Open Heaven*, p. 224, and the literature cited in n. 24, p. 481.

33. H.B. Swete's discussion of the use of the Old Testament in Revelation (*Apocalypse*, pp. cxxxiv-clvii), is still worth consulting. Of the 404 verses in Revelation in the Westcott and Hort New Testament, Swete counted 278 as containing clear references to the Old Testament, and he provides a handy list of the more important ones.

too much to suggest that he was familiar with Old Testament information about the priestly orders and used it to picture what we argue
are heavenly representatives of those made by Christ 'priests to his
God' (1.6).[34]

In the vision scene in Revelation 4, the twenty-four elders appear with
the four living creatures, and this connection of the two groups of beings
may help us further to identify the meaning of the former group. Just as
the living creatures are likely to be heavenly representatives of the
orders of life (so most interpreters), so the elders are likely heavenly represents of the elect. That is, in the two groups we have represented general creation (the living creatures) and the elect (the elders). The elders
are probably not particular saints, such as Old Testament heroes, but are
symbolic representations of the elect. They are heavenly archetypes,
which serve as counterparts and representatives of the earthly saints,
offering the prayers of the saints to God directly in heaven, for example
(5.8), and are intended to show that the promises to the elect are based
on heavenly realities. Thus, as to *nature* these 'elders' are heavenly
figures, whose *significance* is that they are the heavenly representation
of the elect, demonstrating by their proximity to God's throne in the
vision here the close tie of the elect with God's majesty and
sovereignty.[35]

Now if the elders represent in some way the elect, and if their regalia
and position are intended to call to mind the promises to the Christian
elect of their own reward, this would fit with and help explain the
appearance of these figures only in this heavenly vision of John and not
in the analogous visions in Jewish apocalyptic. Thus, the elders appear
here because of the author's conviction that the Christian elect are to
receive the status represented by the twenty-four elders as a result of the
victory of Christ; and the presence of the elders signals the conviction
that Christ's exaltation has in fact happened, even though it is not explicitly celebrated until Revelation 5. That is, we are arguing that it is incorrect to think that only Revelation 5 reflects the writer's Christian views

34. It should be noted that an origin of the twenty-four elders in astrological
thought fails to explain why they are called 'elders'.

35. This suggestion about the significance of the elders has some similarity to the
kind of significance attached by J.J. Collins to the 'son of man' figure in *1 Enoch*:
'The Heavenly Representative: The "Son of Man" in the Similitudes of Enoch', in
Ideal Figures in Ancient Judaism: Profiles and Paradigms (ed. J.J. Collins and
G.W.E. Nickelsburg; Chico, CA: Scholars Press, 1980), pp. 111-34.

and that Revelation 4 is 'conceived throughout on the traditional lines of Hebrew angelology'.[36] In fact, we have found in the twenty-four elders a major item in the vision of Revelation 4 that has no parallel in any example of apocalyptic visions of heaven. We suggest, therefore, that Revelation 4 is profoundly influenced by the Christian convictions of the author, and that Revelation 4–5 is a genuinely integral vision in two scenes, the whole vision reflecting the author's Christian faith and experience.

Thus, the fact that the elders vacate their thrones and cast their crowns toward God, chanting that he alone is worthy of the royal honours given to them (4.11), is to be seen as a moving dramatization both of the richness of God's gifts to the elect and of their powerful awareness that these gifts are theirs solely by his generosity, and in spite of their unworthiness. These dramatic gestures of the elders are intended to show that there is heavenly reality behind the related worship by the elect upon the earth, and that the gifts for which the earthly elect praise God, in anticipation of the full enjoyment of them, are secured in heaven. The adoration of the elders here and in 5.9-14 is intended both to stimulate and to give substance to the corresponding worship by the elect upon the earth. And, this kind of pastoral concern explains why the author does not engage in speculations about heavenly ranks and layers, for to do so would obscure his emphasis upon the twenty-four elders and what they represent. Further, the strongly Christo-centric view of the author may have caused him to avoid discussion of a heavenly hierarchy, fearing that his readers might be distracted from their contemplation of Christ. That is, what might appear at first as a somewhat sparse description of the heavens is a deliberate attempt to focus attention on a few important symbols of heavenly truth.

The worship of the elders mentions God as creator (4.11b), but the eschatological promise is invoked in the chant of the four creatures (ὁ ἐρχόμενος 4.8b), which provokes the elders to fall before God in adoration, indicating that the vision is governed, not only by the sense of God as holy creator, but also by a view of him as the one who brings eschatological salvation.[37] This in itself is obviously not a peculiarly Christian idea, but was taken over by early Christians from Judaism and was a major Christian conviction. It is confirmation of our interpretation

36. *Contra* Beckwith, *Apocalypse*, pp. 498-99.
37. Bietenhard emphasizes that Rev. 4 is an eschatological scene: '...die Thronvision steht am Anfang der Endgerichte' (*Himmlische Welt*, p. 58).

of the elders as representatives of the Christian elect that the description of God as the one who 'is to come' provokes their dramatic actions of praise in 4.11, for it shows further that the scene relates to the eschatological and salvific hopes of the writer and readers, which, though indebted to Jewish tradition, were obviously grounded firmly in their Christian convictions.

Our argument that Revelation 4 shares with Revelation 5 the influence of the writer's Christian faith should not seem strange or unreasonable, for in 4.1 it is the risen Christ who summons John to the heavenly vision described here and in 4.2 John links his vision with the Spirit, for early Christians the agency of Christian experience.[38] Thus, the whole of Revelation 4–5 is introduced by the Christian prophetic experience of the author. However much the author was familiar with and drew upon Jewish apocalyptic traditions, the material before us in Revelation is a fresh rendering of apocalyptic themes under the impact of the writer's own faith and powerful religious experiences.

To turn now to Revelation 5, there is hardly any disagreement with the view that this chapter clearly displays the radical alteration of apocalyptic perspective resulting from early Christian faith. We need not discuss the imagery used to describe the victorious Christ here; the commentaries give ample space to these matters. Instead we will concentrate on only one feature of this passage, the fact that worship is directed both to God and to the Lamb, for perhaps in this as in nothing else in the scene we see the effect of the writer's faith.

To be brief, it is well known that the ancient Jewish fascination with the heavenly world reflected in apocalyptic literature included speculation about the roles and positions of chief angels and/or certain Old Testament worthies such as Enoch or Moses. This speculation about God's chief angel(s) often invoked Exod. 23.20-21, with its mention of an angel in whom God's name dwells. For example, we meet Jaoel in the *Apoc. Abr.* 11, where he is described very much after the fashion of theophanies in the Old Testament. Much later, there is Metatron, in

---

38. Although Jewish literature also refers to the Spirit, elsewhere in Revelation the writer makes it clear that for him the Spirit is the property of Jesus (5.6), points to Jesus (19.10), and is linked with Christian elect (22.17). Bietenhard (*Himmlische Welt*, p. 61) points also to the mention of the 'seven spirits of God' (Rev. 4.5) as evidence of the distinctively Christian tenor of the scene, stating, 'Ich habe in keiner jüdischen Himmelsbeschreibung den Geist Gottes erwähnt gefunden als eine himmlische Wesenheit'.

3 Enoch, there referred to as the 'lesser YHWH' (12.5). But in all the examples of such speculations so far available, the chief angel or Old Testament hero is always finally distinguished from God himself, most importantly by describing the figure as joining in the worship of God, and as refusing the worship of the seers to whom the visions are attributed.[39] Thus, there is no true parallel for the fact that in Revelation 5 'the Lamb' is hymned and adored jointly with God (5.9-14; note especially 5.13).[40]

Elsewhere in Revelation, the writer shows his familiarity with the standard Jewish conviction that angels are not to be worshipped (19.10; 22.8-9). Also, the writer condemns the worship of the beast and the dragon (13.4-8, 11-15; 14.9-12; 16.2; 19.19-20), and calls for the worship of God alone (14.6-7; 15.4; 19.4), his rhetoric reflecting very much the commonly encountered attitude of ancient Jews concerning God's uniqueness (cf. also 9.20). In light of the Jewish apocalyptic background, otherwise so amply reflected in Revelation, the adoration of the Lamb jointly with God by all orders of creation in Rev. 5.13-14 is especially striking. Indeed, it would be mind-boggling but for the fact that other early Christian evidence shows that the scene powerfully dramatizes the beliefs and liturgical practice characteristic of early Christianity (e.g. the well-known 'hymns' in the Pauline corpus, Phil. 2.5-11; Col. 1.15-20;

39. See the excellent study by R. Bauckham, 'The Worship of Jesus in Apocalyptic Christianity', *NTS* 27 (1981), pp. 322-41.

40. *1 En.* 61.8-13 and 62.6-9 are perhaps the closest analogies to Rev. 5, and 61.11-12 *may* describe heavenly praise being offered to 'the Elect One' as well as to God. But we must note a couple of matters in interpreting these passages. First, though sometimes discounted, there is the question of whether this section of *1 Enoch* is affected by Christian hands or reflects a Jewish attempt to counter Christian exaltation of Jesus by offering a competing figure. Most scholars now date the Similitudes in the late first century CE (e.g. E. Isaac, in Charlesworth [ed.], *The Old Testament Pseudepigrapha*, p. 7), which allows ample time for Christian influence, whether direct or indirect. Thus, if the passages in question are properly to be interpreted as showing praise given to the Elect One alongside God, the Christian worship of Jesus may have influenced the writer(s). Secondly, elsewhere in the Similitudes (e.g. 47.2-3; 48.5-6; 63.1-10; 69.27; 71.11-12) worship is directed exclusively to God, thus indicating that the compressed wording of 61.11-12 should perhaps be read as worship of God alone, though it is worship *occasioned* by the revelation of the Elect One. In 62.6-16, the attempt to praise the Elect One is made not by heavenly hosts or the righteous, but by sinners, and it is rejected by God, who sends them to judgment. Thus, even in the Similitudes the Elect One is not treated to the same unrestrained worship that is clearly given to the exalted Jesus in Rev. 5.9-14.

and the striking liturgical fragment in 1 Cor. 16.22). But, however widely shared was the author's exalted view of Christ among other Christians, this does not minimize the fact that it represented a radical mutation of the monotheistic commitment characteristic of most of the ancient Jewish evidence, the heavenly vision of Revelation 5 reflecting what it is now fashionable to call a very 'high' christology.[41]

The recognition that Revelation 5 reflects a profoundly Christian adjustment of the apocalyptic, heavenly-vision tradition suggests again that we are dealing with an author whose Christian faith served to re-arrange and re-orient, not merely to redecorate in a superficial way, his apocalyptic heritage. This being so, the interpretation of Revelation 4 as also reflecting the writer's Christian views, as urged in this essay, is even more plausible. The appearance of the Lamb in Revelation 5 should not be taken to mean that the writer experiences and reflects the effects of the Lamb's exaltation only at this point, and that Revelation 4 is intended as a picture of heaven as yet unaffected by Christ's work, along the lines of traditional Jewish apocalyptic.[42] It should not be forgotten that in Revelation 5 the Lamb is described as already slain and victorious, and hence able to open the sealed book of eschatological triumph. That is, Revelation 5 does not describe the Gospel events but presupposes them as having already happened. The relationship of Revelation 4 to Revelation 5 is not chronological but logical, and the two chapters are not finally contrasts with each other, but complementary scenes in one vision. Revelation 4 gives the picture of the idealized heavenly sovereignty of God, shared by the representatives of the elect, the elders; and Revelation 5 gives the means by which this heavenly reality was secured and is to be made a historical reality upon the earth, the exaltation and triumph of the sacrificed Lamb, and shows that it is this exalted figure who is alone worthy to execute God's eschatological plan.

41. The Christology of Revelation is not, however, a fashionable topic of discussion and is often done less than justice in studies of early Christology. An exception is T. Holz, *Die Christologie der Apokalypse des Johannes* (Berlin: Akademie-Verlag, 1962).

42. *Contra* M. Kiddle, *The Revelation of St John*, pp. 80-81; and Rowland, *The Open Heaven*, p. 222, who sees an intended 'contrast between the description of the divine court in Rev. 4 and the transformation which takes place as the result of the exaltation of the Lamb'.

Conclusion

My purposes in this essay were to study Revelation 4–5 in the context of ancient Jewish apocalyptic visions of heaven, with the intent of testing two theses: (a) that the Christian views of the author are confined to Revelation 5, ch. 4 being thoroughly typical of Jewish apocalyptic heavenly visions and unaffected by the writer's Christian faith; and (b) that Revelation 4 is, therefore, incidental to the rest of the book. We have encountered what are offered as plausible reasons for rejecting the first thesis and for seeing the whole of Revelation 4–5 as an integrally ordered heavenly vision that is significantly influenced by the writer's Christian faith, and as a notable mutation on the pattern of heavenly visions in the Jewish apocalyptic background. The unique features of Revelation 4, especially the description of the twenty-four elders, I have concluded, are indications that the passage is understood best as significantly conditioned by the writer's Christian faith and experience. This conclusion is in turn strong reason to reject the second thesis, and to conclude instead that the writer meant Revelation 4–5 to be an important, first unit in the material stretching from 4.1 to 22.5, and that the whole of these two chapters portrays important Christian truths for the readers. Briefly put, Revelation 4–5 gives the readers the heavenly realities, the sovereignty of God, the pure worship of his majesty, the relationship of the elect to God's throne, the triumph of the Lamb, that govern the rest of the scenes in the book. Before describing the rebellion of the earth, the suffering of the saints, and the measure of God's judgment, the writer gives the readers this unified vision of the heavenly 'logic' that will serve to explain the rest and will show that their cause is God's.

JSNT 33 (1988), pp. 85-95

MARTYR CHRISTOLOGY IN THE APOCALYPSE

Mitchell G. Reddish

The author of 'The Letter of the Churches of Lyons and Vienne', which describes the Christian martyrdoms that occurred in Gaul during the last quarter of the second century, states that those who had suffered persecution and survived refused to be called martyrs. Instead, they yielded that title to Christ alone, 'the faithful and true witness and firstborn of the dead'.[1] The author's indebtedness to the book of Revelation for his characterization of Christ is unmistakable. The descriptions of Christ as 'the faithful and true witness' and as 'the firstborn of the dead' are direct quotations from Rev. 3.14 and 1.5.[2] In addition, the use of the title 'martyr' for Christ was also likely influenced by the Christology of the Apocalypse, for of prime importance to the author of Revelation was his depiction of Christ as the supreme martyr. This paper is an examination of that motif in the Apocalypse.

At the outset two assumptions upon which this study is based need to be delineated. First, the assumed *Sitz im Leben* of the Apocalypse is Asia Minor during the latter part of the first century CE. As evidence from Revelation itself attests, John of Patmos was in a situation in which he perceived the churches of Asia Minor to be threatened by official persecution and martyrdom. John himself had been exiled to Patmos 'on account of the word of God and the testimony of Jesus' (1.9). Antipas had been martyred in Pergamum (2.13). The church at Smyrna is warned of impending imprisonment and testing for some of its members (2.10). The Roman Empire is pictured as a beast that demands worship

1. Eusebius, *H.E.* 5.2.3.
2. Although the phrase 'the firstborn of the dead' is also found in Col. 1.18, the combination of this phrase with 'the faithful and true witness' is evidence that the author was drawing from Revelation.

and that exterminates those who refuse (13.1-18). Whether or not an accurate depiction of the historical situation is given in the Apocalypse, John conveys the impression that he was writing in a time of extreme crisis. The historical validity of this perception is secondary. John perceived the threat to be real and perilous and wrote from the standpoint of that perception.[3]

Secondly, I would posit that the theme of martyrdom is not just an incidental part of the book of Revelation, but is the primary motif of John's writing.[4] Revelation is a book written for and about martyrs. Indeed, as one scholar has described it, the Apocalypse is 'the greatest of all textbooks for martyrs'.[5] In Revelation the martyrs are the central characters. Their sufferings and their rewards are emphasized. Their faithfulness is held up as an example to be followed. Martin Rist aptly summarizes the intent of the book when he states that John

> endeavored to make martyrdom, with its eternal rewards, so attractive, and worship of the emperor, with its eternal punishments, so fearsome, that his

3. Elisabeth Schüssler Fiorenza (*The Book of Revelation: Justice and Judgment* [Philadelphia: Fortress Press, 1985], p. 9) makes the valid point that how we answer the question of whether or not the threat of persecution was real during John's time depends 'on whose perspective we adopt. One could argue from the perspective of well-to-do white Americans that no harassment, denigration, discrimination, or oppression of blacks existed at the time of Martin Luther King, Jr, although King was assassinated. The perspective and experience of blacks would be quite different! Similarly, the author of Revelation had adopted the "perspective from below" and expressed the experiences of those who were powerless, poor, and in constant fear of denunciation.'

4. See Mitchell G. Reddish, 'The Theme of Martyrdom in the Book of Revelation' (PhD dissertation, The Southern Baptist Theological Seminary, 1982). See also Robert H. Mounce ('The Christology of the Apocalypse', *Foundations* 11 [1969], p. 50) who concludes, 'The entire Apocalypse may be called a philosophy of martyrdom'. Major commentators who have strongly emphasized the martyrological concern of Revelation include G.B. Caird, *A Commentary on the Revelation of St John the Divine* (HNTC; New York: Harper & Row, 1966); Martin Rist, 'The Revelation of St John the Divine', *IB* (ed. George A. Buttrick; New York: Abingdon, 1957), XII, pp. 347-613; Martin Kiddle, assisted by M.K. Ross, *The Revelation of John* (MNTC; New York: Harper and Brothers [1940]; E.F. Scott, *The Book of Revelation* (New York: Charles Scribner's Sons, 1940); and R.H. Charles, *A Critical and Exegetical Commentary on the Revelation of St John* (2 vols.; ICC; Edinburgh: T. & T. Clark, 1920).

5. Kiddle, *Revelation*, p. xlix.

readers would quite willingly accept death as martyrs rather than be
disloyal to Almighty God and his Christ by worshipping Roma and the
emperors.[6]

Chief among the martyr figures in the Apocalypse is Jesus. The earliest description of Jesus in Revelation occurs in 1.5 when he is called 'the
faithful witness, the firstborn of the dead, and the ruler of the kings on
earth'. These titles are especially appropriate in a work concerned with
martyrdom. As G.B. Caird has commented,

> The titles of Christ are...carefully chosen for John's pastoral purpose.
> His friends are called to bear the costly witness of martyrdom, trusting that
> in his death Christ has been a *faithful witness* to God's way of overcoming
> evil; to look into the open jaws of death, remembering that he has risen as
> the *firstborn* of many brothers; to defy the authority of Imperial Rome in
> the name of a *ruler* to whom Caesar himself must bow.[7]

Of special significance is the first description of Jesus, 'the faithful
witness', ὁ μάρτυς ὁ πιστός (1.5; cf. also 3.14). As is well known, the
English word 'martyr' is derived from the Greek word used here,
μάρτυς. One is tempted to translate μάρτυς here and elsewhere in
Revelation as 'martyr'. As Allison Trites has shown, however, around
the end of the first century μάρτυς had not yet reached the stage in its
semantic development in which it necessarily included the idea of death.[8]
The idea of witness was still primary. Only the context can determine if
death was associated with that witness.

In what way, then, was Christ the faithful witness? In one sense it is
correct to say that he was the faithful witness throughout his entire
earthly existence as he bore testimony to God. His witness was 'his
whole attestation of God in word and deed, which was consummated on
the cross'.[9] Yet the emphasis in 1.5 is on Christ as the faithful witness
through his suffering and death. He is the faithful μάρτυς because he
has maintained his testimony even through the agony and suffering of

6.   Rist, 'Revelation', p. 354.
7.   Caird, *Revelation*, p. 16.
8.   Allison Trites, 'Μάρτυς and Martyrdom in the Apocalypse: A Semantic
Study', *NovT* 15 (1973), pp. 77-80.
9.   J.P.M. Sweet, 'Maintaining the Testimony of Jesus: The Suffering of
Christians in the Revelation of John', in *Suffering and Martyrdom in the New
Testament* (ed. William Horbury and Brian McNeil; Cambridge: Cambridge
University Press, 1981), p. 104.

the cross. He 'has sealed his witness with his death'.[10] He thus deserves to be labelled not only ὁ πρωτότοκος, the firstborn of the dead, but also ὁ πρωτόμαρτυς. This martyrological interpretation is strengthened by noting that the only other usage of the phrase 'faithful witness' is its application to Antipas (2.13), the only martyr figure who is singled out by name in Revelation. The faithful witness is the one who endures, who 'holds the testimony', even at the cost of his or her life.

Any discussion of the Christology of the Apocalypse must consider the most prominent christological title in John's work—that of the Lamb. Twenty-eight times the term ἀρνίον is used in reference to Christ. Much discussion has occurred over John's use of the term ἀρνίον instead of ἀμνός, the latter being the usual Greek term used in the Gospel of John and elsewhere in the New Testament. If there is any significance to the choice of terms, I would agree with Norman Hillyer that the Seer probably avoided ἀμνός because of its connotation of a sacrificial lamb.[11] In Revelation Christ is more than a sacrificial victim. He is, paradoxically, the powerful, conquering Lamb who leads his army of martyrs to victory.

Four times the Lamb is described as the one who was slain.[12] In addition, three times the effectiveness of the blood of the Lamb is stressed.[13] Scholars are divided over the intention of John's portrayal of the messiah as a lamb. Beckwith believes the primary emphasis is on the lamb as the sacrificial animal of the Jewish cultus.[14] The idea of a lamb offered as a cultic sacrifice certainly contributes to this imagery. Yet one should not too quickly interpret the lamb imagery as solely, or even primarily, cultic-sacrificial terminology. The Lamb who is slain is also the warring Lamb (17.14), who has seven horns and seven eyes, symbolizing his power and knowledge (5.6). Revelation 5, in an unexpected shift of metaphors, reinforces the conqueror motif by showing that the Lamb is at the same time the conquering Lion of the tribe of Judah.

Other interpreters have argued that due to the Exodus typology

10. Akira Satake, *Die Gemeindeordnung in der Johannesapokalypse* (Neukirchen–Vluyn: Neukirchener Verlag, 1966), p. 114.

11. Norman Hillyer, '"The Lamb" in the Apocalypse', *The EvQ* 39 (1967), p. 229.

12. Rev. 5.6; 5.9; 5.12; 13.8.

13. Rev. 5.9; 7.14; 12.11.

14. Isbon T. Beckwith, *The Apocalypse of John* (London: Macmillan, 1919; repr., Grand Rapids: Baker, 1979), p. 315.

prevalent in the Apocalypse, the Lamb should be understood as the new Paschal Lamb.[15] J. Comblin has strongly defended the Suffering Servant figure of Isaiah 53 as the dominant idea behind John's depiction of Christ as a lamb.[16] For C.H. Dodd Jewish apocalyptic traditions provide the clue for the lamb imagery in Revelation.[17] The clearest example of the lamb as a conqueror, similar to John's portrayal, is found in *1 En.* 89–90, which recounts the history of Israel using animal symbolism.[18] The people of God are represented as sheep while some of their leaders are depicted as rams. In a passage which is often interpreted as a reference to Judas Maccabeus, a great horned sheep arises who leads the others to victory. The passage reads:

> Then I kept seeing till one great horn sprouted on one of those sheep; and he opened their eyes; and they had vision in them and their eyes were opened. He cried aloud to the sheep, and all the rams saw him and ran unto him...I saw thereafter the shepherds coming; and those vultures and kites cried aloud to the ravens so that they should smash the horn of that ram. But he battled with them, and they fought each other; and he cried aloud, while battling with them, so that (God's) help should come (90.9-13).[19]

Dodd writes, 'It is clear that we have here a prototype of the militant seven-horned "Lamb" of the Apocalypse'.[20]

Rather than seeing the lamb imagery in Revelation as being drawn from only one source or having one meaning, a better approach is to

15. Traugott Holtz, *Die Christologie der Apokalypse des Johannes* (Berlin: Akademie Verlag, 2nd edn, 1971), pp. 39-47; Schüssler Fiorenza, *Revelation*, pp. 96-97; George R. Beasley-Murray (*The Book of Revelation* [NCB; Greenwood, SC: Attic Press, 1974], pp. 124-26) argues that John has reinterpreted the Jewish apocalyptic imagery of the lamb in light of the Passover Lamb.

16. J. Comblin, *Le Christ dans l'Apocalypse* (Paris: Desclée, 1965), pp. 17-34.

17. C.H. Dodd, *The Interpretation of the Fourth Gospel* (Cambridge: Cambridge University Press, 1953), pp. 231-32. See also J. Massyngberde Ford, *Revelation* (AB, 38; Garden City, NY: Doubleday, 1975), pp. 88-89; Robert A. Mounce, *The Book of Revelation* (NICNT; Grand Rapids: Eerdmans, 1977), p. 145; C.K. Barrett, 'The Lamb of God', *NTS* 1 (1954–55), pp. 215-16; Beasley-Murray, *Revelation*, pp. 124-26; Charles, *Revelation*, I, p. cxiii.

18. Animal symbolism is also prevalent in Daniel. Dan. 8 even has a horned ram figure, although this imagery does not symbolize Israel or a messianic figure. Another possible use of the Lamb imagery in Jewish apocalyptic literature is found in the *T. Jos.* 19.8. This passage is suspected of being a Christian interpolation, however.

19. E. Isaac (trans.), '1 Enoch', in *The Old Testament Pseudepigrapha* (2 vols.; ed. James H. Charlesworth; Garden City, NY: Doubleday, 1983), I, pp. 69-70.

20. Dodd, *Interpretation*, p. 232.

acknowledge the multivalent character of this powerful symbol. During John's time several connotations probably existed concerning the word lamb. John has drawn on all of these, shaping his materials and creating a new symbol—a victorious military figure who conquers by self-sacrifice, who willingly gives up his life to become 'the faithful and true witness'. For John, the lamb was an excellent symbol to convey his understanding of Jesus and his mission.

The warrior Lamb who is always also the slain Lamb is especially appropriate for John's martyrological interest. The message of Revelation is that those who conquer are the ones who remain faithful, who hold the testimony of Jesus, even when confronted with death.[21] These are the ones who 'loved not their lives even unto death' (12.11). That is part of the message contained in the lamb imagery. The conquering Christ conquers not by military force, but through self-sacrifice, through martyrdom. The Lamb figure evokes ideas not only of cultic sacrifice, Paschal Lamb, Suffering Servant, messianic conqueror, but also of the martyr. Jesus the Lamb is Jesus the Martyr. The reference to the Lamb being slain is a reminder of the cross, of Jesus' death—his martyr death.

In a work addressed to potential martyrs it would be important to remind them that their leader, their Savior, was likewise a martyr victim. He was the powerful Lamb, but also the Lamb who had been slain, the martyred Lamb. Indeed it was because of and not in spite of this martyr death, this shed blood, that he was their Savior. Those who would participate in the reign of this Lamb must be willing to follow him wherever he goes, even to martyrdom (14.4).

The major christological title in the Apocalypse, then, is a martyrological title. The slain Lamb is the martyred Christ. The idea of cultic sacrifice, while not absent, is diminished. The victim is a sacrifice, but a martyrological sacrifice more than a cultic sacrifice. The martyr idea is primary.[22]

Elsewhere in Revelation, martyr Christology is important also. One of the dominant roles of Christ, as already suggested, is that of conqueror. Cosmic combat is at the core of John's message. The forces of good are

---

21. As with Caird (*Revelation*, pp. 32-34) I would argue that the conquerors who are promised specific rewards at the end of each of the letters in Rev. 2–3 are to be understood as martyrs.

22. See the excellent discussion of the martyrological interpretation of the Lamb by Massyngberde Ford (*Revelation*, pp. 90-91).

arrayed against the forces of evil; God against Satan, Christians against the Roman Empire. The leader of God's forces is Christ, variably depicted in his warring role as a lamb, as a reaper, as a rider on a white horse. Yet even in his role as victorious warrior, Christ appears as a martyr. In 17.14 it is the Lamb, and implicitly the slain Lamb, who conquers the enemies. In the description of the rider on a white horse in ch. 19, several reminders of Christ as a martyr figure are present. This heavenly avenger is called 'Faithful and True', reminiscent of the designation in 3.14, 'the faithful and true witness', which, as argued above, is martyrological.

He wears a robe 'dipped in blood' (19.13).[23] Borrowed from Isa. 63.3, the imagery of the bloodstained robe has intrigued many commentators. Most interpret the blood as that of Christ's enemies.[24] This is supported by its usage in Isaiah in which the blood sprinkled on the robe of the divine warrior is that of his enemies. In the scene in the Apocalypse, however, the blood is on Christ's robe before he engages in battle, thus lessening the likelihood that it is the blood of his enemies.[25]

---

23. Several textual variants appear in place of βεβαμμένον, all with some meaning of 'sprinkled' instead of 'dipped'. These variants are best explained as assimilation to Isa. 63.3, where the reading 'sprinkled' is found in both the Hebrew and the Septuagint texts.

24. Rist, 'Revelation', p. 514; Kiddle, *Revelation*, pp. 384-85; Beasley-Murray, *Revelation*, p. 280; Beckwith, *Apocalypse*, p. 733; Mounce, *Revelation*, p. 345; Charles, *Revelation*, II, p. 133; T.F. Glasson, *The Revelation of John* (Cambridge Bible Commentary on the New English Bible; Cambridge: Cambridge University Press, 1965), p. 109. In an earlier study ('The Theme of Martyrdom', pp. 157-59) I, too, argued for identifying the blood as belonging to Christ's enemies. Further study, however, has convinced me that the reference is to Christ's blood. Among the commentators who interpret the blood as Christ's own blood are J.P.M. Sweet, *Revelation* (Westminster Pelican; Philadelphia: Westminster Press, 1979), pp. 282-83; Richard L. Jeske, *Revelation for Today* (Philadelphia: Fortress Press, 1983), p. 112; Ronald H. Preston and Anthony T. Hanson, *The Revelation of Saint John the Divine* (Torch Bible; London: SCM Press, 1949), p. 120. Some commentators (Alfred Loisy, *L'Apocalypse de Jean* [Paris: E. Nourry, 1923], p. 339; and Henry Barclay Swete, *Commentary on Revelation* [London: Macmillan, 3rd edn; repr., Grand Rapids: Kregel, 1977], p. 252) see here a double reference—the blood of the enemies and Christ's own blood. Caird (*Revelation*, pp. 242-43), on the other hand, argues that the blood is the blood of the martyrs.

25. The chronological inconsistency involved in interpreting the blood already on the robe as belonging to the enemies yet to be killed is part of Caird's reason for interpreting the blood as that of the martyrs. Admittedly, chronological inconsistency

A better understanding is to view the blood as Christ's own. The blood-stained garment is a reminder of the cross. It serves the same purpose as the repeated description of the Lamb as the one who was slain. Both descriptions remind the reader that the conquering Christ is also the suffering Christ, the Christ of the cross. The bloodstains point to the baptism of blood—martyrdom—which Christ experienced. Ronald Preston and A.T. Hanson were correct in their observation that in the difference between Isaiah's use of this imagery and John's use of it 'lies the whole Christian gospel'.[26] In the Apocalypse, Christ conquers not by shedding the blood of his enemies but by shedding his own blood for his enemies.

Related to this is the description of the weapon of the conquering Christ. His sword is the word of his mouth (19.15), his testimony. He brings judgment upon an idolatrous world by maintaining his witness to God. In several places in Revelation the effectiveness of the Christian martyrs is stressed. They are the ones who hold the testimony of Jesus (6.9; 11.7; 12.17; 20.4). They conquer 'by the blood of the Lamb, and by the word of their testimony' (12.11). These are the ones who compose the armies of heaven who follow the rider on the white horse—an army of martyrs commanded by the Supreme Martyr. That image is central to John's message. The forces of evil are overcome through faithful witness, not through violent resistance nor through acquiescence and denial. Christ won the victory with the sword of his mouth and the cross. His followers continue the battle in the same way.

The book of Revelation recognizes that a conflict exists between God and the world, and whoever ventures to be God's spokesperson, God's witness, to the world risks death. The intent of John's writing was to encourage the Christians of his day to be faithful witnesses, and if necessary, to prove their faithfulness by enduring death. By so doing they would be maintaining the conquest of the cross. John achieved this goal by identifying the conquering Christ as the martyred Christ.

In the Apocalypse Christ is also presented as the exalted and glorified

---

is evidenced throughout the Apocalypse and thus is not impossible here. An interpretation, however, that adheres to the normal sequence of events is preferable unless overwhelming reasons demand otherwise. Additionally, the dependence of this passage on Isa. 63 does not decide the question of interpretation. Whereas in Isa. 63 the blood is that of the enemies, such an identification is not required in Rev. 19.13. Throughout the Apocalypse John has demonstrated his creative ability in reinterpreting older symbols.

26. Preston and Hanson, *Revelation*, p. 120.

Lord. His praises are sung by the heavenly hosts and by the martyrs. Even these acclamations, however, are related to his martyrological work. In 5.9 the heavenly chorus sings, 'Worthy art thou to take the scroll and to open its seals, for thou wast slain and by thy blood didst ransom men for God'. Later, in v. 12, it is 'the Lamb who was slain' who is worthy 'to receive power and wealth and wisdom and might and honor and glory and blessing'. As noted earlier, the image of the slain Lamb, while partially indebted to sacrificial practices, is also a reminder of Christ's martyr death. He is worthy of praise and honor because he is the faithful and true witness who maintained his testimony to the Father even through death. Throughout John's presentation he holds before his readers the image of Christ as a martyr figure. Regardless of whether Christ is presented as the faithful witness, the slain Lamb, the conquering warrior, the heavenly avenger, or the exalted and glorified Lord, he is always at the same time the martyred Christ.

Of particular importance to John in his portrayal of Christ as a martyr was the imitation value. Jesus is the proto-martyr. His followers are to follow in his path, being willing to suffer and die on account of their witness. Jesus, the faithful witness, is their example. This, more than any other reason, explains John's emphasis on Christ as a martyr. The situation for John and his readers was perilous, while the temptation to compromise with Rome was great. Into this tense climate John projected the image of the martyred Christ who was not afraid to pay the ultimate price of death for his testimony. The martyred Christ, the faithful and true witness, is the one who addresses the seven churches. The martyred Christ is the one who battles the forces of evil; and the martyred Christ is the one who reigns. The importance of the example of Christ is recognized by Adela Yarbro Collins who writes, 'The model of Christ who suffered, died and rose from the dead makes suffering and death tolerable, gives them value, and allows hope which transcends death'.[27]

John instructed his readers that as Christ was willing to suffer and die they too must endure in their faith in the face of persecution. They too are to be faithful and true witnesses. It is no accident that listed among those who will suffer the second death are the cowardly and the faithless—the ones who are not willing to endure, to be faithful witnesses (21.8). For John of Patmos, to be a follower of Jesus Christ meant following in the way of the cross, through suffering and death.

27. Adela Yarbro Collins, 'The Political Perspective of the Revelation to John', *JBL* 96 (1977), p. 254.

Donald W. Riddle has written that the functional purpose of both apocalyptic literature and martyrologies is social control of the group in a time of persecution.[28] The book of Revelation, as a type of apocalyptic literature which at the same time is concerned with martyrs and martyrdom, shares in this purpose. John's writing sought to control the behavior of the believers during the coming days of persecution, preventing them from yielding to the temptation to deny their faith. No other christological motif could have served John's purposes better than the characterization of Christ as the Supreme Martyr. By showing his readers the faithful and true μάρτυς, John called his readers to perseverance and obedience. By pointing them to the Lamb that was slain, he urged passive resistance. By offering them the bloodstained, conquering warrior, he assured them of victory.

More recently, scholars have spoken of the purpose of the writing of Revelation to be the construction of an alternative symbolic universe for John's readers.[29] This new understanding of reality was needed because the old order had collapsed. To John's readers God no longer seemed in control. The dragon and his cohorts were the dominant forces in the universe. Evil, not good, was triumphant. Rome was viewed as the monstrous beast who had authority 'over every tribe and people and tongue and nation' (13.7). Schüssler Fiorenza describes well the crisis that must have confronted John's readers:

> [The] experience of harassment, persecution, and hostility challenged Christians' faith in Christ as Lord. Their experience of hunger, deprivation, pestilence, and war undermined their belief in God's good creation and providence. Christians experienced painfully that their situation in no way substantiated their faith conviction that they already participated in Christ's kingship and power.[30]

Through the Apocalypse, John sought to lead his readers to a deeper understanding of reality, to help them see that the power structures of the world were illusory and temporal. The true course of history resides

28. Donald W. Riddle, 'From Apocalypse to Martyrology', *ATR* 9 (1926–27), pp. 264-65.

29. Paul D. Hanson, *The Dawn of Apocalyptic* (Philadelphia: Fortress Press, rev. edn, 1979), p. 434; Schüssler Fiorenza, *Revelation*, pp. 187-99. Also cf. Adela Yarbro Collins; *Crisis and Catharsis: The Power of the Apocalypse* (Philadelphia: Westminster Press, 1984), p. 141, who speaks of the task of Revelation to be the overcoming of 'the intolerable tension between reality and hopeful faith'.

30. Schüssler Fiorenza, *Revelation*, p. 194.

in the one 'who is and who was and who is to come, the almighty' (1.8; 4.8). Appearance is not reality, for the one who appears 'as though it had been slain' is in actuality the true victor. The martyred Christ has conquered by his act of self-sacrifice. A part of the new symbolic universe, the higher vision, which John creates is that martyrdom is not defeat but victory. This is true not only for the Supreme Martyr, but also for his followers.

In constructing this new symbolic universe John was attempting not only to provide a clearer vision, but through that vision to lead his readers to proper action.[31] He sought to motivate them to faithful endurance in the midst of persecution. One of his primary means of accomplishing this task was by holding before them the image of the martyred Christ. The extent of John's success with his early audience is unknown. The evidence, however, from a later martyrology—'The Letter of the Churches of Lyons and Vienne'—demonstrates the value of such Christology to those who are potential victims.

---

31. Cf. Schüssler Fiorenza, *Revelation*, pp. 187-88, who states that Revelation is not just a symbolic-poetic work, but also a rhetorical work which provides 'the vision of an "alternative world" in order to encourage Christians and to enhance their staying power in the face of persecution and possible execution'.

JSNT 35 (1989), pp. 111-20

POLEMICAL PARALLELISM:
SOME FURTHER REFLECTIONS ON THE APOCALYPSE

Paul Barnett

It was with characteristic insight that, in 1910, Adolph Deissmann commented:

> The cult of Christ goes forth into the world of the Mediterranean and soon displays the endeavour to reserve for Christ the words already in use for worship in that world, words that had just been transferred to the deified emperors or had perhaps been invented in emperor worship. Thus there arises a *polemical parallelism* between the cult of the emperor and the cult of Christ, which makes itself felt where ancient words derived by Christianity from the treasury of the Septuagint and the gospels happen to coincide with solemn concepts of the Imperial cult which sounded the same or similar.[1]

Immediately post-war E. Stauffer developed this theme of parallelism in the chapter 'Domitian and John' in his semi-popular *Christ and the Caesars*.[2] More recently, as the Apocalypse has been subjected to extensive scrutiny in light of its context in contemporary Graeco-Roman history, Deissmann's descriptive phrase has become even more appealing.

1. *Parallelism in the Apocalypse*

Once the idea is recognized it can be seen at many points by a straight-forward reading of the text of the Apocalypse, especially in chs. 12–22.

1. A. Deissmann, *Light from the Ancient East* (New York and London: Hodder & Stoughton, 1910), p. 346.
2. E. Stauffer, *Christ and the Caesars* (ET London: SCM Press, 1952), pp. 174-91.

The evil element in the parallel is probably to be identified in specific ways. Clearly Babylon is Rome. The 'great harlot' is perhaps Messalina, promiscuous wife of Claudius.[3] (Cf. Juvenal, *Satire* 6.116-124; Tacitus, *Ann.* 9.31). The beast from the sea is Caesar and the beast from the earth = the false prophet is the high priest of the Roman cult in Asia. The parallels are as follows:

a. The imagery of the godly woman—persecuted in ch. 12, the wife of the Lamb in ch. 21—is paralleled by the 'great harlot' in ch. 17.

b. The new Jerusalem, the holy city in chs. 21–22 corresponds with but surpasses by far Babylon the great in ch. 18.

c. 'The Lamb...as though slain' (ὡς ἐσφαγμένον, 5.6, 12; 13.8) is paralleled by 'the [sea] beast', one of whose heads 'seemed to have a mortal wound' (ὡς ἐσφαγμένην, 13.3). The beast is taken to be the Roman Emperor, perhaps represented in the province of Asia in the persona of the Proconsul.

d. The beast has an image and those who worship him have the mark of his name on their foreheads (13.15-17; 14.9, 11; 16.2; 19.20; 20.4). In parallel but by contrast the servants of the Lamb who worship him, and who refuse to worship the beast, will bear the name of the Lamb on their foreheads (22.3-4).

e. The community of Christ, the bride of the Lamb, characterized by chastity, truthfulness and endurance (14.4-5), is paralleled by the community of the beast, the great harlot, characterized by murder, fornication, sorcery and falsehood (21.8).

2. The Message of the Apocalypse: Worship God

The most urgent challenge by the writer of the Apocalypse to his readers is that men worship God the creator and judge and the redeemer-Lamb, not the pseudo- and pretentious counterpart, the Roman Emperor, by means of the Imperial Cult which had spread rapidly throughout the dozens of cities of Roman Asia.

It is well known that Domitian sought to be called 'Lord and God' and that a large statue of the emperor had recently been erected in a specially constructed temple in Ephesus, the leading city in the province

---

3.   J.E. Bruns, 'The Contrasted Women of Apocalypse 12 and 17', *CBQ* 26 (1964), p. 462.

of Asia (Suetonius, *Dom.* 13; Dio Cassius, *Roman History* 67.5.7).[4]

R. Bauckham comments that 'the conflict between God and Satan takes historical form in the conflict of human allegiances manifest in *worship*. The Apocalypse divides mankind into the worshippers of the dragon and the beast...and those who will worship God in the heavenly Jerusalem.'[5] The eternal gospel, as declared by the Apocalypse, is: 'Fear God and give him glory...worship [God]' (14.7). John says, repeatedly: Do not worship the beast (14.9, 11; 16.2; 19.20; 20.4); worship God (15.4; 19.4, 10; 22.8).

What is meant by worship? Ritual and ceremony are clearly intended by John. The many passages in the Apocalypse where evangelic proclamation is followed by worshipful response are suggestive of congregation proclamation echoed by worshipful praise. In governor Pliny's account of the trial of Christians in nearby Bithynia a few years later we have a description of the worship of Caesar used as a test of the beliefs of Christians:

> They...repeated after me a formula of invocation to the gods and...made offerings of wine and incense to your statue (which I had brought into court for this purpose along with images of the gods) and moreover had reviled the name of Christ: none of which things any genuine Christian can be induced to do (*Epistle* 96 LCL).

The passage from Pliny's Epistle to the Emperor shows that ritual was used to ascertain the true loyalties of those involved. To affirm Caesar as god was to deny Christ as Lord. To affirm Christ as Lord was to deny Caesar as god. Worship, whether pagan or Christian, gave expression to one's deepest convictions. The many expressions of worship in the Apocalypse affirm from the heart and with the mouth that God Almighty and the Lamb were worthy to entrust one's all to, but that Caesar and his image were not. Worship is the mind's conviction and the mouth's confession that reality, truth and goodness are to be found in God and the Lamb and not in any other.

4.   S.R.F. Price, *Rituals and Power* (Cambridge: Cambridge University Press, 1984), p. 197; B.F. Harris, 'Domitian, the Emperor Cult and Revelation', *Prudentia* 11 (1979), p. 22.

5.   R. Bauckham, 'The Worship of Jesus in Apocalyptic Christianity', *NTS* 27 (1981), p. 329.

3. *Parallelism in Roman Ritual and the Apocalypse*

D.E. Aune has explored several areas in which ideas in the Apocalypse run parallel with thought and practice in the Graeco-Roman world. In one article he argues that much of the symbolism in the Apocalypse has been influenced by the Roman Imperial Court Ceremonial. It is not, however, that the author, John, has merely copied from his political and cultural environment. In Aune's words:

> The author of the Apocalypse was thoroughly convinced that the claims of Caesar were antithetical to those of Christ. So convinced that he regarded any compromise as impossible and any accommodation as blasphemy. So convinced that he produced an elaborately designed and ingeniously crafted literary work in which he both heightened and schematized that antithesis to persuade his wavering readers that his perceptions were not only right, they coincided with the perspectives of God himself. Basic to the structure of his thought is his perception of the dragon and the beast...as a diabolic duo who function as counterfeit counterparts to God and the Lamb.[6]

Aune is especially interested in 'the heavenly ceremonial practised in the throne room of God' which, he says, 'bears such a striking resemblance to the ceremonial of the imperial court and cult that the latter can only be a parody of the former'.[7] He notices parallels in a number of areas.

First, the role of God in the Apocalypse, which is passive and concerned with 'dispensing justice', corresponds with the 'primary role of the Roman emperor, which from the time of Julius Caesar on, was that of rendering justice'.[8]

Secondly, the outer encirclement of the Enthroned One by the Twenty-Four Elders, the inner encirclement by the four living creatures and the overarching vaulted rainbow (ch. 4) may parallel, yet infinitely surpass the Golden House built by Nero after the great fire of AD 64. According to Suetonius 'The main banquet hall was circular and constantly revolved day and night, like the heavens' (*Nero* 31.2). That the face of the one like a son of man 'shone like the sun shining in full strength' (1.16) may suggest a parodying of Nero, who depicted

---

6.   D. Aune, 'The Influence of Roman Imperial Court Ceremonial on the Apocalpyse of John', *BR* 38 (1983), p. 5.
7.   Aune, 'Influence', p. 5.
8.   Aune, 'Influence', p. 8.

himself as Apollo Helios (cf. Suetonius, *Nero* 25).[9]

Thirdly, the fifteen or so hymn-like passages in the Apocalypse, which are usually in a two-beat format (evangelic declaration and worshipful response) are now not thought to have been adapted from church liturgies, but to have been John's own composition. Aune points out that hymns and acclamations, often antiphonal or responsive in form, were frequently directed to Hellenistic rulers and that the practice had become common in the west by New Testament times. Tacitus reports that Nero was accompanied everywhere by 5000 equestrians called *Augustiani* who continually acclaimed the emperor:

> Then it was that Roman knights were enrolled under the title of Augustiani, men in their prime and remarkable for their strength...Day and night they kept up a thunder of applause, and applied to the emperor's person the voice and epithet of deities (*Ann.* 14.15).

Fourthly, it is noted that a further characteristic of the Apocalypse is the praise of the Lord God Almighty and of the Lamb by vast throngs of the redeemed and of angels (5.13; 7.9-12; 19.6-8). Aune links this with the ancient *argumentum e consensu omnium*, that is, the very serious place given to the governed in the making of emperors and the legitimating of their taking power. Aune refers to a formulaic phrase in the *Res Gestae* 34: *per consenum universorum potitus rerum omnium*: 'by universal consent taking control of all things', a concept that would be repeated many times during the principate of Augustus and his successors.

According to Aune[10] the *consensus omnium* became very important in the period after Nero and not only to legitimate a Princeps's imperial accession but also at the time of his *adventus*, that is, his arrival at a place with all due pomp and pageantry. The same applied to the arrival of a provincial governor or visiting dignitary, though with lesser ceremony. The third-century rhetorician Menander stated, in an imperial panegyric:

> [You say]...'We have gone out to meet you for your welcome, with our whole families, children, old men and men in their prime, the priestly families, the city council and people at large. We were all glad in our hearts (and expressed) it with acclamations calling you our saviour

9.   Aune, 'Influence', p. 11.
10.   Aune, 'Influence', p. 19.

and wall, a most radiant star, and children called you their nourisher and saviour of their parents.'[11]

Aune shows that the *argumentum e consensu omnium* had become very important by the end of the first century in imperial propaganda. This may explain the pointedness of the universal, cosmic and eternal acclamation of the Lord God and of the Lamb.

Fifthly, Aune and many others, including Deissmann, note the critical parallel between the honorific titles of Christ and Caesar. Terms used of both include 'son of god', 'god', 'lord', 'saviour'.

Aune concludes that:

> For the most part the individual constituents of [Roman Imperial] cere-monial used by John in his depiction of the heavenly ceremonial have been heightened, expanded and give even greater cosmic significance. The result is that the sovereignty of God and of the Lamb have been elevated so far above the pretensions and claims of earthly rulers that the latter, upon comparison, become only pale, even diabolical imitations of the transcen-dent majesty of the King of kings and Lord of lords.[12]

4. *Who is the True Prophet?*

A further example of parallelism between the Apocalypse and Roman society has been raised by D. Georgi's question, which is the title of his important article: 'Who is the true prophet?'[13] The precise answer is that John is the true prophet and that what he has written is true prophecy. John refers repeatedly to 'the book of this prophecy' (1.1-4; 22.6-9). If John is the true prophet, who then is the *false* prophet about whom we read in the Apocalypse?

Against the opinion of Georgi, which we will outline below, it must be said that strict historical exegesis requires that we identify the 'false prophet' with 'the beast...out of the earth' (19.20; 13.11-18). Recent study in the Imperial Cult in Asia makes it clear that John means his readers to think of the false prophet as the High Priest (*archiereus*) of the Province.[14] The *archiereus* officiated at the numerous and diverse cultic activities and also presided at the Provincial Assembly of Asia

11. Quoted by Aune, 'Influence', pp. 19-20.
12. Aune, 'Influence', p. 22.
13. D. Georgi, 'Who is the True Prophet?', *HTR* 79 (1986), pp. 100-26.
14. Price, *Rituals*, p. 197.

(*Koinon Asias*).[15] It was the *archiereus* of Asia, a local dignitary, who, according to John,

> exercises all the authority of the first beast…and makes all the inhabitants worship the first beast…works signs…causes all…to be marked…so that no one can buy or sell unless he has the mark…(13.12-17).

Georgi, however, may be correct in identifying the false prophet more broadly. Georgi expresses surprise that New Testament students, in their preoccupation with eschatology, have neglected an obvious field of enquiry, one that is contemporary with the New Testament, namely Roman texts. Virgil's *Fourth Eclogue* is well known to Christians as expressing a striking parallel to the gospel of Christ:

> Now the last age by Cumae's Sibyl sung
> Has come and gone, and the majestic roll
> Of circling centuries begins anew:
> Justice returns, returns old Saturn's reign,
> With a new breed of men sent down from heaven.
> Only do thou, at the boy's birth in whom
> The iron shall cease, the golden age arise…
> Apollo reigns. And in thy consulate
> Tis glorious age, O Pollio, shall begin,
> And the months enter on their mighty march.

According to Virgil, with the birth of Augustus, a new breed came down from heaven, a new, golden age began in which the god Apollo now reigns.

Georgi points out that Virgil's *Fourth Eclogue* is by no means alone as a text of the Augustan age which promises that the new age has now come.[16] He refers in particular to Horace's *Carmen saeculare*, commissioned for the celebration of the Secular Games, the official jubilee for the foundation of the Republic. The Secular Games were an instrument for dividing the epochs. (Stauffer, however, had anticipated this line of thought, though uncritically and without references.)[17] Horace wrote:

> Already the Parthian fears the hosts mighty on land and sea and
> fears the Alban axes.
> Already the Indians and Scythians, but recently disdainful, are
> asking for our answer.

15. *OGIS* 458.
16. Georgi, 'True Prophet', p. 101.
17. Stauffer, *Christ*, pp. 152-59.

> Already Faith and Peace and Honour and ancient Modesty and neglected
> Virtue have courage and have come back, and blessed Plenty with her horn
> is seen...
> May Phoebus, the prophet...prolong the Roman power and Latium's
> prosperity to cycles ever new and ages ever better!
> (*Carmen Saeculare* 37–52 LCL)

Georgi argues that the word *vates* used by both Virgil and Horace
means much more than 'poet'; as used by these authors it means
'inspired singers of ancient times'.[18] Horace portrays Aeneas, the hero
of ancient Troy, as a contemporary saviour who brings world peace.
Clearly Augustus is in mind; the heroic past is now incarnate in the
person of the Princeps.[19]

According to Georgi the prophet John, who is the true prophet,

> sees in the gigantic machinery of the *Imperium Romanum* the demonstra-
> tion of a prophetic religion fascinating the world. Rev. 13.17 and 18 testify
> to the correctness of the analysis of Horace given above, namely, that the
> political ideology of the principate possessed religious integrity, relevance
> and attraction. John is aware of the eschatological dimension of the
> intentions and actions of the principate although he protests them. For him
> the Caesar religion is cult and theology of the devil which apes the
> authentic eschatological conviction, that which is caused by Jesus... [John]
> feels himself in dramatic competition with the prophet(s) of the Caesar
> religion, people like Horace and Virgil and lesser ones. The religion they
> represent and propagate is a world religion, the religion of a world empire.
> Therefore the battle with them has to be seen in cosmic proportions.[20]

Whether John was aware of the eschatological poems of Virgil and
Horace is open to question. Direct evidence is lacking. As a person living
in Proconsular Asia, however, John would almost certainly have known
of the decree issued in 9 BC by the *Koinon Asias* changing the local calendar so that Augustus's birthday (23 September) became New Year's
Day. The decree, which was inscribed in temples of Caesar in Asia,
speaks about Augustus in ways that resemble the references of the poets
Virgil and Horace:

> whereas the providence which divinely ordered our lives created with zeal
> and munificence the most perfect good for our lives by producing
> Augustus and filling him with virtue for the benefaction of mankind,
> blessing us and those after us with a saviour who put an end to war and

18. Georgi, 'True Prophet', p. 105.
19. Georgi, 'True Prophet', p. 116.
20. Georgi, 'True Prophet', pp. 123-24.

established peace...and whereas the birthday of the god marked for the world the beginning of good tidings through his coming...Paullus Fabius Maximus, proconsul of the province...suggested for the honour of Augustus a thing hitherto unknown by the Greeks, namely, beginning their calendar with the god's nativity.[21]

Scholars have long puzzled over John's reference to the child in Revelation 12. It is here suggested that the '...male child...who is to rule the nations with a rod of iron...[who] was caught up to God and to his throne' (12.5) is John's deliberately made declaration about the nativity of true saviour and God, Jesus the Messiah, in comparison with whom Augustus, as described by Virgil, is a false and pretentious ruler.

John the servant of God and witness to Jesus is the true prophet. He who testifies to and promotes the cult of Caesar is a false prophet, to be overthrown along with the beast whom he serves and the dragon who makes war against God, his Christ and his people. This evil trinity is paralleled by the Lord God Almighty, the Lamb and...?

Who is the third person in God's trinity in the Apocalypse?

It is well known that the Spirit does not figure significantly in this book. The prophet John, the true prophet in parallel with the false prophet, however, is very important (1.3; 19.10; 22.6, 7, 9, 10, 18; cf. 16.3; 19.20; 20.10). But John does not operate in his own right but only 'in the Spirit', ἐν πνεύματι (1.10; 4.2; 17.3; 21.10). The true trinity, then, is completed after all by the Spirit. But in John's presentation the role of the Spirit is to inspire the true prophet John to prophesy. In particular, the message of the Spirit-inspired prophet is: Do not worship the beast or its image; worship God, follow the Lamb wherever he goes.

As such a prophet, this John is a polemicist, one whose assault on the enemies of God in the world of his time resembles the prophets of the Old Testament in their assault on the world of their times. The more we know of John's Graeco-Roman context, which is now seen to correspond polemically with the Apocalypse, the higher our estimate of John's audacity becomes. John the prophet of Patmos became for the Christians of Asia what the classic prophets of Israel had been centuries before in their denunciations of the nations surrounding Israel.

---

21. *OGIS* 458 (trans. N. Lewis and M. Reinhold; Roman Civilization, 2; New York; Harper & Row, 1964), p. 64.

JSNT 34 (1988), pp. 105-23

PLINY'S PROSECUTIONS OF CHRISTIANS:
REVELATION AND 1 PETER

F. Gerald Downing

There was no large-scale action against Christians in the courts of those parts of Asia Minor addressed in Revelation and 1 Peter before the cases heard by Pliny and referred to in his letter, 10.96, and in his copy of Trajan's reply, 10.97. If Revelation and/or 1 Peter were occasioned by the commencement of official judicial action, their 'publication' dates from this time; and this is most likely. Their respective attitudes to the human world around, however, are in all probability much less 'occasional', and are based on mature though divergent analyses of human society in the light of early Christian life and faith.

I shall primarily be discussing the implications of Pliny's letters 10.96 and 10.97.[1] The case I hope to make has in my mind a number of ramifications and these I now list, along with some already introduced. I do not intend to argue all these supposed implications in detail; nor do I expect my primary argument on its own to be sufficient to settle these other issues, even if the main argument is itself persuasive. There may be, however, a certain amount of mutual support among the theses if a coherent picture of popular and official Roman reactions to the nascent Christian movement emerges.

I list my points in reverse order to which I shall consider them:

1. Revelation may contain material that pre-dates 70 CE, but Rome has now by its destruction of the Temple become a second 'Babylon', and Domitian has propagated the cults of Rome and the Emperor.

---

1.   I refer to the LCL (Betty Radice, *Pliny, Letters and Panegyricus* [Cambridge, MA: Harvard University Press; London: Heinemann, 1969]), though I have looked at others. There do not seem to be any textual difficulties affecting the arguments of this paper.

Revelation knows of past martyrs (6.9-11—in Nero's time?) but only one recent one (2.13).

2. There was no co-ordinated persecution/prosecution of Christians qua Christians under Domitian: not in Ireneaus, nor Luke (if so dated).

3. The 'fiscus iudaicus' issue is a red herring. Non-payment was no capital offence, Christians delated as 'Jewish non-payers' were not on that count executed, nor are they recorded as having been on any other count arising out of such prosecutions.

4. Ignatius of Antioch is fixated on 'martyrdom', yet is apparently unaware of any such witness offered by members of the Christian communities of Ephesus, Smyrna, Philadelphia (addressed in Revelation); nor Tralles nor Magnesia; nor his home Antioch; nor even in Rome, in his own generation.

5. There is no danger for anyone else in these churches in being in touch with Ignatius, even though he is apparently already under sentence.

6. 1 Peter suggests a rather sudden ('unexpected') new intensity of opposition. The theoretical possibility of 'suffering' has all at once become actual. What Christians face is described in very much the same terms as are used in Pliny 10.96, yet this provides no precedent for Pliny to look back to (see below). It seems to be the same situation.

7. There is no evidence for early persecution/prosecution involving executions, no evidence available to Christian writers later, other than in Tacitus and Suetonius, in 1 Clement, Revelation, and 1 Peter, and in Pliny. There may have been little documentation because there was little to tell.

8a. Pliny it is who prompts the alarm we may discern in Revelation as we now have it, and in 1 Peter. The Beast seems to be waking up.

8b. If Pliny had had precedents, formal or informal, he would have used them, or at least referred to them, even if he also asked for confirmation of his use or innovation from Trajan.

8c. Neither Pliny (10.96) nor Trajan (10.97) uses any precedents to guide them, either formally or informally: nothing from their general knowledge of the courts and procedure elsewhere, and nothing from the local records or the memories of local officials. And the 'lapsed Christians' have not lapsed in response to any significant official pressure: Pliny draws from them no precedent, nor pointer to where a precedent might be sought.

So now to this last point in more detail (and then back through the list):

8c. Pliny seems to be under the impression that there have been *cognitiones de Christianis*, somewhere, sometime, somehow, in his adult lifetime. Some such impression must be implied by his note that he has not been present at any. But in gaining the impression that some such cases have occurred he seems to have picked up no information as to how, no hints to guide him, and no likely sources of information to follow up before troubling the emperor Trajan. At least, he claims none.

I want to be very guarded in my claims at this point, because the ground has been very well trampled-over, and lots of quite diverse conclusions have seemed very obvious to different historians. At this stage I am only pointing out that Pliny does not in fact *claim* to be basing his procedure on anything in the past other than a conviction that Christians have been subject to official court action somewhere, sometime, somehow. Of course, he could have had more information, and it could have been accurate, and he could just have been kidding Trajan, perhaps flattering him by asking for advice. He could even have been present at such court proceedings, and have here been lying. But none of that seems very likely.

A.N. Sherwin-White has distinguished three approaches to the issue,[2] and subsequent writers have seemed happy to follow him in this division.[3]

(1)   Some would argue that there was a general enactment, forbidding the practice of the Christian religion: most recently, Marta Soldi: 'The decision had been taken to allow the Christians to be accused of *superstitio illicita*, so that from now onwards they could be incriminated for their religious persuasion alone. Again [and] far more serious was the fact that the state authorities had allowed and even encouraged the spreading of slanderous rumour against the Christians...'[4] Sherwin-White details some of the difficulties involved in any such reconstruction: for instance, that any such enactment would have

2.   A.N. Sherwin-White, 'The Early Persecutions and Roman Law Again', *JTS* NS 3 (1952), pp. 199-213; *The Letters of Pliny* (London: Oxford University Press, 1966); and also *Roman Society and Roman Law in the New Testament* (London: Oxford University Press, 1963).

3.   The division is accepted by M. Sordi, *The Christians and the Roman Empire* (1983; ET London: Croom Helm, 1986); and by P. Keresztes, 'Rome and the Christian Church I', *ANRW* II.23.1.

4.   Sordi, *Christians*, p. 35.

had to have been renewed at the start of each Principate, and so, I take it, brought to the notice of imperial officials relatively recently.[5] At this stage I only want to point out that Pliny does not mention any such enactment, does not say, 'Unfortunately I haven't a copy of the text, could you have it sent to me', nothing like that. He seems to be asking Trajan to create a ruling.

(2)   There is then what Sherwin-White calls the '*coercitio*' theory.[6] In this it is argued that there was officially instigated police action (as it were) against Christians as '*hostes humani generis*', on some sort of 'common law' basis. Sherwin-White can readily point out how unlikely that is, both in terms of the availability of 'police' (who would have to be soldiers), and in terms of normal procedures for which we have evidence. Rather was it the case that court action would be taken on information lodged (as in Pliny's letter, *deferebantur*) by some individual or individuals; whether private or by chance holding some civic office was immaterial. Certainly Pliny makes no mention of any such supposed 'police' action (let alone noting that any had been going on, or alleging, say, it had been done so badly as to need sorting out by the Emperor). It is private and now anonymous informers who have been bringing cases to his attention.

(3)   Sherwin-White himself prefers, then, the third position just referred to, for which I feel he certainly adduces convincing general procedural evidence. Here the Christians are vulnerable to public accusation, as having an established reputation for anti-social behaviour—the '*flagitia*' Pliny refers to without specifying them. Up to this point, I would suggest Sherwin-White has the best of the argument. But he then claims—well, I think, takes it for granted—that such delation on this basis has been going on regularly. The locals are just getting the new governor to keep the pot boiling the way it has been over the years. And for now, I would only point out that Pliny makes no mention of any such action by his predecessors, nor of the

---

5.   Sherwin-White, 'Early Persecutions', p. 201 (but contrast Pliny 10.58, and the comment on it below).

6.   Sc. action to confine, restrain or punish: Sherwin-White, 'Early Persecutions', pp. 199, 203.

accusers referring him to any such action. Pliny does mention people who claim to have apostatized, recently or in the distant past, and that is taken as evidence by most for their own particular interpretation. But Pliny shows no sign of considering that these supposed past cases might afford him some guidance. He does not even say that they present him with conflicting possibilities.

I would suggest that Pliny refers to no precedents because neither he nor anyone else around has any that would be of any use. No kind of court action has been happening in his province or anywhere in the neighbourhood or in Rome, either. In the many cases to be reviewed below, where there are precedents he wants to follow or wants to change he makes them explicit. But here he does not refer to any search for precedents, nor ask for any such search to be made for central archive copies. He asks Trajan to create a ruling.

Pliny's own actions to date against Christians brought before him have been made up out of his own head. At no point does he suggest that he is using tried procedures. He exercises his *ius gladii*, but starts to have qualms when he seems likely to be faced with lots of cases. It is within his discretion, but he is supposed to be discrete (he could be arraigned for *saevitia*).[7] He does not excuse his action as following established custom, asking if he was right to follow it. He is asking if he did right in inventing it.

He tells Trajan that his procedure has been to ask those brought before him on suspicion of being Christians, if they were. Those who admitted it were warned of the penalty for persistence in such allegiance, and were asked a second and, if need be, and again with a warning, a third time. If anyone persisted, Pliny had them executed, on the basis of the suspicion that being a confessed Christian warranted it, but also consoling himself with the thought that the obstinate disobedience to a magistrate's command to desist (*pertinacia*) was sufficient warrant on its own.[8] Those of the accused who denied ever having been Christians,

---

7.   Cruel and pointless severity: Sherwin-White, *Roman Society*, pp. 14-17; *Letters*, p. 698.

8.   Sherwin-White places a great deal of stress on the Christians' '*pertinacia*', paraphrasing it very soon by '*contumacia*'. He is taken to task for this by G.E.M. de Ste. Croix 'Why Were the Early Christians Persecuted?', *Past and Present* 26 (1963), pp. 18-21, to which Sherwin-White replied, 'Why Were the Early Christians Persecuted?—An Amendment', *Past and Present*, 27 (1964), pp. 23-27, with a

and those who claimed to have desisted from such allegiance, were invited to offer incense and a libation to statues of the Roman gods and of the Emperor, and to curse Christ. Pliny had gathered that this was likely to be a decisive test. He does not say that anyone had told him it or any other part of the procedure had been used in court before.

Sherwin-White and Hugh Last, for instance, are surely right that it is only a test.[9] It is not presented by Pliny as the basis for his action, nor taken by Trajan as the basis for prosecution, and in fact he drops the use of his statue from it. But there is no law that says people must do this sort of thing publicly. It is just that refusal is a sufficient if not necessary sign that these are Christians—and, I would add, that they are perhaps sufficiently disaffected to demand attention. There is certainly no sign that Christians have been ostentatiously refusing to join in the annual celebrations of the Emperor's accession or birthday or whatever, no sign that this is the whole or even a part of an initial charge. As Lucian shows later, it is probably quite widely believed that Christians, like Epicureans, are a godless and irreligious lot, and likely to show it.[10] But my main point is that, as said, there is no suggestion that this test has been established as part of court procedure. Our efficient and humane financial administrator and his humane and efficient Emperor establish the pattern for the first time.

It is also worth noting that none of the information laid has suggested or adduced evidence (however shaky) for the *flagitia*, nor is there any past court record of convictions or even of investigation in this area, to guide Pliny. The informants have themselves given him no guidance here either.

The Christians who have maintained their allegiance say they have given up meeting since the ban on *collegia/hetaeriae* (10.96.7). They do

---

rejoinder by St Croix, *Past and Present* 27 (1964), pp. 28-33. Despite the firm agreement of both Keresztes and Sordi with the latter, it certainly appears to me that Sherwin-White does more justice to Pliny's actual words: 'If they persist, I order them to be led away to execution; for whatever it is they are admitting to, I am convinced that the stubbornness and unshakeable obstinacy (sc. of their persistence in refusing to renounce their Christian allegiance) ought not to go unpunished' (10.96.3): *perseverantes duci iussi. neque enim dubitabam, qualecumque esset quod faterentur, pertinaciam certe et inflexibilem obstinationem debere puniri*. Sherwin-White maintained his position in his commentary (*Letters*, pp. 698-99).

    9.   Sherwin-White, 'Early Persecutions', pp. 207-208; H. Last, 'The Study of the Persecutions', *JRS* 27 (1937), pp. 80-92.

    10. Pliny, *Letters* 10.35, 52, etc.; Lucian, *Alexander*, pp. 25, 38, etc.

not seem to have been aware of any other court action (still less, any central enactment) that would have amounted to a prohibition. The ban on *collegia* was the first, and as law abiding subjects, they complied.

8b. Sherwin-White argues that there must have been more precise precedent of some kind for Pliny to go ahead, even granted all this independent authority: just suspicion and intransigence would not have been enough.[11] But in the many instances where Pliny for other matters has precedents on which he has acted, but about which he is unsure, he makes that very clear. And even where he has not yet taken action, he again makes it clear that he has tried to find out what precedent there might be. His silence on this score in this single instance of the Christians must surely be significant. This is the longest letter of those he preserves addressed to Trajan. He may bother the Emperor sufficiently to get the occasional testy reply; he shows no sign of willingness to appear lazy or incompetent.

At 10.6, Pliny has asked for Roman citizenship for a freedman—but has been reminded there are special rules applying to natives of Egypt and apologizes for not having checked or followed them as laid down.

At 10.8, Pliny is very punctilious in noting the rules about leave of absence, as Trajan acknowledges, 10.9.

(At 10.18 he is rebuked for not getting other kinds of advice locally; and compare 40; at 42 he is told he should have tried Lower Moesia first.)

At 10.19, he has found a custom, changed it for the moment, but checks with Trajan (using slaves as prison warders).

At 10.29, he is presented with a problem: two slaves have enlisted as soldiers. Pliny makes it very clear that he does understand most of the rules, but just does not know what to do now they have got as far as taking the oath, though have not actually been enrolled. He wants to know, because any action of his might well create a precedent (*exemplum*). Everyone knows slaves must not offer for the army: if the fault lies with them, says Trajan, they are to be executed.

At 10.31, he has found a precedent, is loathe to change what his predecessors have left undisturbed, but knows it infringes explicitly authorized procedure: condemned criminals have been allowed to work as public slaves. Records of sentences from many years back are available

---

11. Sherwin-White, *Letters*, pp. 694-95, on 10.96.1; 'Early Persecutions', pp. 208-209.

for consultation. Pliny has asked searchingly how this situation arose, found no documentation for their release to these less exacting duties, but the assurance that previous governors had allowed it. He clearly expects to make this kind of investigation of past records before consulting the Emperor, even though he is still going to consult him.

At 10.47, he expresses unease at being faced with breaching long established custom; Trajan replies that he is to, but establish explicitly that this action [inspecting a free city's accounts; *plus ça change!*] is *not* to create a precedent.

At 10.56, an action by a previous governor [rescinding a banishment order of his own] has been brought to his attention. The documents are all available for inspection. Previous orders are not supposed to be contravened, Pliny says he is well aware of that. Trajan is so sure of that, he will not allow the rescinding by the man himself to stand till he has found out from him why he did it. (In a related case, in the same letter, Trajan also stresses the seriousness of *contumacia*: 10.57.)

At 10.58 (despite what Sherwin-White says about '*damnatio memoriae*'),[12] letters and decisions of Domitian had been accepted as entirely relevant by Nerva, and so were presumed to be by Trajan, too. If decisions and actions had not been rescinded, they were still in order—and were presumed to be accessible.

At 10.65 Pliny writes, 'There is a serious problem (concerning the support of foundlings)...I was unable to find a particular case or a general rule which could apply to Bythinia...I felt it was not sufficient to be guided only by precedents' (it is a financial welfare-benefits matter). But even here, where he doubts the validity of precedents, he quotes them. An edict relating to Andania in the Peloponnese and letters to Sparta and to the province of Achaia from all three Flavian emperors, including Domitian, have been brought to his attention as possibly relevant. He expects Trajan to have copies (if the examples are genuine) in the files in Rome. Trajan accepts that items that have been traced have force, but decides they do not in fact affect the legal situation in Bythinia (10.56).

At 10.68, Pliny quotes previous practice in proconsular provinces, and is told to follow ancient local precedent, even if people there have not of late been following it themselves (10.69).

At 10.72, Pliny talks of looking up other Senatorial decrees relating to proconsular provinces for guidance, as well as local precedent in

---

12. 'Early Persecutions', pp. 201-202: 'Imperial edicts, especially of emperors who suffered *damnatio memoriae*, died with their authors'.

Domitian's time; only he forgets to give Trajan the reference for him to check the copies in the central archives.

At 10.78, he again talks of following the practice of previous reigns, but is unwilling to do anything that would set a further precedent for others, unless he has Trajan's confirmation.

At 10.110 and 111, recent practice is not to be undone: but, while querying it, Pliny still details it.

At 10.114/115, where established law and custom clash, again both are explained, as a basis for Pliny's query; the decision is similar to the previous one. The law Trajan wants re-enforcing dates from Pompey; (compare 10.79, 10.112).

At 10.117, Trajan says a little testily that Pliny can surely decide for himself whether the custom of the rich handing out small sums of money to mark a wedding is likely to be a cover for political corruption. But Pliny (10.96) has thought fit to detail the custom.

In the light of these instances it seems to me very unlikely indeed that Pliny would have failed to mention that he had tried to find some guidance from past rulings or court decisions, and used them, had there been any. Sherwin-White is surely right to insist that he would not have been absolutely bound, even had they been available. But by this juncture if not sooner Pliny must have been fully aware that Trajan was very much averse to innovation unless it were clearly needed; even had he felt precedent was a poor guide, he would have felt duty bound to look for it, important to mention his search, if need be explain why it was fruitless, and imperative to justify in detail any new procedure on his part. It is much the most likely that he would have stated and followed established custom, had there been one, and either have asked permission to change, had he felt change necessary, or retain, if that seemed best. In fact he is neither claiming precedent nor asking for permission to vary established procedures. He must be taken to be doing what his words most naturally state: he has been employing an *ad hoc* set of procedures that he has had to think up from scratch.

There have been no cases of Christians being brought to the courts in his province—ever. He does not simply fail to refer to them—there are none, none for him in Bythinia and Pontus, but also none in Trajan's archives, and none in any other context that he or Trajan might think relevant, no sign of 'this is what has been done or x or y, and it seems a good idea'. There has been no action in the courts against Christians for their allegiance in Pontus or Bythinia, and none in the provinces around for his local advisers to bring to his attention.

8a. So Pliny and Trajan are taking the first steps in opening the courts to informers against Christians. Christians have already got a bad reputation, and they are clearly not Jews, who still have privileges, however much controverted by local communities.[13] Christians are vulnerable to local enemies when a governor arrives who is intent on imposing order and law. It is very likely appropriate to describe the informers as 'trying it on' with the new governor; but this is the first occasion for such a 'try on'—or, at least, the first successful attempt.[14]

And despite Sherwin-White's rejection of E.T. Merrill's suggestion, it does seem worth taking the decree against *collegia* into account.[15] Pliny notes that the continuing Christians had seen it as having a very direct relevance for themselves. Its importance to the administration can be judged by other well-known letters between Pliny and Trajan: the refusal of permission to form a fire-brigade for Nicaea (10.33/34), the guarded permission for the free city of Amisus to retain a 'benefit society', so long as no suspicion of political unrest attaches to its meetings; but point-blank refusal to extend that to any other town (10.92/93).

Pliny is there to tidy things up and settle things down, and the Christians are inconvenient, untidy. Their 'pertinacia' shows they must be taken seriously.[16] If the Revelation to John and 1 Peter in particular are occasioned by some crisis in Asia Minor then this is it, and it is the

---

13. Compare Josephus, *Ant.* 14.219-267, as evidence. I write, be it said, with no claim to expertise in Roman Law, basing my case on Pliny's letters in the main, along with other evidence adduced in the works here referred to; but also noting Quintilian, *Institutes* 5.2 (and 12.4.2), on precedent.

14. Ste. Croix, 'Why Were the Early Christians Persecuted?', p. 9; Sherwin-White, 'Early Persecutions', p. 209.

15. 10.96.7; E.T. Merrill, *Essays in Early Christian History* (London, 1924), ch. 7, cited by Sherwin-White, 'Early Persecutions', pp. 205-206.

16. See above, n. 8. The ideology of Trajan's reign is usefully summed up by Dio of Prusa as follows: 'The good emperor...regards moral virtue as the true sanctity and any wickedness as the real sacrilege. It is not just temple-robbers and those who blaspheme the Gods who are in his view accursed sinners: much more serious still is the offence of cowardly and unrighteous people with no self-control, stupidly running counter to the Gods' purposeful power' (3.52-53, LCL, amended). It is that purposeful power, as exercised by Pliny on behalf of Trajan, that the Christians are obstinately and contumaciously resisting.

first in that part of the world, very likely the first anywhere since Nero's action in Rome. The Beast is waking up.

We now take the next step back to consider other possible evidence.

7. There is in fact very little more evidence available to Christian writers in the succeeding centuries, for any other persecution or prosecution of Christians. Eusebius tells of one Cleophas suffering under 'Atticus' (*H.E.* 3.127),[17] and refers to Ignatius. Relying on Hegesippus (*H.E.* 4.19-20) he refers to '*Caesar Domitianus*' interrogating members of the family of Jesus, in Palestine. That story suggests no worry about Christian allegiance, only about royal pretensions. It seems clear that Tertullian had no other source than our letters of Pliny, and the notes of Nero's actions in Rome, as recorded by Tacitus and Suetonius.[18] One likely reason for the scant data later available is that there was anyway little to record.

L.W. Barnard has argued that *1 Clem.* 1 and 5–7 must refer to some persecution, with 7.1 saying 'we are in the same arena' (σκάμματι) as Peter and Paul and the host of their immediate contemporaries. It was directed, however, Barnard argues, only against eminent individual Christians: Flavius Clemens, Domitilla, etc. But their deaths had been a severe loss, a shock and a threat to the Roman Christian community. If one were convinced on other grounds that such persecution had been going on, then one might feel justified in reading *1 Clement* this way. But it is very difficult to see the athletic imagery of 7.1, the struggle in the arena, as other than conventional metaphor (in Cynic tradition at least).[19] If the Roman Christian community were feeling it was facing real danger, but Corinth were not, it would seem very odd for Clement to refer to this so allusively. 'In your much happier situation you ought to behave yourselves better' is what we might in that case have expected. If 7.1 looks very nonchalant as a reference to being in precisely the kind of situation recalled in 5–6, then 60–61, with their happy reliance on divine guidance of their splendid rulers, would also seem very odd, if Domitian had just been picking off eminent and even

---

17. Sherwin-White, *Letters*, p. 695; Sordi, *Christians, ad loc.*

18. In a paper presented to the Ehrhardt Seminar earlier in 1986, Professor A.A. Birley made a strong case for Tertullian (in *Apologiticum, Ad Nationes, De Spectaculis*, etc.) having no other sources than those listed here.

19. L.W. Barnard, 'Clement of Rome and the Persecution of Domitian', *NTS* 10 (1964), pp. 251-60. For the metaphor, see e.g. Diogenes in Dio of Prusa 8 and 9.

leading members of the community. (I suppose one might suggest that 1 Peter seems able to maintain a similar paradox; but we come to that in a moment.)

Hebrews, wherever we date and place it, talks of losing property, not blood (10.33; 12.4). If it is later than 70 CE, this might be a reference to being forced to pay the *fiscus iudaicus*. But executions are explicitly excluded.[20]

6. On one reading (albeit disputed) 1 Peter initially records a conviction that the Empire is a good thing, pretty effectively in God's hands (2.13-17), even though Christians have a bad public reputation (2.12; 3.16). Suffering (3.17) is something that might possibly happen, though probably only to slaves (2.18-25). And then (4.12), the fiery trial descends in a manner and force that could well appear unexpected (ξένος). The theoretical possibility of general suffering has become actual, and has occasioned the publication of this reminder of what the community had always been taught.[21] If this 'fiery trial' that has descended on the community involves the courts, it must be Pliny's doing. There has been no other in the provinces (or areas) of Pontus and Bythinia or, in all likelihood, the rest, to which the letter is addressed (1 Pet. 1.1).

Admittedly, the letter does not say in so many words that the fiery trial has involved court appearances. It could have amounted to no more than hostility, maybe economic and social oppression, the odd beating up, or death, even, at the hands of an angry mob.[22] Yet, as John Knox pointed out some thirty-five years ago,[23] the issues facing the Christians

20. Heb. 9.8 must make any attempt to date the work in relation to the fall of the Temple (before or after) quite impossible. The writer is not concerned with it.

21. F.W. Beare, *The First Epistle of Peter* (Oxford: Oxford University Press, 1958), pp. 7-9; *per contra* e.g. E. Best, *1 Peter* (London: Oliphants, 1971), pp. 25-27.

22. The general social situation presupposed by the letter is well analysed by J.H. Elliott, *A Home for the Homeless* (Philadelphia: Fortress Press, 1981). He argues against seeing the book's theology as formed by overt official prosecutions (e.g. pp. 143-45). Accepting that, I would still argue for its appearance having been occasioned by Pliny's response to the informers.

23. J. Knox, 'Pliny and 1 Peter: A Note on 1 Pet. 4.14-16 and 3.15', *JBL* 72 (1953), pp. 187-89. Knox's suggestion, following J. Moffatt and F.W. Beare, of 'revolutionary' for '*allotriepiskopos*' (1 Pet. 4.15), is less convincing, and 'informer' might even be preferable, if the other arguments here seem persuasive. Among other earlier scholars who would accept this sort of dating, note F.W. Beare, as above; and also H. Lietzmann, *A History of the Early Church*. II. *The Founding of*

addressed in 1 Peter do seem to be very like those in Pliny: Are they to suffer for 'the name' alone, or for some other accusation of wrong doing? Pliny does not specify the 'flagitia' Christians are popularly supposed guilty of, but seems to take 'no theft, robbery, adultery, or fraud' as relevant: 1 Peter lists among suspicions to be avoided, 'murder, theft, and other wrong-doing'. Christians brought before the court are to make it clear (as Pliny has found they do) that there is no substance in such popular accusations. (In line with 1 Pet. 2.13 they have even obediently given up meetings that might contravene the edict against *collegia*.)

If the terms are much the same, the situation must be precisely that of Pliny's letter 10.96, for, as we have seen, nothing like it has occurred in the area before.[24] It must have been official action through the courts that was in question: it is very unlikely that the writer of 1 Peter would expect Christians faced by a lynch mob to be able to insist on making this kind of distinction. It is also worth considering the unlikelihood of a town mob feeling it could get away with even an occasional lynching;[25] but also the unlikelihood of it feeling the need to. If (as in Pliny's letter) it was thought that there were charges against an unpopular group that could be made to stick, then the most obvious move would be through the governor's court: there would be the stigma of a criminal conviction borne by the whole movement, in addition to penalties imposed, and all at no risk of the town being held responsible for a riot (rather might it be 'commended for doing right'—1 Pet. 2.14!).[26]

(Another possibility to be discounted is the suggestion that 1 Peter

---

the Church Universal (ET London: Lutterworth, 1961).

24. The situation presupposed in 1 Peter cannot have provided the long-term lapsed who turned up among those accused by Pliny: as we have seen, they provide him with no precedent, while what 1 Peter describes would have.

25. A realization of the risks involved in riotous behaviour is plain in Dio 46.14, and others of his addresses to townsfolk, just as it is in Acts, written not long before; and it is important to note the general lawfulness presupposed in Pliny's letters (he has no riots to deal with, even though he has very few troops at his disposal, and seditious fire-brigades are a worry).

26. Lucian, *Demonax* 16, for instance, shows how readily an appeal could in fact be made to a governor, on even a small issue, as, again, does Acts; and how ready crowds were to attempt to use governors and others to secure their vengeance for them (and compare Philo, *De Legatione* and *In Flaccum*). I think this must be accepted, despite the valid point with which Sherwin-White ends his 'Early Persecutions', pp. 212-13, regarding the limited availability of governors.

was facing—maybe two, maybe five decades earlier—a threat of official action that never materialised to provide Pliny with a precedent. The terms are too close, the testing is too astonishingly real.)[27]

There is, then, nothing in 1 Peter to count against the conclusions drawn from Pliny's and Trajan's letters, and a great deal to corroborate them. There has been no prior action against Christians in the courts; and 1 Peter is most likely concerned with the identical situation—from the other side.

5. It is puzzling to find how little cross-reference there seems to be between people writing on Revelation and people writing on Ignatius. The only at all extensive coverage I have been made aware of is in Heinrich Kraft's commentary—and though that makes a case for linking the ecclesiastical situation in the Seven Letters of Revelation with that in Ignatius, to the issue of comparing the political situations of each I can find no allusion.[28] Yet it does seem to me that if any frequent action had been taken in recent years against Christians as Christians, 'for the name', it is extremely odd to see how little danger Ignatius feels he is putting other Christians in, and how little trouble they actually suffer. Christians in touch with him would be publicly confessing, delating themselves to authorities actually concerned with the issue. You would expect a whole host of corpses en route and others packed off to die alongside the bishop. Yet he remains in solitary splendour—and expects to.

4. Ignatius, then, is doing something special. That seems clear. Suffering for Christ is special in itself. But his acceptance of this call is special. There is no sign of it being in any way commonplace. He is not joining a mass movement to martyrdom, he is joining Christ, and his act is quite distinctive. With this in mind it would be very odd for him not at least to note that the churches addressed in Revelation and also addressed by him—Ephesus, Smyrna, Philadelphia—had a tradition of producing such

---

27. See further below (4), on the significant silence of Ignatius on any previous 'martyrdoms' in the province of Asia, also addressed in 1 Peter.

28. H. Kraft, *Die Offenbarung Johannes* (Tübingen: Mohr, 1974), pp. 87-94. C.J. Hemer, *The Letters to the Seven Churches of Asia in their Local Setting* (JSNTSup, 11; Sheffield: JSOT Press, 1986), arguing for a date under Domitian, has a number of incidental references to Ignatius, but none, I find, to the bearing on Revelation of Ignatius's own major concern: 'Martyrdom'.

heroes. If Revelation had been about a recent conflict with the state in which, say, many more were going to die, as many had, we would expect at least some reference to their past example, which Ignatius would be encouraging them to renew—or telling them to leave it to specially chosen individuals like themselves. But there is complete silence. (The Roman province of Asia is also, of course, addressed in 1 Pet. 1.1: and the situation being faced in 1 Peter has also, it seems, failed to produce any martyrs in his generation for Ignatius to refer to.)

However egocentric we may judge Ignatius to have been (and I must confess a not uncritical fondness for him), it does seem hard to imagine him getting away—or expecting to get away—with such neglect of past martyrs in the churches of Asia Minor that he addresses on that very topic. And if we judge him sincere, such silence does seem very implausible. There can have been no martyrs in that part of the world for him to acknowledge. His is a pioneer ministry, around 108–110 CE.

Rome, and Rome only, is where martyrdom happens, according to Ignatius (*Rom.* 10.1; *Eph.* 12.2). The only general opposition he faces locally is from 'a few fools' (*Trall.* 8.2). Yet even in Rome there have been no recent martyrdoms, and it is to Peter and Paul only that he looks back (see also *Rom.* 4.3).

William R. Schoedel argues that Ignatius has been picked on by the authorities in Antioch, either in a situation of internal strife in the Christian community, or with the effect of creating internal tensions.[29] His arrest as such has certainly left the church in Antioch in some disarray, he may well have hoped his prospective 'martyrdom' would resettle the Christian community there, re-establishing his authority, albeit at a distance, and he is much relieved when good news does arrive (*Phld.* 10.1, etc.). His arrest had not, however, brought an automatically favourable response. There is no tradition of respect for those facing death for their faith. Neither actions from outside the community nor the publication of John's Revelation in this area has yet made an expectation of widespread 'martyrdom' an established part of Christian culture.

In the light of what has been accepted from Sherwin-White, we should question Schoedel's assumption that Ignatius's arrest would have been at the instigation of the authorities, rather than arising from a private delation.[30] But over all the picture in Schoedel of the situation that

29. W.R. Schoedel, *Ignatius* (Philadelphia: Fortress Press, 1985), pp. 10-14.
30. Schoedel, *Ignatius* , p. 11.

faced Ignatius's picture fits that in Pliny, as I have argued it. Prosecution is a new and spectacular thing.

G.B. Caird notes that by the time of Polycarp's death, his is 'only' the twelfth for both Smyrna and Philadelphia together (*Mart. Pol.* 19.1)—that is another thirty years on.[31]

It is also worth mentioning again Heinrich Kraft's case that the ecclesiastical situation in Revelation is similar to that presupposed by Ignatius. There is some Judaizing with a threat of a split, some gnosticizing that has resulted in a split; and he notes some details, such as Ephesus remaining faithful in both, in both in face of intruders from elsewhere, but a bit cool on churchgoing; and there is the one link quite often noted between the stylos in Rev. 3.12 and the stele in *Phld.* 6.1, with the note about men's names being inscribed. (I would add, there seems also to be a very similar interpretation of the cultic assembly: compare Rev. 4–5 with, for example, *Magn.* 6–7).

3. Some writers on Revelation make considerable play with Domitian's severe exaction of the Jewish Tax.[32] It would, they say, have split Christians from Jews, and would have removed the last vestige of tolerance Christians might have enjoyed as a kind of Jew. But there is no Roman evidence to suggest that action to obtain payment resulted in people being put to death[33] (to afford Pliny a precedent).

2. Dio Chrysostom has harsh things, too, to say about Domitian, having been exiled by him (45.1); but there is no reference to persecution of provincial dissidents. It is noted that Iraeneus, who dates Revelation in Domitian's time, does not link it with any persecution.[34] The people

---

31. G.B. Caird, *The Revelation of St John the Divine* (BNTC; London: A. & C. Black, 1964), p. 35.

32. J. Sweet, *Revelation* (London: SCM Press, 1979), p. 30; Elisabeth Schüssler Fiorenza, *The Book of Revelation: Justice and Judgment* (Philadelphia: Fortress Press, 1985), p. 194 (despite claiming [p. 19] to be much persuaded by H. Kraft's dating in Ignatius's time); compare more recently her 'The Followers of the Lamb', *Semeia* 36 (1986), p. 135 (linking Pliny 10.96 still more closely with Revelation, yet as illustrating conditions under the Flavians, without offering any argument for the latter conclusion); compare also Hemer, *The Letters*, pp. 9-11.

33. None seems forthcoming; Suetonius's *Domitian* 12.2 does not suggest the abused old man was on trial for his life.

34. Cf. B. Newman, 'The Fallacy of the Domitian Hypothesis', *NTS* 10 (1964), pp. 133-39 (accepting Irenaeus's date); and A.J. Bell, Jr, 'The Date of John's

Pliny encountered who had given up their Christian allegiance in Domitian's time had simply given it up. As we noted, they afforded Pliny no clue to lead him to a precedent. And if Luke is for other good reasons dated in Domitian's time, he shows every sign of expecting Imperial officials to be neutral or favourable to his movement, despite Jesus' crucifixion and Paul's imprisonment.

1. Most commentators that I have consulted seem convinced that Rev. 11.1 must originally have been uttered during the siege of Jerusalem but prior to its fall. But, as Adela Yarbro Collins argues, the use of the code-name 'Babylon' (in preference to 'Edom') indicates that Rome has already played the part of destroyer of God's Temple.[35] 13.4 is widely argued to post-date the boost given by Domitian in particular to the cult of Rome and the Emperor. 11.1, then, is re-used with a metaphorical sense to refer to the Christian community as God's 'sanctuary' (for myself I do not see why it should not have had that sense from the start).

The various 'heads' of 17.9-10 are awkward for any attempt to attach them to one of the preferred dates, and I would agree with Caird, for instance, that the sequence of seven is taken over as a given symbol, only slightly adapted.[36] Even if it did once have Nero in mind under Galba (seven plus one from Julius Caesar), one can find a similar sequence of seven plus one from Galba to Trajan—including a wounded sixth: if one wants to. But I would think the explanation that these are also the hills of Rome should keep us from over-pressing the issue.

There is no clear evidence that John has been exiled to Patmos, none that it was a place for exile or a penal colony. Past martyrs are known (under Nero, 6.9-11) and there has been just one, recently (Antipas, Pergamum, 2.13). The author expects worse to come. The work seems to have been occasioned by the threat of physical violence, related to response to the cult of the Emperor, the situation first met with under Pliny. But Revelation comes out of a much deeper and more penetrating analysis than this forecast of physical suffering. It is not primarily about the clash of symbols: that only constitutes the symptoms of the real disease. It is about a clash of total cultures, a clash of life-styles. The

---

Apocalypse', *NTS* 25 (1969), pp. 93-102 (though arguing for a date under Nero).

35. Adela Yarbro Collins, *Crisis and Catharsis: The Power of the Apocalypse* (Philadelphia: Westminster Press, 1984), pp. 57-58.

36. Caird, *Revelation*, pp. 216-19; H. Kraft, *Offenbarung*, pp. 219-22, etc.

heart of Revelation's concern is displayed in ch. 18, with its picture of the oppression of a society given over to the acquisition of wealth by the few, with their ostentatious consumption. That system is the real beast, the real enemy. Caesar and Rome are merely the obscene figureheads for an underlying and incurable corruption, one that remains as hostile to Christian life and faith whether or not it demands formal cultic homage.[37]

The author of 1 Peter is in favour of a much more quiescent subservience, even though the cost may be high.[38] It should not surprise us to find two such divergent views among early Christians. A single individual such as Dio of Prusa, from this same area and period, could at times adopt a Cynic anarchism, and at others a touching trust in a high-minded and divinely inspired and authorized Emperor.[39]

There was no official action taken against Christians in the courts in the provinces of Syria, Asia, Pontus, Bythinia, and around, before a conscientious governor attempted to establish on a firmer basis the order and efficiency and prosperity of the two provinces committed to his charge by an enlightened Emperor. The author of 1 Peter appreciated the high-minded ideals; the author of Revelation discerned, maybe long before, the underlying evil that now revealed its true colours. Perhaps the blood of the martyrs proves the latter was the more perceptive.

37. Something of this emerges in the work of J. Sweet and E. Schüssler Fiorenza, but particularly that of A.Y. Collins; and compare also L. Thompson, 'A Sociological Analysis of the Apocalypse of John', and E Schüssler Fiorenza, 'The Followers of the Lamb', both in *Semeia* 36 (1986).

38. Compare Elliott, *Home for the Homeless*, pp. 142-44, again.

39. Contrast the Diogenes Discourses (4, 6, 8, 9, especially) with the first three on Kingship.

INDEXES

INDEX OF REFERENCES

OLD TESTAMENT

PSEUDEPIGRAPHA

CHRISTIAN AUTHORS

INDEX OF AUTHORS